The Illustrated
Guide to
BLACKJACK

The Illustrated Guide to
BLACKJACK

150 Situations and Solutions to Make Winners out of Beginners!

DENNIS PURDY

LYLE STUART
Kensington Publishing Corp.
www.kensingtonbooks.com

LYLE STUART BOOKS are published by

Kensington Publishing Corp.
850 Third Avenue
New York, NY 10022

All Kensington titles, imprints, and distributed lines are available at special quantity discounts for bulk purchases for sales promotions, premiums, fund-raising, educational, or institutional use. Special book excerpts or customized printings can also be created to fit specific needs. For details, write or phone the office of the Kensington special sales manager: Kensington Publishing Corp., 850 Third Avenue, New York, NY 10022, attn: Special Sales Department; phone 1-800-221-2647.

Lyle Stuart is a trademark of Kensington Publishing Corp.

First printing: March 2007

10 9 8 7 6 5 4 3 2 1

Printed in the United States of America

ISBN-13: 978-0-8184-0708-6
ISBN-10: 0-8184-0708-5

Dedication

Shortly after finishing my last midnight shift of the week at Fisher Controls in Marshalltown, Iowa, in the winter of 1977, I had a breakfast meeting with Al Burgess, a former poker-room manager from Nevada. Although he was considerably older than I was, we had become friends at the local bowling alley and played together in a Friday-morning poker game every week. Over the previous nine months, I had developed what I believed was a system that would consistently win at baseball wagering, and I wanted to move to Las Vegas to try it out. I told Al of my system and my belief in it, but he was skeptical.

"Dennis," he said, "I used to make my living in the gambling world, and one thing I know is that Vegas just loves to see guys like you come to town to try your systems. She always sends them all home broke."

Unfazed, I persisted in telling (annoying) Al about my system. He finally agreed to meet with me about it, even telling me that if I could prove to him I could consistently beat baseball, he would sell his house and business and move to Las Vegas with me, bankrolling the whole endeavor. Two hours later he was convinced. Al was as good as his word. Within a month he sold his home, sold this business, cashed in his stocks and bonds, and raised our grubstake. I quit my good-paying factory job of five years and we were off.

Once in Vegas, the baseball system—much to my delight—did prove out, but after the bets were placed each morning, we had a lot of free time on our hands. We filled this void by playing blackjack. I learned how to count cards and tried to teach A1, but his vision was so poor that he never could master counting, so I did the counting for both of us. We later met and became friends with some other gamblers, forming blackjack teams. While I wouldn't give you a nickel to live that lifestyle again, I wouldn't take a million dollars for the memories and experiences of that time in my life.

Al eventually got tired of the Vegas lifestyle and moved to Oregon to be closer to his family. Although I never heard from him again and he's probably passed away by now, I'd still like to thank him for believing in a young man and his baseball system thirty years ago and putting it all on the line for our adventure. You don't find many friends like Al.

Contents

The Illustrated
Guide to
BLACKJACK

What This Book Is . . . and Isn't

So, you want to play **blackjack,** huh? All right, then, let's play it together and let's play it to win.

If you're like most players, you've read (or skimmed) at least a book or two on blackjack. Most players, though, read just enough to get themselves into trouble. At first glance it's basically a simple game: just get closer to 21 than the **dealer**. Or at least that's what the house dealers would have you believe. But blackjack involves much more than just trying to get closer to 21 than the dealer. In fact, it's often the *wrong* move to try to get closer to 21 than the dealer.

If you haven't yet actually played at the tables, you're most likely nervous about doing so. I know I was. You might even be a bit confused by some of the terminology. Don't worry, I've included a comprehensive glossary in the back of this book that should cover any term you're likely to come across at a blackjack table.

One of the nice aspects of blackjack is that there's a correct, predetermined course of play no matter what **hand** you get or what card the dealer has showing. There's no need to guess which of several plays might be your best option as in other games such as poker. I call this predetermined course of play *perfect basic strategy*. If you learn to play perfect **basic strategy**, not only will you have yourself a game that is on a level playing field with the house, but you'll actually have a slight advantage. And you don't have to become a card **counter** to make use of perfect basic strategy, you just have to learn (and memorize) the correct plays, something the average player should be able to do in one afternoon of practice.

Before I moved to Nevada and became a full-time professional gambler in the 1970s, I bought and read many books on blackjack. Some dealt with basic playing strategy, while others were very sophisticated (and expensive!) books on card counting systems. At the end of the day, however, it still came down first to learning to play perfect basic strategy. Once you've accomplished that goal, you can move on to learning a card counting system, but it's not necessary in order to win at blackjack.

What I've done in *The Illustrated Guide to Blackjack* is present a learning system that is different from any other book on blackjack. While virtually every other book on blackjack is organized by topic, such as **surrender**, **doubling down**, **splitting** pairs, and so on, this book is organized by situation: 150 to be exact. I used this same teaching approach in my two poker books, *The Illustrated Guide to Texas Hold 'em* and *The Illustrated Guide to No-Limit Texas Hold 'em*, and the feedback I received from readers through letters, e-mails, and phone calls was overwhelmingly consistent: readers loved the illustrated situational approach because it allowed them to *visualize* the hand and move back and forth between the question and answer of each situation until they grasped the concept. This format also lends itself to making this book an excellent study guide when you feel the need to *refresh* yourself on the game's proper plays.

The 150 situations I present within these pages represent the meat of this book. Rather than instructing you by topic, I've chosen to teach you how to play winning blackjack by analyzing various situations—the same way they'll come at you in a casino—and then making the correct play. As you read through the situations in this book, you'll notice that I show you how to think about the hand you've been dealt and how to mentally consider your options. In many cases I also present you with the numbers, **odds**, and percentages that back up each correct decision. By the time you get to the end of the 150 situations, you should know both how to approach the analysis of any hand you receive and how to decide what move to make.

One last item: I realize that dealers and players are as likely to be female as male, but in the interest of avoiding awkward constructions such as "he or she," and so on, I have referred to the players as being male and the dealers as being female throughout.

CHAPTER 1

The Basics of Blackjack

Technically speaking, the game that's played in casinos around the world is actually 21, not **blackjack**. In actual blackjack, the deal is supposed to rotate to a new player whenever that player catches a blackjack. Since the deal never rotates from the **house dealer** in a casino, the game isn't blackjack, even though it's commonly known by that name, including in this book.

The rules of blackjack are quite simple. Each of the 13 ranks in a deck of cards (2 through Ace) has a numeric value. The numbers 2 through 10 are worth their face value, that is, a 3 is worth 3, an 8 is worth 8, and so on. All Jacks, Queens, and Kings are worth 10. Aces are a special case in that they are worth either 1 or 11, your choice (at least initially), but more on that later. The four suits (clubs, diamonds, spades, and hearts) mean nothing in normal blackjack, although in some exotic bonus plays at a few casinos a particular suit may come into play in the bonus payoff.

There are two basic ways in which to win: either you have to be closer to 21 than the dealer if neither of you **break** (exceed 21) or the dealer has to break, whereas you do not, regardless of your hand's total. While the casino dealer may tell you that the object of the game is to get closer to 21 than she does, that isn't the whole truth. You only have to *beat the dealer*, which in some cases means holding a live hand while she breaks, even if your hand is a 12.

When play begins, the dealer will deal out two cards to all players and herself. Depending on the casino, the players' cards will be dealt either face up or face down. The dealer will always have one card face up, the other face down. The card facing up is known as—surprise—the **up card**, or the showing card, and the face-down card is known as the **hole card**. This down card is one of the two advantages the house holds over the player. The second comes when the players act on their hands. After the deal, all players act first—in turn—followed by the dealer. You have the option of taking cards or not, and as many as you want, until you either break or get as close to 21 as you wish to try. Once all the players have acted on their hands, the dealer will play her hand according to the required rules. If a player breaks (or **busts** out) before the dealer later breaks as well, the house still keeps the breaking player's money, which, hence, is the second advantage. This breaking second aspect while still keeping the players' money gives the house a built-in advantage of about 4 percent (52–48 percent). That may not sound like much, but in casino terms it is huge given the speed with which hands are dealt. Thus, all things being equal, the house will, on average, win about 52 times out of every 100 hands in which the player plays by the same rule that is required of the house.

That required house rule is this: the dealer must **hit** (**draw** one or more cards) to a hand of 16 or less and **stand** (take no more cards) once she has 17 or more. Therefore, if a player played by this same rule, he would be at a 4 percent disadvantage to the house because about 4 times in 100 both the dealer and player will break *on the same hand*.

So, how do we turn the tables on the house and actually win at this game? Simple. We take full advantage of special rules only allowed to the player, some of which are major and some of which are minor. The first of the major rules allows players to stand whenever they want to. Players do not have to hit a breaking hand (12 through 16) like the dealer does. The hands of 12, 13, 14, 15, and 16 are known as breaking hands because the player could (and oftentimes does) potentially break by drawing one more card. The house dealer does not have the option of standing on a 16 if she wants to. She must hit, and any of the eight card ranks from a 6 through a King will break her, making you the automatic winner no matter what your hand's total, so long as you don't break first. Simply put, by not hitting a breaking hand when the dealer shows a 2 through a 6 as her up card (potential breaking hands for the dealer assuming she has a 10-count card in the hole), the player gains back a little of the aforementioned **house advantage.**

A second major rule that only the players can take advantage of is known as **doubling down**. What this means is that if, after getting your first two cards, you like your total in relation to the dealer's up card, you may double your wager and receive only one more card. So, if you received a 7 and a 4 for an 11 total and the dealer had a 6 showing (for a possible 16 total), you would be smart to double down. The reason: more cards in the deck are worth 10 (all 10s, Jacks, Queens, and Kings) than any other number, meaning that your best shot for improving your 11 will be a 21. Also, since more cards are worth 10 than any other total, the dealer stands a good chance of having a 10-count card in the hole, giving her a 16 total, and any of the eight ranks from 6 through King will break her, giving you double the win (or in blackjack parlance, two **units** instead of one).

A third major **player advantage** is the rule that allows the player to **split** any pair and play two new hands if he chooses to. For example, if you were dealt a pair of 8s and the dealer had a 7 up, you would be wise to split your 8s into two new hands. (Don't worry, I will discuss the strategy behind these and other moves as we work our way through the 150 situations.) This requires placing a new wager equal to your original wager. If you win both hands, then you pick up two units instead of one. The player, however, is not required to split all pairs; he has the option of splitting only those he wants to. Thus, once a player has considered his own hand against the dealer's up card, he can decide whether it would be advantageous to split his hand into two new hands. Once again, this rule allows the player to gain back some of the lost **edge** to the *break-first* rule of the game.

A fourth rule of profound advantage to the player is the one that says players collect 3-to-2 payoffs on blackjacks. A blackjack is an Ace and 10-count card as the first two cards dealt to the player. The house, conversely, does not collect a 3-to-2 bonus payoff when the dealer gets a blackjack, only the original money wagered by the player. Since players will, on average, make a blackjack once in about every twenty-one hands played, this effectively means the player will gain back a half-unit **bet** every twenty-one hands, once again eroding the house advantage.

A fifth option that's advantageous to the player is one called **surrender**. Although not offered in every casino, this option allows a player to forfeit half of his original bet if he doesn't want to play the hand. This is possible, for example, if the player is dealt a 16 total and the dealer has an Ace or 10-count card showing (assuming the dealer didn't have a blackjack).

Another option that is offered (although it is *disadvantageous* to the player) is called **insurance**. Essentially what you do, when the dealer shows an Ace up, is bet 50 percent of your original wager as insurance against a dealer blackjack. Insurance pays 2 to 1. So if the dealer has the blackjack, you lose your original bet (unless you also had a blackjack) but collect 2 to 1 on your insurance bet, effectively breaking even. If the dealer doesn't have the blackjack, you lose your insurance bet and then play out the hand (maybe losing that one, too!). I'll discuss this more in depth within the 150 situations as well, but always play with the knowledge that the insurance option you see displayed on the blackjack table cover isn't a good bet for the player. Ever.

CHAPTER 2

Pre-Game Preparations

Before you head for the casino, there are some things to consider. Are you in the proper mind-set? If you're angry, tired, depressed, have had too much to drink, or are otherwise distracted, you should not play. That goes for any gambling game of any kind, but particularly blackjack because you can lose a lot of money in short order, unlike, for example, poker in which it takes a while to lose your grubstake because of the limited betting structure. In blackjack, you can lose it all on one hand, and I've seen it done many times.

If your mind is right, then you need to consider your **bankroll**. Over the next three hundred-plus pages, I'm going to teach you how to play winning blackjack, but you can't win if you aren't properly bankrolled. A proper bankroll for a **session** of blackjack is fifty times your single-unit bet. If you walk into a casino with a $100 blackjack bankroll, your single-unit bet should be no more than $2, and frankly, there aren't many casinos that take such a small bet anymore. If you're going to play $5 hands, you need to have $250 at your disposal. Now, this doesn't mean you're always going to need the whole $250. In fact, you should never need the whole amount, but what a fixed betting amount does in relation to your bankroll is keep you from getting wiped out quickly when the cards turn on you for eight or ten hands in a row. It's very important that you always bet in proportion to your bankroll. I can confidently say that if you have fifty times your single-unit bet, you'll never lose your bankroll, providing you play perfect **basic strategy**. I remember a time in 1998 when I lost 23 straight hands at $25 a hand and yet, I came back to have a winning session because I had enough of a bankroll to back up a tough losing streak. Had I been betting $25 hands on a $500 bankroll (only 20 times my single-unit bet), I'd have been wiped out.

Once you know what your bankroll and single-bet units are, you need to establish a **loss limit**. This means the point you will stop playing because of your losses. If, for example, you start with a $500 bankroll and will be playing $10 hands, your loss limit should be around $200. This would represent a 20-unit loss. If you're down that much in any one session, the danger of playing longer is that you might get angry or begin to chase, upping your bets to a higher and riskier level than initially planned for, and thereby jeopardize your entire bankroll. If you have the discipline not to let it affect you, okay, but for the most part, you should protect yourself against yourself.

If you know you're going to be spending the night out at the tables, be sure to bring anything of a personal nature you might need with you so that you don't have to cut your night short in case you're doing well. These would be things such as medications, eye drops, throat lozenges, dental floss, and so on. While some of these things may be available in the casino, many, such as medications, are not. I learned a long time ago to take a jacket with me that has a large inner pocket that can hold all these things. You never know when you may want or need your nasal spray, a Q-tip, or an aspirin.

Bring your **study charts** (or this book) with you and study for a few minutes in your car each time just before you play. Eventually the perfect basic strategy presented in this book will become second nature, but until it does, keep studying and memorizing. I even made up some laminated credit-card-sized study charts on problem hands (for me) that I could keep in my wallet and study in the casino's restroom or lounge until I had them fully memorized. If you ever become a professional blackjack player, you'll be past the point of needing reminders of how to play perfect basic strategy. Until then, however, you always need to refresh your memory on the correct plays because if you're like most people, you aren't going to play blackjack every night. And if it's two months between playing sessions, your memory will start to fade on many of the borderline plays.

Another consideration before you sit down at the tables is which casino to give your action to. Many of you will not have the option (or many options) of where to play. But if you do, be sure to play at the casino with the most liberal rules for the player. For example, some casinos only allow doubling down on 10 and 11, while others allow this move on any two cards. Clearly, it is in your best interest to play at casinos that allow the latter. Other casinos allow players to double down after they split a pair, while more restrictive establishments do not. Still other casinos allow the **surrender** option (**early surrender** and/or late surrender), while most do not. Some casinos require the dealer to stand on all 17s (a player advantage), while others require the dealer to hit soft 17s (a 17 made by counting an Ace as worth 11, a casino advantage). Some casinos offer a blackjack spin-off game called Spanish 21 in which all the number 10s are removed from the deck (a huge player disadvantage), but the players are paid for all 21s before the dealer resolves her hand (a small player advantage). Be sure you know the variable rules at play in your casinos of choice, and play where it is to your advantage.

Once you have decided on your casino, you should look for a favorable table. The most favorable table is one with the most liberal playing rules and the use of a single deck. For the record, a single-deck game is better than a **double-deck** game, which is better than a six- or eight-deck **shoe game**. It is also advantageous for a player to sit in the seat to the dealer's extreme right, also called **third base**. The reason for this is that you get to see all the player action in front of you before you have to make the final decision on your hand. Every once in a while your play will be altered by what the other players do in front of you. For example, if you hold a Jack and a 4 for a 14 total and the dealer has a King showing (possible 20), the only way you will likely beat her is if you draw a 7 to your hand. While normally you would hit this hand, if you are playing in a single-deck game and all four 7s come on the board before you act, you would now stand on the hand rather than hit.

CHAPTER 3

Let the Game Begin

Okay, your mind-set is good, you've got a proper bankroll for the amount you're going to be betting, you've chosen the casino with the most liberal playing rules, and you've succeeded in getting the third-base seat. Now it's time to play. What happens next? First, you'll need **chips** to play. I personally like to have 40 units in front of me. This means that if I'm playing $5 hands, I'll want $200 worth of $5 chips. If I'm playing $25 hands, I'll want $1,000 worth of $25 chips. In either case, the base chip ($5 or $25) is my one-unit bet. It certainly isn't necessary for you to have this many chips in front of you, but because I'm a card **counter**, I actually use my chip stacks to help keep track of certain things, such as the number of Aces, 10-count cards, and 5s played, or the overall count/condition of the deck/shoe. You won't have to worry about any of that, however, since this book deals only with learning perfect basic strategy.

You should buy in for at least 20 units of whatever your betting level is going to be, keeping the other 30 units in reserve if you want to. To buy chips from the dealer, you wait until the current hand is finished and then place your cash in front of you. Do not put your cash on the betting space in front of you lest the dealer mistake it for a large cash bet. The dealer will take your cash and drop it into a slot on the table. The money is collected into a **drop box** that is exchanged for an empty box every so often by casino security personnel. The dealer will also drop receipts and other paperwork into the drop box during the course of play. Once you secure your chips, pull them back directly in front of you. Place one chip on the betting space and wait for your cards. (You should always bet the minimum at the beginning of a session so that you can get a feel for the table, the other players, and a sense of the deck or shoe, which could be in mid-shoe when you arrive.)

Since you are in the last position, you will watch all the other players at the table play out their hands in front of you. When it is finally your turn to act, you will indicate your intention to the dealer. If the cards are dealt face down, you will have to pick them up to look at them. If this is the case, you will need to slide them under your wagered chip if you intend to stand or scrape them across the felt toward yourself if you want the dealer to give you another card. If you go over 21, you will have to turn your cards face up and give them to the dealer because you have busted. If you intend to stand, then slide your two cards face down under your wagered chip. If you want to split your hand, you will turn your cards face up, and using your index finger and middle finger (as if you were indicating the number two), tap the table so the dealer can see you. She will then split the hand, deal one card to the first new hand, and then await your decision on that hand. Once that hand is complete, she will deal one card to the second new hand and await your decision again. If you want to double down, you will turn your two cards over, tell the dealer, "Double," and then you will place another bet (equal to the first) out on the table. The dealer will give you one more card and then play out her own hand. Once the dealer completes the play on her own hand, she will turn over your face-down cards to determine the winner, and either take your money, give you your winnings, or tap the table (indicating a tie, or **push**).

If you receive your cards face up, you are not allowed to touch them in most casinos. To indicate that you want to stand (take no more cards), you will take your open hand and wave it, palm down, back and forth over your cards. If you want another card, you will take your index finger and scrape it across the felt toward you, repeating this each time you want another card. To split a pair, use the same two-finger motion as just mentioned. To double down, simply put another bet out and tell the dealer, "Double."

In the event that surrender is offered and you decide to take it, simply tell the dealer you want to surrender. She'll take half of your bet and remove your cards. You'll occasionally see players placing money on the insurance betting line, but this is something you should *never* do because it's always a poor bet.

Once the dealer completes the action on her own hand, she will go around the table and pay off the winning hands and collect the money from the losing hands. She will place all the played cards into a discard tray on her right-hand side. She will then wait until all players have placed their next bets and then deal the next hand, either from the single or double deck in her hand or the multiple-deck shoe (a plastic box containing usually six or eight decks) on her left-hand side.

Each casino has its own rules about how far into a deck or shoe the dealer will deal before **shuffling** up, but generally speaking, she will deal about half to two thirds of the way through a single or double deck and about 60 percent of the way through a shoe. The reason they do not deal all the way through a deck or shoe is because it is one of the casino countermeasures used to thwart card counters who can skillfully keep track of all the cards played, thereby altering their betting patterns in ways advantageous to them (and disadvantageous to the casinos!).

As an aside, I should mention that blackjack has become increasingly popular on the Internet. Based on my own experience, however, I would avoid online blackjack. Why? Because I have doubts about the integrity of online blackjack. Online poker is fine, but not blackjack, and here's why I believe this: When playing online poker, you're playing against other players, not the house, so the house has no real vested interest in who actually wins at the poker tables. They take their *rake* (percentage) out of every winning pot regardless of who wins it. Blackjack is different. You're playing against the house, so they *do* have a vested interest in who wins.

One night, after winning $1,400 in an online poker tournament, I decided to try my luck at the site's blackjack side. I started off betting small, just $2 a hand until I got the feel of the game. After an hour or so, I was up about $100, so I increased my bets to $5 a hand and played all five spots on the table, meaning that the game was just between the dealer and me. After another hour, I was up nearly $300. Feeling at ease, I decided to break out in a big way. I played five hands for $100 a hand. I got four 20s and a 19. The dealer got a blackjack and wiped me out for $500 on one hand. Stinging, but still up around $1,200 for the night because of my poker win, I again bet $100 on all five **betting spots.** This time I got three 20s, a 19, and a 17. Not bad. In the last 10 hands in which I bet big money, I didn't break once. But for the second hand in a row, the dealer got a blackjack and wiped me out for another

$500. I then lowered my bets back to $2 and returned to my winning ways. About 10 minutes later, I decided to try the $100 per hand bet again on all five spots. Once again, I received five made hands (didn't bust on any hand) and the dealer got a blackjack, costing me another $500. That ended my online blackjack career. Scientific evidence? No. Anecdotal? Yes. I suppose it wouldn't be inconceivable for a crooked website designer to include something in the gaming software that allowed the house to hit a blackjack whenever there was a large amount bet or a large increase in the betting level of a player or players. They do, as I pointed out earlier, have a vested interest in who wins the hand in blackjack. Call me cynical, but I will never again play online blackjack.

And so it goes, 24 hours a day, seven days a week in a bazillion casinos all over the world. Your playing session can last as long as you want, so long as you aren't tired, are winning (slowly but surely), or don't have to baby-sit on your wife's bowling night. Barring any of those possibilities, good luck, and have a profitably good time!

CHAPTER 4

The Rules of Playing Perfect Basic Strategy

The concept of playing perfect basic strategy was developed more than forty years ago, and not much has changed since. What makes this book different is the manner in which that basic strategy is taught. Rather than just utilizing a bunch of charts and requiring you to memorize them like virtually all other blackjack books (although both concepts are included in this book, too), I've added the visual element of the dealer's hands and yours along with a situational problem for you to resolve. It's been said that people remember 10 percent of what they hear, 20 percent of what they see, and 70 percent of what they do. That principle alone makes this book a better way to learn how to play winning blackjack. While the meat of the information will be presented within the 150 situations, I'll first provide you with all the basic rules you'll need for playing perfect basic strategy as well as a few charts that illustrate some of the percentages in play. Once you master the concepts and rules of these several charts, you'll be able to walk into a casino and hold your own against the house, and even have a bit of an advantage. Should you become proficient at playing perfect basic strategy, you might decide to take the next step and enter the world of card counting, an advanced concept that can be truly rewarding.

♥ ♠ ♣ ♦

Chart 1: Perfect Basic Strategy

Chart 1 includes every correct move for playing perfect basic strategy, whether the game is single-deck or multiple-deck shoe. *Important note:* The listed strategy is for a single-deck game; exceptions for correct play in a shoe game are listed as *Shoe Exceptions*.

WHEN YOU HOLD: 5, 6, or 7 (without an Ace)
  You must always hit.

WHEN YOU HOLD: 8 (with a 6-2 combination)
  You must always hit.

WHEN YOU HOLD: 8 (with a 5-3 combination)
  Double down against a dealer's 5 or 6; hit against any other up card.
  Shoe Exception: Do not double down on this combination in a shoe game.

WHEN YOU HOLD: 9
  Double down against the dealer's 2, 3, 4, 5, or 6; hit against everything else.
  Shoe Exception: Do not double down against a 2.

WHEN YOU HOLD: 10
  Double down against the dealer's 2, 3, 4, 5, 6, 7, 8, or 9; hit against everything else.

WHEN YOU HOLD: 11
  Double down against any dealer up card.
  Shoe Exception: Do not double down against an Ace.

WHEN YOU HOLD: 12
  Stand against the dealer's 4, 5, or 6; hit against everything else.

WHEN YOU HOLD: 13
  Stand against the dealer's 2, 3, 4, 5, or 6; hit against everything else.

WHEN YOU HOLD: 14
  Stand against the dealer's 2, 3, 4, 5, or 6; hit against everything else.

WHEN YOU HOLD: 15
  Stand against the dealer's 2, 3, 4, 5, or 6; hit against everything else.

WHEN YOU HOLD: 16
Stand against the dealer's 2, 3, 4, 5, or 6; hit against everything else.

WHEN YOU HOLD: 17
You should always stand.

WHEN YOU HOLD: 18
You should always stand.

WHEN YOU HOLD: 19
You should always stand.

WHEN YOU HOLD: 20
You should always stand.

WHEN YOU HOLD: Ace-2 (soft 13)
Double down against the dealer's 4, 5, or 6; hit against everything else.
Shoe Exception: Do not double down against a 4.

WHEN YOU HOLD: Ace-3 (soft 14)
Double down against the dealer's 4, 5, or 6; hit against everything else.
Shoe Exception: Do not double down against a 4.

WHEN YOU HOLD: Ace-4 (soft 15)
Double down against the dealer's 4, 5, or 6; hit against everything else.

WHEN YOU HOLD: Ace-5 (soft 16)
Double down against the dealer's 4, 5, or 6; hit against everything else.

WHEN YOU HOLD: Ace-6 (soft 17)
Double down against the dealer's 2, 3, 4, 5, or 6; hit against everything else.
Shoe Exception: Do not double down against a 2.

WHEN YOU HOLD: Ace-7 (soft 18)
Double down against the dealer's 3, 4, 5, or 6; hit against the dealer's 9 or 10-count card; stand against the dealer's Ace, 2, 7, or 8.
Shoe Exception: Hit against the dealer's Ace.

WHEN YOU HOLD: Ace-8 (soft 19)
Double down against the dealer's 6; stand against everything else.
Shoe Exception: Stand against everything.

WHEN YOU HOLD: Ace-9 (soft 20)
You should always stand.

WHEN YOU HOLD: A pair of Aces:
You should always split.

WHEN YOU HOLD: A pair of 2s:
You should split against the dealer's 3, 4, 5, 6, or 7; hit against
everything else.
Shoe Exception: Do not split against a 3.

WHEN YOU HOLD: A pair of 3s:
You should split against the dealer's 4, 5, 6, or 7; hit against
everything else.

WHEN YOU HOLD: A pair of 4s:
You should double down against the dealer's 5 or 6; hit against
everything else.
Shoe Exception: Do not double down against a 5 or 6, just hit
against everything.

WHEN YOU HOLD: A pair of 5s:
You should double down against the dealer's 2, 3, 4, 5, 6, 7, 8, or 9;
hit against an Ace or any 10-count card.

WHEN YOU HOLD: A pair of 6s:
You should split against the dealer's 2, 3, 4, 5, or 6; hit against
everything else.
Shoe Exception: Do not split against a 2.

WHEN YOU HOLD: A pair of 7s:
You should split against the dealer's 2, 3, 4, 5, 6, or 7; hit against an
Ace, 8, or 9; stand against any 10-count card.
Shoe Exception: Hit against any 10-count card.

WHEN YOU HOLD: A pair of 8s:
You should always split.

WHEN YOU HOLD: A pair of 9s:
  You should stand against the dealer's Ace, 7, or 10-count card; split
    against everything else.

WHEN YOU HOLD: A pair of 10-count cards:
  You should always stand.

Chart 2: Expected Dealer Performance

Chart 2 gives you an idea of what to expect from the dealer in the way of busting or making a made hand (17 or more) with each of the listed up cards. Notice the jump in performance from 6 to 7. This is why you must not stand on a hand of 16 or less against dealer's 7 through Ace.

Up Card	Made Hand (%)	Break (%)
2	65	35
3	62	38
4	60	40
5	57	43
6	58	42
7	74	26
8	76	24
9	77	23
10/J/Q/K	76	24
Ace	83	17

Chart 3: Why We Make the Moves We Do, Part 1

Chart 3, while not all-inclusive (I didn't include the percentages for doubling down on a 5, for example, because it's nothing you would seriously entertain), is intended to give you an idea of the percentage gain by making some of the double-down moves we do in playing perfect basic strategy or the loss we suffer by incorrectly doubling down. It's not necessary to memorize this chart, but it should help you visualize just how good or bad a particular move is. Notice, for example, the drop in gain when you hold a 10 and you double against a 6 (+16.2%) compared to a 7 (+8.5%). Reason being, when the dealer shows a 7, she will often make a made hand, while you will sometimes hit a small card to your 10 when you double and don't have the option of hitting again, which results in a losing hand for twice the units. You should still double on a 10 against a 7, but your return won't be as great. Also, notice when you have an 8 against the dealer's 5 or 6 how small your gain is when you double. It wouldn't be the end of the world if you didn't double on this hand, but every little bit helps. Notice, too, how large your loss is when you incorrectly double on an 8 against an Ace.

Percentage Gain (or Loss) by Doubling Down

Your Hand	Dealer Up Card	Gain over Just Hitting (%)
8	2	(-7.5)
8	3	(-5.1)
8	4	(-2.6)
8	5	+0.4
8	6	+0.5
8	7	(-12.7)
8	8	(-18.8)
8	9	(-24.3)
8	10	(-24.6)
8	Ace	(-28.8)
9	2	+1.2
9	3	+2.8

Your Hand	Dealer Up Card	Gain over Just Hitting (%)
9	4	+5.2
9	5	+7.7
9	6	+8.0
9	7	(-1.0)
9	8	(-5.2)
9	9	(-11.5)
9	10	(-14.8)
9	Ace	(-16.1)
10	2	+10.8
10	3	+12.3
10	4	+13.9
10	5	+15.4
10	6	+16.2
10	7	+8.5
10	8	+5.0
10	9	+2.3
10	10	(-1.0)
10	Ace	(-2.3)
11	2	+13.5
11	3	+14.8
11	4	+16.3
11	5	+18.0
11	6	+18.1
11	7	+9.3
11	8	+6.0
11	9	+3.9
11	10	+2.6
11	Ace	+2.1

Your Hand	Dealer Up Card	Gain over Just Hitting (%)
A-2	2	(-4.1)
A-2	3	(-2.1)
A-2	4	+0.3
A-2	5	+2.7
A-2	6	+3.1
A-2	7	(-13.2)
A-2	8	(-17.6)
A-2	9	(-18.0)
A-2	10	(-19.5)
A-2	Ace	(-26.3)
A-3	2	(-3.2)
A-3	3	(-1.6)
A-3	4	+0.9
A-3	5	+3.4
A-3	6	+3.8
A-3	7	(-11.8)
A-3	8	(-14.5)
A-3	9	(-16.7)
A-3	10	(-17.8)
A-3	Ace	(-24.8)
A-4	2	(-2.9)
A-4	3	(-1.1)
A-4	4	+1.2
A-4	5	+3.4
A-4	6	+4.0
A-4	7	(-8.8)
A-4	8	(-13.9)
A-4	9	(-15.4)

Your Hand	Dealer Up Card	Gain over Just Hitting (%)
A-4	10	(-16.3)
A-4	Ace	(-23.3)
A-5	2	(-2.5)
A-5	3	(-0.9)
A-5	4	+1.3
A-5	5	+3.3
A-5	6	+5.1
A-5	7	(-8.3)
A-5	8	(-12.4)
A-5	9	(-14.3)
A-5	10	(-15.7)
A-5	Ace	(-22.5)
A-6	2	+0.3
A-6	3	+1.9
A-6	4	+3.9
A-6	5	+7.0
A-6	6	+6.7
A-6	7	(-2.3)
A-6	8	(-8.3)
A-6	9	(-10.5)
A-6	10	(-12.2)
A-6	Ace	(-16.4)
A-7	2	(-0.4)
A-7	3	+1.1
A-7	4	+5.5
A-7	5	+6.4
A-7	6	+6.2

Your Hand	Dealer Up Card	Gain over Just Hitting (%)
A-7	7	(-8.6)
A-7	8	(-6.8)
A-7	9	(-8.4)
A-7	10	(-9.2)
A-7	Ace	(-12.9)
A-8	2	(-8.2)
A-8	3	(-3.7)
A-8	4	(-2.1)
A-8	5	(-0.4)
A-8	6	0
A-8	7	(-14.5)
A-8	8	(-20.9)
A-8	9	(-17.4)
A-8	10	(-14.5)
A-8	Ace	(-24.1)
A-9	2	(-13.8)
A-9	3	(-12.6)
A-9	4	(-9.8)
A-9	5	(-7.3)
A-9	6	(-6.7)
A-9	7	(-21.1)
A-9	8	(-27.8)
A-9	9	(-32.8)
A-9	10	(-30.4)
A-9	Ace	(-36.1)

A-10 should never be counted as an 11 for double down purposes. Be content with your 3-to-2 payoff for a blackjack.

Chart 4: Why We Make the Moves We Do, Part 2

Chart 4 is intended to give you an idea of the percentage gain by making some of the pair splitting moves we do in playing perfect basic strategy or the loss we suffer by incorrectly splitting a hand. Again, it is not necessary to memorize this chart, but it should help you visualize just how good or bad a particular move is. As you will notice, you always improve your situation by splitting a pair of Aces or 8s. Notice, too, how you always worsen your position when you split a pair of 4s and how badly you suffer whenever you split 10-count cards.

Percentage Gain (or Loss) by Splitting Pairs

Your Hand	Dealer Up Card	Gain or Loss by Splitting (%)
A-A	2	+23.6
A-A	3	+24.6
A-A	4	+26.3
A-A	5	+27.5
A-A	6	+28.0
A-A	7	+19.1
A-A	8	+15.7
A-A	9	+14.6
A-A	10	+12.1
A-A	Ace	+12.8
2-2	2	(-1.2)
2-2	3	+0.2
2-2	4	+1.5
2-2	5	+3.3
2-2	6	+3.3
2-2	7	+1.7
2-2	8	(-3.9)
2-2	9	(-8.4)

Your Hand	Dealer Up Card	Gain or Loss by Splitting (%)
2-2	10	(-8.8)
2-2	Ace	(-8.2)
3-3	2	(-2.4)
3-3	3	(-0.7)
3-3	4	+1.4
3-3	5	+3.5
3-3	6	+2.9
3-3	7	+2.1
3-3	8	(-2.1)
3-3	9	(-5.1)
3-3	10	(-7.7)
3-3	Ace	(-6.8)
4-4	2	(-11.3)
4-4	3	(-8.8)
4-4	4	(-7.4)
4-4	5	(-5.2)
4-4	6	(-6.9)
4-4	7	(-16.8)
4-4	8	(-13.7)
4-4	9	(-13.4)
4-4	10	(-15.6)
4-4	Ace	(-16.4)

A pair of 5s should never be split. Double down if appropriate.

Your Hand	Dealer Up Card	Gain or Loss by Splitting (%)
6-6	2	+0.2
6-6	3	+1.8
6-6	4	+3.7
6-6	5	+6.1
6-6	6	+7.7
6-6	7	(-0.5)
6-6	8	(-4.6)
6-6	9	(-8.9)
6-6	10	(-13.0)
6-6	Ace	(-12.2)
7-7	2	+3.9
7-7	3	+5.2
7-7	4	+7.1
7-7	5	+10.0
7-7	6	+11.9
7-7	7	+13.8
7-7	8	(-0.3)
7-7	9	(-3.9)
7-7	10	(-5.3)
7-7	Ace	(-6.4)
8-8	2	+13.4
8-8	3	+14.2
8-8	4	+16.8
8-8	5	+18.5
8-8	6	+21.2
8-8	7	+28.5
8-8	8	+16.9

Your Hand	Dealer Up Card	Gain or Loss by Splitting (%)
8-8	9	+4.3
8-8	10	+2.9
8-8	Ace	+6.3
9-9	2	+0.9
9-9	3	+3.7
9-9	4	+5.2
9-9	5	+7.8
9-9	6	+5.7
9-9	7	(-3.4)
9-9	8	+6.2
9-9	9	+4.6
9-9	10	(-6.8)
9-9	Ace	(-3.1)
10-10	2	(-14.8)
10-10	3	(-12.7)
10-10	4	(-10.1)
10-10	5	(-7.7)
10-10	6	(-7.7)
10-10	7	(-14.4)
10-10	8	(-21.9)
10-10	9	(-28.6)
10-10	10	(-27.5)
10-10	Ace	(-27.7)

CHAPTER 5

The 150 Practice Situations

The time has come for the main event: the 150 practice situations. These situations are quite self-explanatory. On each left-hand page I present you with your hand, the dealer's hand, and a set of variable house rules and other game information that apply to that hand only. On the top of the right-hand page I present you with a situation and end it with a question for you to answer regarding the hand on the left-hand page. Most of the situations will be multiple choice, but a few near the back of the book will ask you to answer questions of a more advanced nature (since you are supposed to be getting smarter as you go through the book!). On the bottom of each right-hand page I provide you with the correct/best answer to the situation presented and the rationale behind the answer. Within these 150 situations, you will encounter not only every basic blackjack play but virtually every borderline play as well. By the time you finish this book, you will have been exposed to every basic strategy concept that exists in the game of blackjack as it is played in casinos. It is my sincere wish that this book will help you experience the enlightenment of mastering this game as you unravel the 150 situations and become a winning blackjack player.

♥ ♠ ♣ ♦

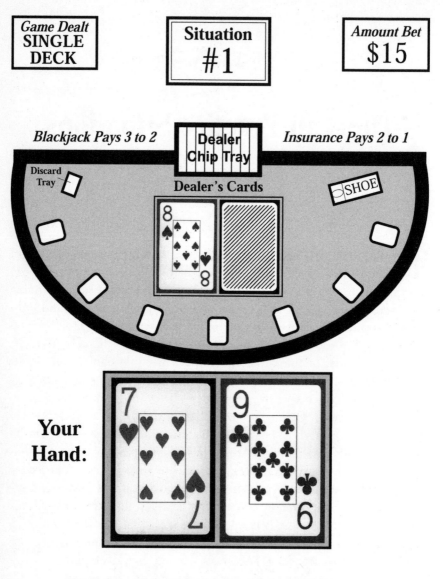

Variable House Rules in Play This Hand:

1. Double Down: Any 2 cards
2. Double Down After Splitting: Yes
3. Surrender Allowed: No
4. Dealer Soft 17s: Must stand

Situation #1

You are playing in a single-deck game. You have been dealt a 9 and a 7 for 16 total. The dealer's up card is an 8. You have several options. Which of the options listed below is your best choice, and why?

My Options

    A)   Stand
    B)   Hit
    C)   Double down
    D)   Split
    E)   Surrender

Situation #1 Answer

The first principle of playing perfect basic strategy is to assume that any unseen card is worth 10, since more cards in the deck are worth 10 than any other number (all 10s, Jacks, Queens, and Kings are worth 10). In this case, the unseen card is the dealer's down card. Since we must assume that the dealer has 18—a made hand—we must hit our 16, as standing will leave us short most of the time because the dealer will break only 24 percent of the time when showing an 8 up. We are at a decided disadvantage on this poor hand, and splitting and surrendering are not options to bail us out. Odds are we are going to break ourselves when we hit this hand since only five cards (Ace–5) keep us in the hand, while eight cards (6–King) put us over 21. Still, hitting (rather than standing) lessens our overall losing propositions for the hand.

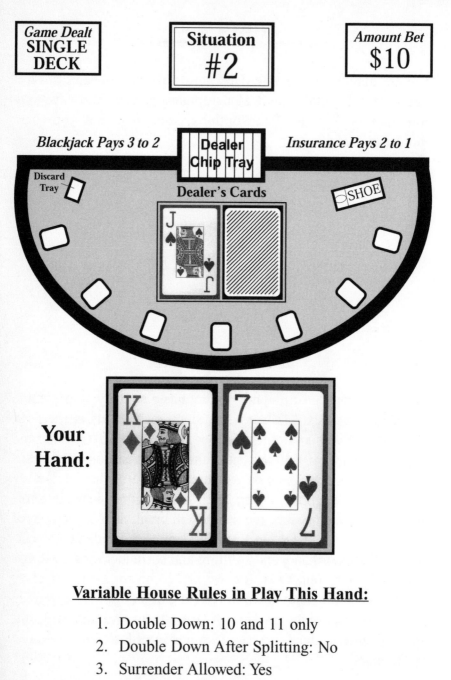

| Game Dealt SINGLE DECK | Situation #2 | Amount Bet $10 |

Blackjack Pays 3 to 2   *Insurance Pays 2 to 1*

Dealer Chip Tray

Discard Tray

Dealer's Cards

SHOE

Your Hand:

Variable House Rules in Play This Hand:

1. Double Down: 10 and 11 only
2. Double Down After Splitting: No
3. Surrender Allowed: Yes
4. Dealer Soft 17s: Must stand

Situation #2

You are playing in a single-deck game. You have been dealt a King and a 7 for 17 total. The dealer's up card is a Jack. You have several options. Which of the options listed below is your best choice, and why?

My Options

A)   Stand
B)   Hit
C)   Double down
D)   Split
E)   Surrender

Situation #2 Answer

The second principle of playing perfect basic strategy is to stand whenever you have a hard 17 or more, regardless of the dealer's up card. As you learned in situation #1, the first principle of playing perfect basic strategy is to assume that any unseen card is worth 10. That being the case, we have to work under the assumption that the dealer has a 20. If this turns out to be true, we are going to lose this hand; *however*, we would lose more by trying to hit a small card here. Realistically, we need a 4 to win. An Ace or 2 likely leaves us short of a winning hand, and a 3 will likely only get us a push. So, since only a 3 or 4 can be viewed as potentially helping us and the other 11 ranks as either not helping us or outright hurting us by making us break, we have to stand on this hand and take our probable lumps.

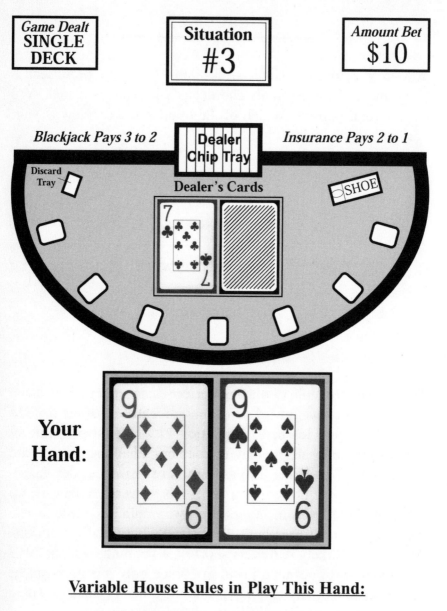

Variable House Rules in Play This Hand:

1. Double Down: Any two cards
2. Double Down After Splitting: No
3. Surrender Allowed: No
4. Dealer Soft 17s: Must hit

Situation #3

You are playing in a single-deck game. You have been dealt a pair of 9s for 18 total. The dealer's up card is a 7. You have several options. Which of the options listed below is your best choice, and why?

My Options

A) Stand
B) Hit
C) Double down
D) Split
E) Surrender

Situation #3 Answer

A third principle of playing perfect basic strategy is to stand when you have a **hard total** that is better than a dealer's likely hard total. In this case you have a hard 18 and the dealer has a likely hard 17, which would make you a sure winner. Yes, you could split the two 9s and try to win two hands at $10 each, but chances are, you will catch one solid hand and one breaking hand, leaving you in the position of scrambling to break even. You might even catch two poor hands (from 12–16 total) and end up losing both hands. Better to take the probable one-unit win now than risk losing two units or breaking even when you hold a clear advantage at this point.

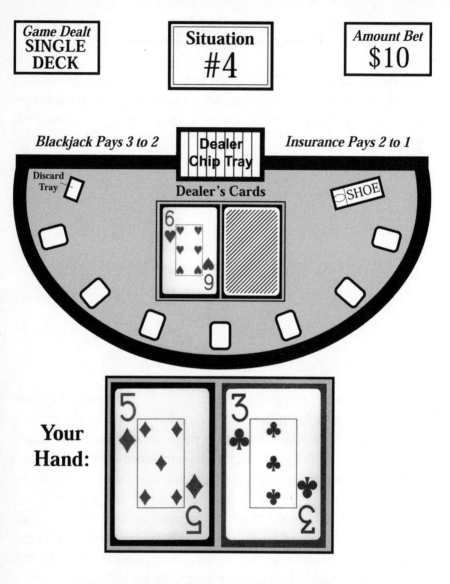

Game Dealt
SINGLE
DECK

Situation
#4

Amount Bet
$10

Blackjack Pays 3 to 2

Dealer
Chip Tray

Insurance Pays 2 to 1

Discard Tray

Dealer's Cards

SHOE

Your
Hand:

Variable House Rules in Play This Hand:

1. Double Down: Any two cards
2. Double Down After Splitting: No
3. Surrender Allowed: Yes
4. Dealer Soft 17s: Must hit

Situation #4

You are playing in a single-deck game. You have been dealt a 5 and a 3 for 8 total. The dealer's up card is a 6. You have several options. Which of the options listed below is your best choice, and why?

My Options

    A) Stand
    B) Hit
    C) Double down
    D) Split
    E) Surrender

Situation #4 Answer

This hand illustrates one elemental and one finer point of basic blackjack strategy. The elemental principle at play here is to hit your hand—regardless of its total—until you have at least a hard 12, and then reassess the situation. In this case, you hold an 8 against the dealer's horrible up card of 6 and cannot break no matter what you draw. Now, the finer point. The dealer's 6 will lead to many breaking hands for her (42 percent of the time). You hold an 8 with a 5-3 combination, which is better than if you held an 8 with a 6-2 combination. While it's far too complex to get into in a basic strategy book, just remember that 5-3 is better than 6-2 in a *single-deck game* (I remember it by equating it to age, 53 being better than 62). You should double down on this 5-3 hand against a 6 to increase your win rate, but only hit a 6-2 hand.

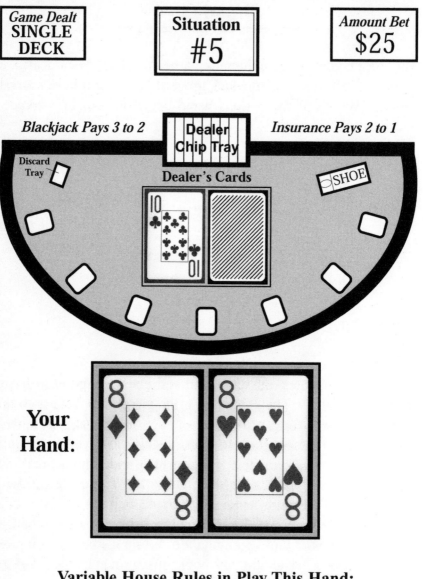

Game Dealt
SINGLE DECK

Situation #5

Amount Bet
$25

Blackjack Pays 3 to 2

Dealer Chip Tray

Insurance Pays 2 to 1

Discard Tray

Dealer's Cards

SHOE

Your Hand:

Variable House Rules in Play This Hand:

1. Double Down: Any two cards
2. Double Down After Splitting: Yes
3. Surrender Allowed: No
4. Dealer Soft 17s: Must hit

Situation #5

You are playing in a single-deck game. You have been dealt a pair of 8s for 16 total. The dealer's up card is a 10. You have several options. Which of the options listed below is your best choice, and why?

My options

    A) Stand
    B) Hit
    C) Double down
    D) Split
    E) Surrender

Situation #5 Answer

This hand represents another core principle of playing perfect basic strategy. When you receive a pair of 8s, you *always* split them, regardless of the dealer's up card. Yes, I know, in the previous situations I taught you to view any unseen card as being worth 10, which would give the dealer a likely 20 against your two 18s, and on the surface, that's correct. However, in the *long term*, by always splitting a pair of 8s, you will come up with enough other combinations to make this a winner. In fact, a pair of 8s against a 10 yields about a 3% increase in units won over the long term so long as you split them. This is one of the correct moves you just have to get into the habit of playing virtually without thinking. Always split 8s in playing perfect basic strategy, whether in a single-deck or shoe game. No exceptions.

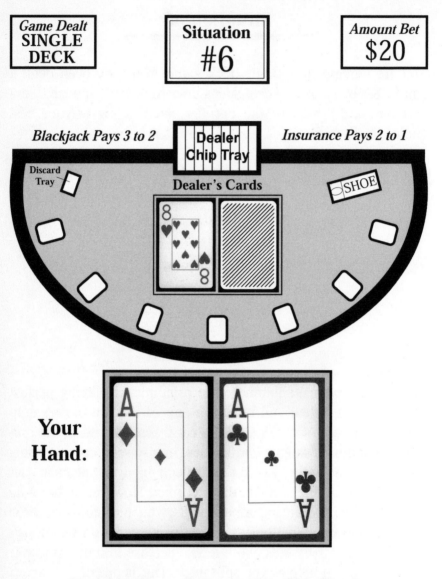

| Game Dealt SINGLE DECK | Situation #6 | Amount Bet $20 |

Blackjack Pays 3 to 2   **Dealer Chip Tray**   Insurance Pays 2 to 1

Discard Tray

Dealer's Cards

SHOE

Your Hand:

Variable House Rules in Play This Hand:

1. Double Down: Any two cards
2. Double Down After Splitting: Yes
3. Surrender Allowed: Yes
4. Dealer Soft 17s: Must hit

Situation #6

You are playing in a single-deck game. You have been dealt a pair of Aces. The dealer's up card is an 8. You have several options. Which of the options listed below is your best choice, and why?

My Options

A) Stand
B) Hit
C) Double down
D) Split
E) Surrender

Situation #6 Answer

This hand represents another *always* perfect basic strategy play. Whenever you get a pair of Aces, you *always* split them, *no exceptions*. A pair of Aces, in fact, is *the* power hand in blackjack next to a blackjack itself, as it lends itself to winning more units over the long run than any other two-card hand, made or not. Get in the habit of telling yourself, "Always split Aces and 8s." And splitting this hand is critical in terms of winning units over the long haul. If you fail to split this hand, you are giving back to the dealer one of your player advantages. The only house advantage is that if the dealer breaks after you break, the house still keeps your money. The player has many advantages at his disposal to counteract this one house advantage, and splitting (when beneficial to do so) is one of them.

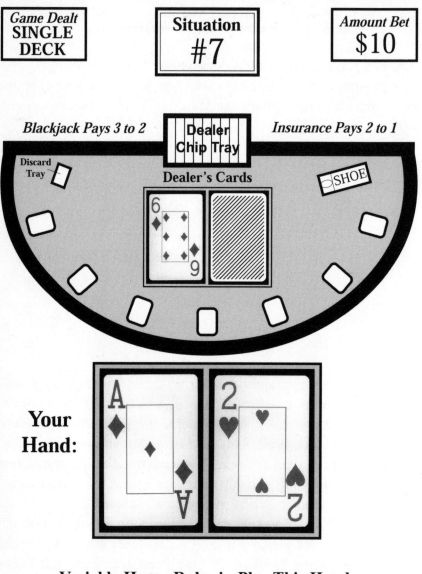

**Situation
#7**

Amount Bet
$10

Blackjack Pays 3 to 2   *Insurance Pays 2 to 1*

Dealer
Chip Tray

Discard
Tray

Dealer's Cards

SHOE

Your
Hand:

Variable House Rules in Play This Hand:

1. Double Down: 10 and 11 only
2. Double Down After Splitting: No
3. Surrender Allowed: No
4. Dealer Soft 17s: Must hit

Situation #7

You are playing in a single-deck game, in Reno, Nevada. You have been dealt an Ace and a 2 for a soft 13 total. The dealer's up card is a 6. You have several options. Which of the options listed below is your best choice, and why?

My Options

A) Stand
B) Hit
C) Double down
D) Split
E) Surrender

Situation #7 Answer

This is a bad break for you. Why? Because you're playing in a casino that doesn't allow a player to double down on any two cards. Many Northern Nevada casinos (and some casinos elsewhere) allow a player to double down only on hands of 10 or 11. This player disadvantage is known as *Northern Nevada rules*. Optimally, you would double down on this hand, mainly based on the dealer's poor up card and secondarily because you can't break no matter what card you draw. Since you can't double, just hit until you get a hard total of 12 or more, then stand. What this hand illustrates is the varying rules at play in today's casinos. Remember, it's to the player's advantage to play where he can double down on any two cards, not just 10 or 11 as in this casino. Check the rules before you play.

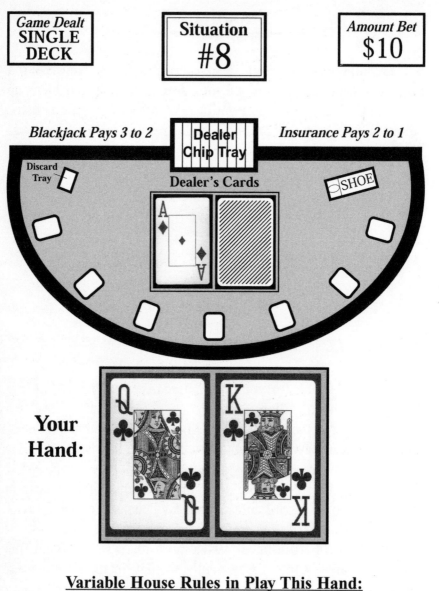

Variable House Rules in Play This Hand:

1. Double Down: Any two cards
2. Double Down After Splitting: No
3. Surrender Allowed: No
4. Dealer Soft 17s: Must stand

Situation #8

You are playing in a single-deck game, and it is the first hand dealt. You have been dealt a Queen and a King for a 20 total. The dealer's up card is an Ace. Before the hand is played out, she asks if you would like to take insurance. Do you take insurance or not?

My Options

    A)   Take insurance.

    B)   Do not take insurance.

Situation #8 Answer

While some dealers would have you believe that what they are offering you is a chance to protect your good hand, what's really going on here is that you're faced with betting whether the dealer has a 10-count card in the hole for a blackjack. Let's figure it out. Assuming you're alone at the table, there are 49 unseen cards. Of these 49 cards, only 14 of them could be a 10-count card, since you hold two of them in your hand. This means that 35 of the unseen cards aren't worth 10. So the ratio of non-10s to 10s on this hand is 35 to 14, or 2.5 to 1. Insurance pays 2 to 1. Thus, insurance is a bad bet on this hand. Don't take it. Also, even if you hold one or no 10-count cards in your hand, insurance is still a bad percentage bet. Unless you're a proficient card counter, *never take insurance.*

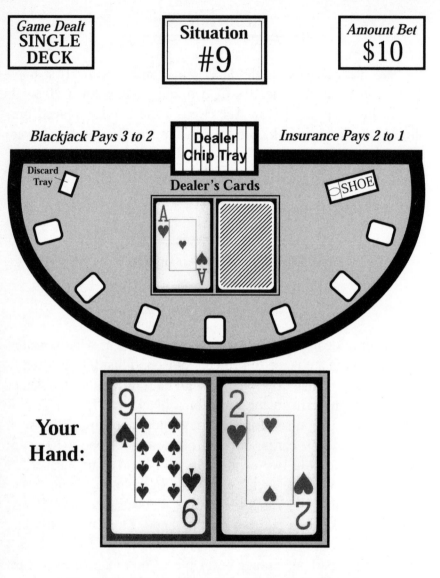

Variable House Rules in Play This Hand:

1. Double Down: Any two cards
2. Double Down After Splitting: No
3. Surrender Allowed: No
4. Dealer Soft 17s: Must hit

Situation #9

You are playing in a single-deck game. You have been dealt a 9 and a 2 for an 11 total. The dealer's up card is an Ace and she has already checked for a blackjack, which she does not have. Which option below should you exercise, and why?

My Options

A)   Stand

B)   Hit

C)   Double down

D)   Split

E)   Surrender

Situation #9 Answer

Obviously, you won't stand or surrender and can't split. That leaves you the choice of hitting or doubling down. This hand represents another cardinal principle of perfect basic strategy play. When you've an 11 total, and the rules allow double down against any dealer up card in a single-deck game, even an Ace as in this case. While the Ace is a powerful card and will turn into many made hands (the dealer will make a made hand—a hard 17 or more—88 percent of the time with an Ace up), you're still better off to double down on this hand in a *single-deck* game because the units picked up in the long term will more than make up for the dealer's high made-hand rate.

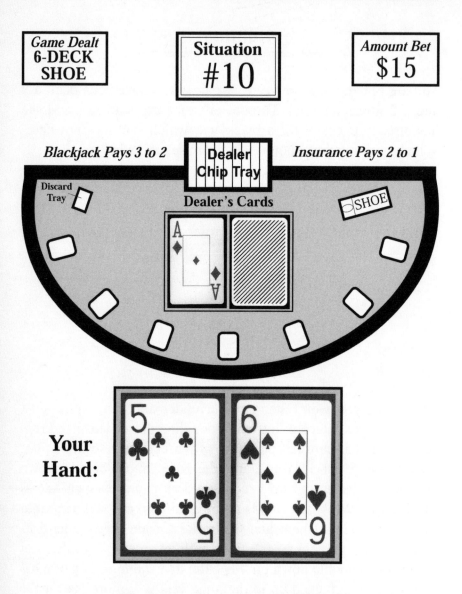

Variable House Rules in Play This Hand:

1. Double Down: Any two cards
2. Double Down After Splitting: No
3. Surrender Allowed: No
4. Dealer Soft 17s: Must hit

Situation #10

You are playing in a 6-deck shoe game. You have been dealt a 5 and a 6 for an 11 total. The dealer's up card is an Ace, and she has already checked for a blackjack, which she does not have. Which option below should you exercise, and why?

My Options

    A)   Stand

    B)   Hit

    C)   Double down

    D)   Split

    E)   Surrender

Situation #10 Answer

The only difference between this situation and the last one is that you are now playing in a multiple-deck game, specifically a 6-deck shoe game. So, does that have any bearing on how you play this hand? Yes. While it is a cardinal rule to double down on an 11 against any dealer up card in a single-deck game, when playing in a **multiple-deck game** such as this one, you only double down on an 11 against any dealer up card *except* an Ace. Statistics show that over the long run, a player will win more units by only hitting an 11 against an Ace in a multiple-deck game rather than doubling. This is another one of the finer points of playing perfect basic strategy and another reason players can beat the house if they follow that proven strategy, *perfectly*.

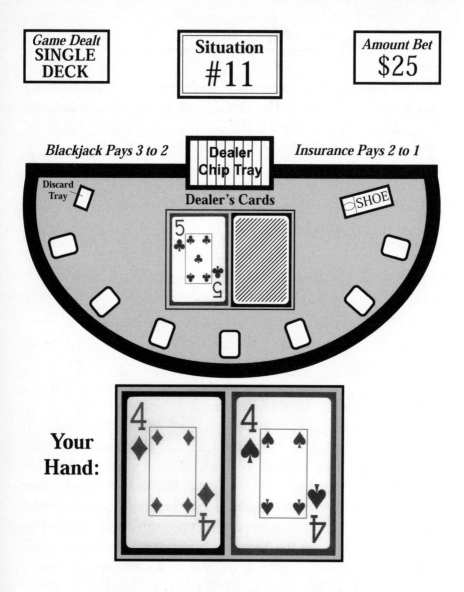

Your Hand:

Variable House Rules in Play This Hand:

1. Double Down: Any two cards
2. Double Down After Splitting: Yes
3. Surrender Allowed: No
4. Dealer Soft 17s: Must hit

Situation #11

You are playing in a single-deck game. You have been dealt a pair of 4s. The dealer's up card is 5. Which of the options listed below is your best choice, and why?

My Options

A) Stand
B) Hit
C) Double down
D) Split
E) Surrender

Situation #11 Answer

You really like to see a dealer catch a 5 as an up card since it's virtually every bit as bad for her (and good for you!) as a 6. Of course, you won't surrender or stand, so the choice for you is whether to hit, split, or double. While hitting this hand would be okay, you're clearly leaving money on the table since you're playing as much on the dealer's bad hand as your two 4s. By splitting or doubling, you're getting twice as much money on the table in a situation where the dealer is highly vulnerable. If you split this pair, you'll be setting yourself up for two bad hands (potential 14s) against the dealer. If you double down (the correct choice here), you'll still be getting twice as much money on the table and you'll be setting yourself up for one potentially good hand (18) against the dealer's poor hand.

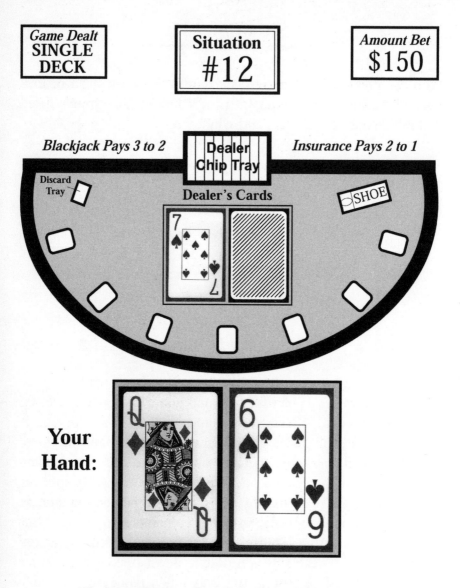

Game Dealt
SINGLE
DECK

Situation
#12

Amount Bet
$150

Blackjack Pays 3 to 2   Dealer Chip Tray   *Insurance Pays 2 to 1*

Discard Tray

Dealer's Cards

SHOE

Your Hand:

Variable House Rules in Play This Hand:

1. Double Down: Any two cards
2. Double Down After Splitting: Yes
3. Surrender Allowed: Yes
4. Dealer Soft 17s: Must hit

Situation #12

You have received a Queen and a 6 for a hard 16 in a single-deck game. The dealer shows a 7. In lieu of your extraordinarily large bet, which of the options listed below is your best choice, and why?

My Options

A) Stand because of the large bet.
B) Hit.
C) Double down.
D) Split.
E) Surrender.

Situation #12 Answer

So, why *did* you make this much larger-than-usual bet? Feeling lucky? Too much to drink? The cards were talking to you? In any event, you're in a pickle here. You've got the worst possible hand (16) against a probable made hand (the dealer will make a made hand—17 or more—74 percent of the time with a 7 showing). So, what do you do? You hit the hand. While it might be hard to do because of the size of your bet, the right move is still the right move. If you stand on this hand, you'll lose (over the long term, on average) 48 units in each 100 hands, and if you hit this hand, you'll lose 37 units in each 100 hands. An 11-unit improvement in 100 blackjack hands is a huge gain, considering the built-in house edge at blackjack is around 4 units per 100 hands. And stop drinking so much when you play, it makes you stupid.

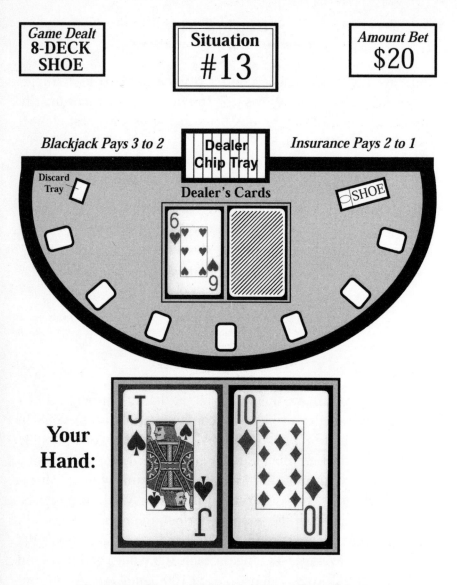

Game Dealt
8-DECK SHOE

Situation
#13

Amount Bet
$20

Blackjack Pays 3 to 2

Dealer Chip Tray

Insurance Pays 2 to 1

Discard Tray

Dealer's Cards

SHOE

Your Hand:

Variable House Rules in Play This Hand:

1. Double Down: Any two cards
2. Double Down After Splitting: Yes
3. Surrender Allowed: Yes
4. Dealer Soft 17s: Must hit

Situation #13

You have been dealt a Jack and a 10 for a 20 total in mid-shoe of an 8-deck shoe game at a full table against the dealer's 6 up card. You notice that no 10-count cards were dealt on the last hand. Which of the options listed below is your best choice, and why?

My Options

A)   Stand.

B)   Hit.

C)   Double down.

D)   Split because of the chance for two good hands against a 6 up card.

E)   Surrender.

Situation #13 Answer

Obviously, you're not going to hit, double down, or surrender on this hand, so the question seems to be whether you stand with your 20 or try to take advantage of what you think is a 10-**rich shoe** against a terrible up card for the dealer. This is where amateurs get themselves into trouble. Yes, the previous hand may indeed have had no 10-count cards, but have you been watching the whole shoe or did you just notice this? While **trends** do occur in a shoe-dealt game, unless you've been keeping close track of the shoe (as in counting the cards) from the beginning, you can't really say whether an inordinately high number of 10-count cards went out early in the shoe and things are just now evening out. Don't mess around with an almost sure winner by splitting this hand. Stand.

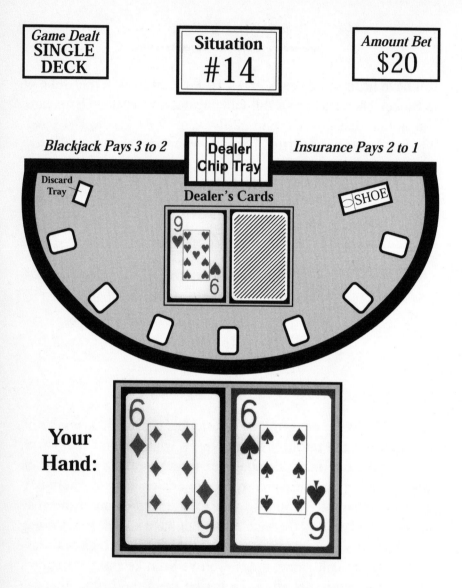

**Game Dealt
SINGLE
DECK**

**Situation
#14**

**Amount Bet
$20**

Blackjack Pays 3 to 2

**Dealer
Chip Tray**

Insurance Pays 2 to 1

**Discard
Tray**

Dealer's Cards

SHOE

**Your
Hand:**

Variable House Rules in Play This Hand:

1. Double Down: Any two cards
2. Double Down After Splitting: Yes
3. Surrender Allowed: No
4. Dealer Soft 17s: Must stand

Situation #14

You have been dealt a pair of 6s in a single-deck game against the dealer's 9 up. Which of the options listed below is your best choice, and why?

My Options

    A) Stand
    B) Hit
    C) Double down
    D) Split
    E) Surrender

Situation #14 Answer

You can't surrender, so you must choose between the other four options. Doubling down would be silly since you could break with a 10-count card and lose twice as much money. You can't very well stand on a 12 against a powerful up card. That leaves you with the options of hitting or splitting. As ugly as a pair of 6s might seem, it would only get uglier if you split this hand, since you'd be setting yourself up for two bad hands (potential 16s) against one good potential dealer hand (19). Just hit the hand until you get to 17 or more, or bust trying. The dealer has a probable made hand, so you have to try for the same thing.

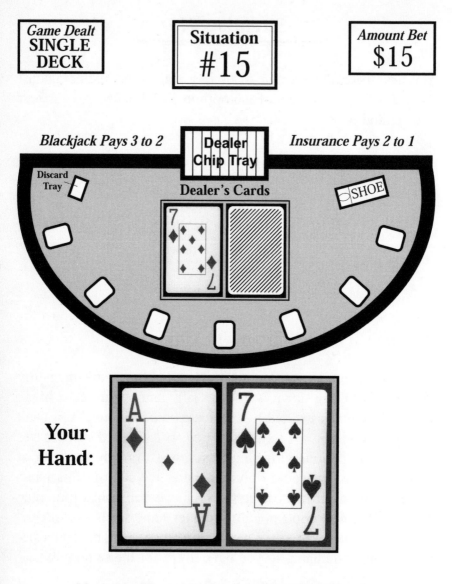

Variable House Rules in Play This Hand:

1. Double Down: Any two cards
2. Double Down After Splitting: Yes
3. Surrender Allowed: Yes
4. Dealer Soft 17s: Must stand

Situation #15

In a single-deck game, you have been dealt an Ace and a 7 for a total of soft 18. The dealer has a 7 showing. Which of the options listed below is your best choice, and why?

My Options

A) Stand
B) Hit
C) Double down
D) Split
E) Surrender

Situation #15 Answer

You can't split and won't surrender, so your options are either hit, stand, or double down. Perfect basic strategy says you have to figure the dealer for a 17 and play your hand accordingly. You have a soft 18, which means that you can count it as 8 or 18, your choice. To hit this hand would mean that you're trying to improve on it, and only an Ace through a 3 will do that, long odds to say the least, and it won't gain you anything since your 18 already beats her probable 17 if you just stand. If you double, you only get one more card, and is it worth it to double your bet and possibly end up with a 12–16 total for a double-unit loss, or a 17 for a push? No, of course not. When the dealer shows a 7, the player holds a 14 percent advantage over the long term. The correct play is to stand.

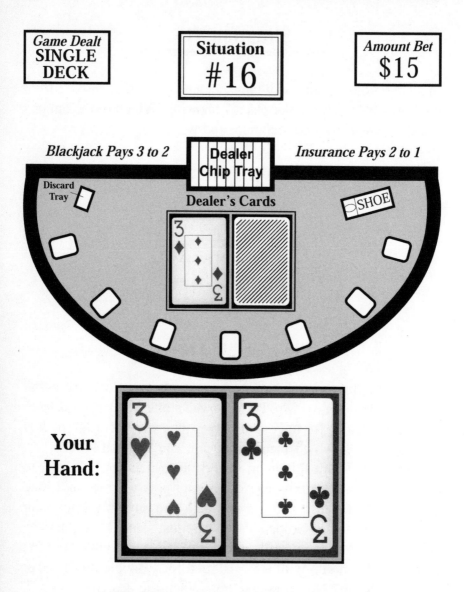

| Game Dealt SINGLE DECK | Situation #16 | Amount Bet $15 |

Your Hand:

Variable House Rules in Play This Hand:

1. Double Down: Any two cards
2. Double Down After Splitting: Yes
3. Surrender Allowed: Yes
4. Dealer Soft 17s: Must stand

Situation #16

In a single-deck game, you have been dealt a pair of 3s against the dealer's 3 up. Which of the options listed below is your best choice, and why?

My Options

A) Stand
B) Hit
C) Double down
D) Split
E) Surrender

Situation #16 Answer

Surrender is out because the dealer has a poor up card and there's no reason to give anything away in this instance. You're not going to double down because the best you can come up with is a soft 17 with an Ace, hardly anything to be proud of. Anything less leaves you with an unmade hand, and the dealer will make a made hand 62 percent of the time with a 3 showing. If you split this hand, you'll be playing two poor hands (potential 13s) against the dealer instead of one. Obviously, you're not going to stand on a 6 total, so the only option left—and the correct one— is to hit your hand and try to improve it. Since the dealer has a potential breaking hand (a hand that could exceed 21 with one more card, i.e., a 10-count card in the hole for 13 and a hit for 23), you should hit until you have 12 or more and then stand.

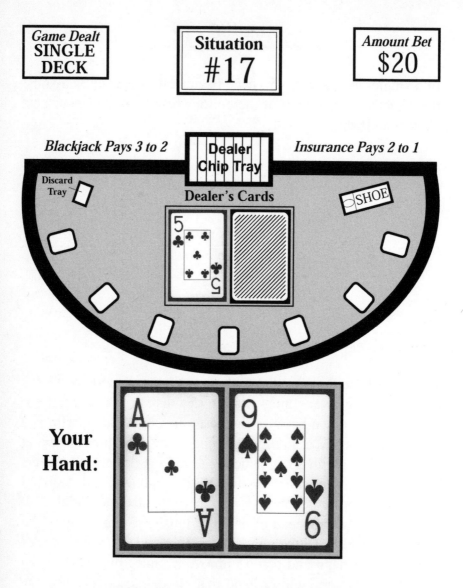

| Game Dealt SINGLE DECK | Situation #17 | Amount Bet $20 |

Variable House Rules in Play This Hand:

1. Double Down: Any two cards
2. Double Down After Splitting: Yes
3. Surrender Allowed: Yes
4. Dealer Soft 17s: Must stand

Situation #17

In a single-deck game, you have been dealt an Ace and a 9 for a soft 20 total. The dealer shows a 5 as her up card. Which of the options listed below is your best choice, and why?

My Options

A) Stand

B) Hit

C) Double down

D) Split

E) Surrender

Situation #17 Answer

You aren't going to surrender a 20, to be sure, and neither will you hit the hand in an effort to improve it, since only another Ace will make your hand better (21 instead of 20). You can't split this hand, so that leaves only standing or doubling down as your remaining options. If you double your bet from $20 to $40 in an effort to win more money, you might actually gum up the works. When a dealer shows a 5 up, she will make a made hand (17 or more) 57 percent of the time. If you double down, any card from a 2 through a 6 will give you a loss 57 percent of the time, and it will be a double unit loss. If a 7 comes, you'll only push a certain number of times as well, meaning 6 of the 13 ranks will either hurt you or positively not help you. And of the other 7 ranks, only one (the Ace) will improve your hand. Don't monkey with success here, just stand, the correct move anytime you have an Ace-9 against any up card.

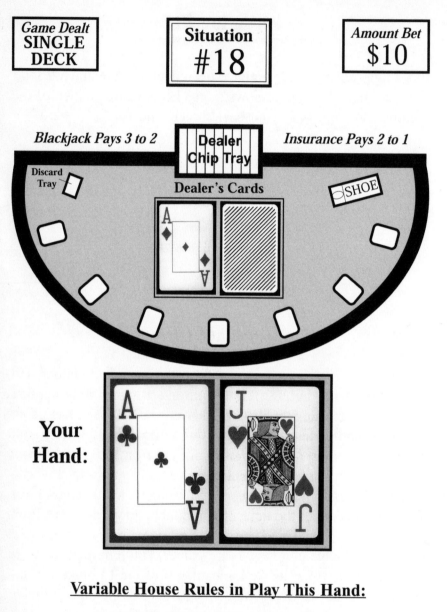

| Game Dealt SINGLE DECK | Situation #18 | Amount Bet $10 |

Variable House Rules in Play This Hand:

1. Double Down: Any two cards
2. Double Down After Splitting: Yes
3. Surrender Allowed: Yes
4. Dealer Soft 17s: Must stand

Situation #18

In a single-deck game, you have been dealt a blackjack, but the dealer has received an Ace up. The dealer asks if you want insurance. Should you take it in this instance, since you have a guaranteed winner, or not?

My Options

A)   Take insurance.

B)   Do not take insurance.

Situation #18 Answer

If you take the insurance—which will cost you $5 (half of your original bet)—and the dealer has a blackjack, your original hand will be a push (tie) and you will win $10 on your insurance bet for a total profit of $10 on the hand. If the dealer doesn't have the blackjack, you will win $15 for your blackjack and lose your $5 insurance bet for a total profit of $10 on the hand. Huh? Yes it's the same either way. So the determining factor here, then, is what the **true odds** are of the dealer having a blackjack (i.e., a 10-count card in the hole). There are 49 unseen cards, and 15 of them are 10-count cards (you hold one Jack in your hand). This makes the ratio of non-10s to 10s exactly 34 to 15, or greater than 2 to 1. Since the payoff is only 2 to 1 and the payoff is the same either way you play the hand, once again we see that insurance is a bad bet, even when you hold a blackjack in your hand. Don't take it.

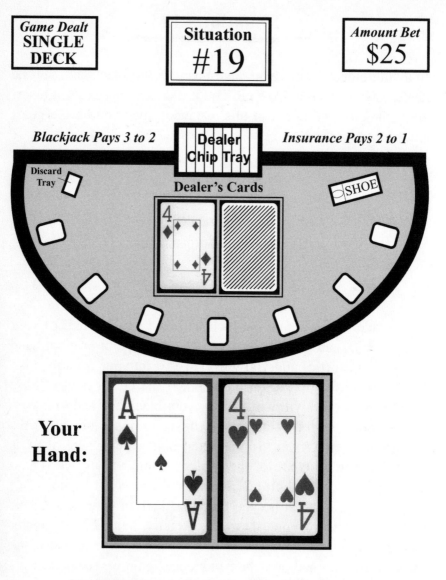

Variable House Rules in Play This Hand:

1. Double Down: Any two cards
2. Double Down After Splitting: No
3. Surrender Allowed: Yes
4. Dealer Soft 17s: Must stand

Situation #19

You are playing in a single-deck game, have been dealt an Ace and a 4 for a soft 15 total. The dealer has a 4 up card. Which of the options below represents the best course of action for you?

My Options

- A) Stand
- B) Hit
- C) Double down
- D) Split
- E) Surrender

Situation #19 Answer

You can't split and you won't surrender, so that leaves hit, stand, or double down as your options to consider. You've a **soft total**, so you won't stand since there's no way to break on the hand. To hit or double, that's the question. Sometimes the correct move in perfect basic strategy is determined by your hand, sometimes by the dealers up card, and sometimes by both factors. This hand is one of the latter. You almost can't help but improve your hand by hitting. The dealer has a breaking card up and will, in fact, break 40 percent of the time with a 4 showing. The correct move here is to double down, maximizing your units of profit. If you just hit the hand, you're ceding one of your weapons to the dealer. Whenever the dealer shows a 4, 5, or 6 up, she's in a very weak position, and you need to make her pay as much as possible, whenever possible. This is one of those times.

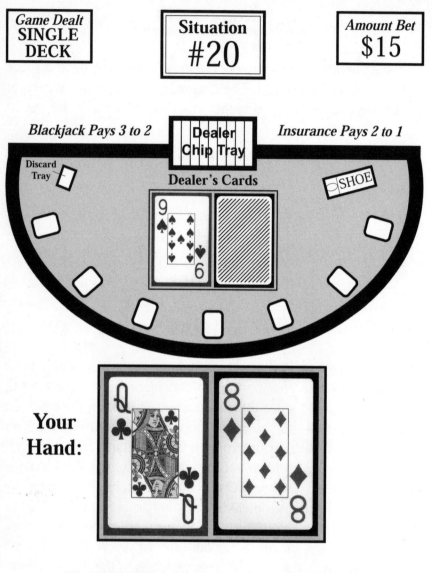

Game Dealt
SINGLE DECK

Situation #20

Amount Bet $15

Blackjack Pays 3 to 2

Dealer Chip Tray

Insurance Pays 2 to 1

Discard Tray

Dealer's Cards

SHOE

9♠

6

Your Hand:

Q♣

8♦

Variable House Rules in Play This Hand:

1. Double Down: Any two cards
2. Double Down After Splitting: No
3. Surrender Allowed: Yes
4. Dealer Soft 17s: Must stand

Situation #20

You are playing in a single-deck game, and have been dealt a Queen and an 8 for an 18 total. The dealer's up card is a 9. Which of the options below should you choose?

My Options

A) Stand

B) Hit

C) Double down

D) Split

E) Surrender

Situation #20 Answer

Often in blackjack you'll catch a hand like this in which there's nothing you can do except take what you're dealt and hope for the best. You can figure the dealer for a 19, since you should assume any card you can't see is worth 10, which leaves you a bit short with your 18. However, there is a bright side. Even though you assume that the dealer has a 10 in the hole, actually more cards are worth something other than a 10 than there are 10-count cards. Of those, only the Aces (besides the 10s) beat you. If the dealer has a 9 in the hole, you push. If she has an 8, you win. If she has a 2 through a 7, she must hit and could break. So, even though there is nothing you can really do with this hand except stand and hope, it isn't always a lost cause. Similarly, even if you're a card counter, 85 percent of the time you'll still be playing perfect basic strategy, the same strategy you're learning in this book.

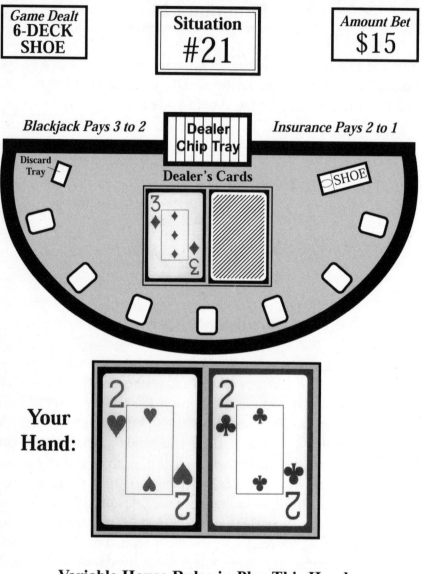

Game Dealt
6-DECK SHOE

Situation #21

Amount Bet
$15

Blackjack Pays 3 to 2

Dealer Chip Tray

Insurance Pays 2 to 1

Discard Tray

Dealer's Cards

SHOE

Your Hand:

Variable House Rules in Play This Hand:

1. Double Down: Any two cards
2. Double Down After Splitting: Yes
3. Surrender Allowed: No
4. Dealer Soft 17s: Must hit

Situation #21

You are playing in a 6-deck shoe game, and have been dealt a pair of 2s. The dealer's up card is a 3. Which of the options below represents the best move on your part?

My Options

A) Stand

B) Hit

C) Double down

D) Split

E) Surrender

Situation #21 Answer

Well, you're definitely not going to stand or surrender, so those two options are out. That leaves hit, double, or split. If you double down, you'll have—at best—a hard 14 or soft 15, hardly scintillating hands. That leaves hit or split. While a 3 up is not a very good card for the dealer, she will make a made hand 62 percent of the time, so if you split this hand you're playing two poor hands (potential 12s) against a hand the dealer will make more than six times in ten. You can't make a silk purse out of this sow's ear of a hand, so the best move is to suck it up and just hit and hope you can make a made hand of some sort. Because you're in a 6-deck shoe game, many small cards could come in clumps, helping the dealer more than you. If this were a single-deck game, with its truer outcomes (and more busting hands) for the dealer with her 3 up, you would split the 2s, but in a shoe game, just hit.

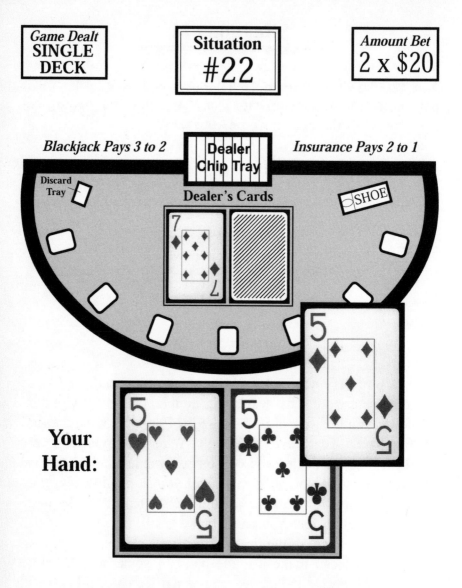

Variable House Rules in Play This Hand:

1. Double Down: Any two cards
2. Double Down After Splitting: Yes
3. Surrender Allowed: Yes
4. Dealer Soft 17s: Must hit

Situation #22

You are playing in a single-deck game. You have received a pair of 5s against the dealer's 7. You carelessly signal that you want to split your 5s instead of doubling—your actual intent. After receiving another 5 on your new first hand, what should you do with this hand, given the variable rules shown on the opposite page?

My Options

A) Hit.
B) Double down and play the next hand out.
C) Double down on this hand and surrender the other hand.
D) Split again and play three hands.
E) Surrender.
F) Stand.

Situation #22 Answer

Well, standing would be about as stupid as your original move in splitting the 5s, something you should *never* do under any circumstances. Next on the list of "stupid things I could still do" would be to split this into a third hand. The third 5 actually bails you out. Now you have a 10, so you should double, as was your original intent on the first two 5s. By getting another $20 out there on this first hand, you might offset the damage that will likely come on the second hand. You might also catch a small card on the second hand, make a made hand, and still win both.

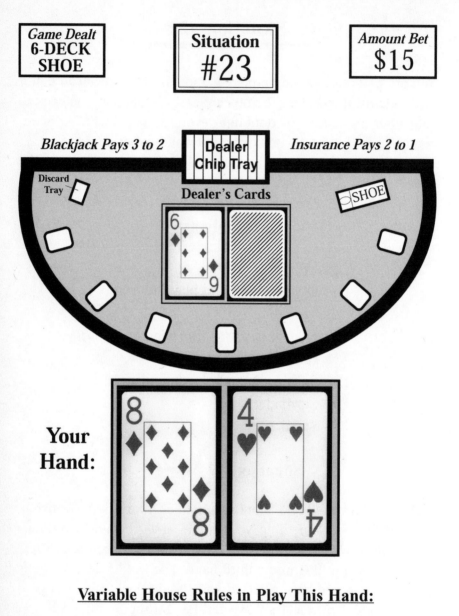

Variable House Rules in Play This Hand:

1. Double Down: Any two cards
2. Double Down After Splitting: Yes
3. Surrender Allowed: No
4. Dealer Soft 17s: Must hit

Situation #23

You are playing in a 6-deck shoe game, and have been dealt a hard 12 total. The dealer's up card is a 6. Which of the options below represents the correct move?

My Options

A) Stand

B) Hit

C) Double down

D) Split

E) Surrender

Situation #23 Answer

You have a breaking hand and so (probably) does the dealer. A breaking hand means that if you take one more card you could conceivably break. In your case, any 10-count card will break you. In the dealer's case, she could have any card from a 6 through a King in the hole and break with one more card. Strong possibility. That is why a 6 up is so hazardous for a dealer. Thus, another cardinal principle of playing perfect basic strategy dictates that when the dealer and you both have a breaking hand, you should stand and let the dealer take her required chances at breaking. The dealer will only make a made hand 58 percent of the time with a 6 up, and you will increase your losses by hitting this hand in this situation because some of the time you will break (and needlessly so) when the dealer will often break after you.

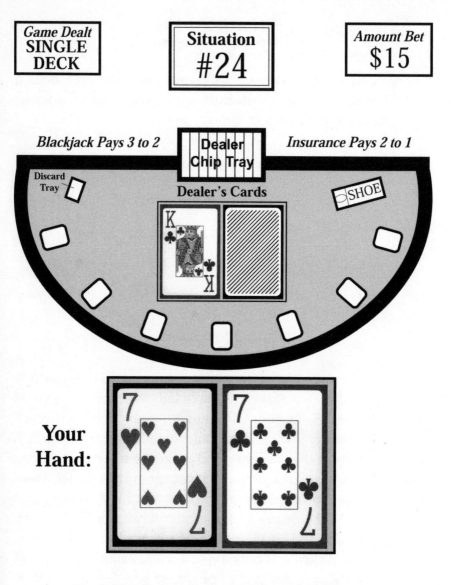

| Game Dealt SINGLE DECK | Situation #24 | Amount Bet $15 |

Blackjack Pays 3 to 2   Insurance Pays 2 to 1

Your Hand:

Variable House Rules in Play This Hand:

1. Double Down: 10 or 11 only
2. Double Down After Splitting: Yes
3. Surrender Allowed: Yes
4. Dealer Soft 17s: Must hit

Situation #24

You are playing in a single-deck game, and have been dealt a pair of 7s for a hard 14 total. The dealer's up card is a King. Which of the options below represents the correct move?

My Options

A) Stand

B) Hit

C) Double down

D) Split

E) Surrender

Situation #24 Answer

Obviously, we won't double on this hand. If we split it, we'll have two underdog hands instead of one, since we have to assume the dealer has a 10-count card down and we'll draw the same to our hands, so splitting is out. Normally you should hit this hand, playing it like a 14 against a 10. *However*, since this is a single-deck game, and you probably need to hit 21 to win the hand because the dealer has a likely 20, this effectively means that you need to catch another 7 to make your 21. Not too likely, since you already hold two 7s in your hand. As strange as it may seem, you should stand on this hand if surrender is not an option, and surrender if it is. If your hard 14 was composed of a 10-4, 9-5, or 8-6, then by all means you will hit instead of stand. Standing on a pair of 7s against a 10 in a single-deck game is one of the finer points of perfect basic strategy play.

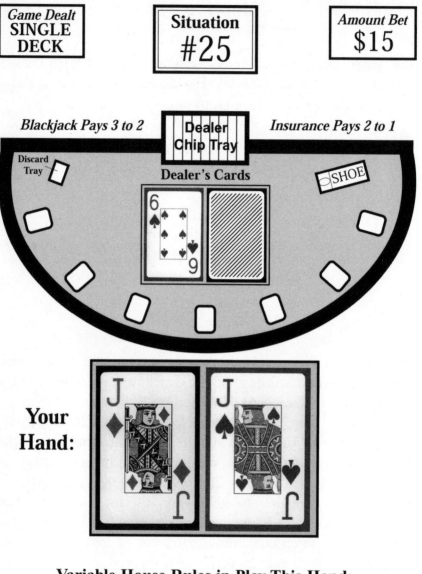

Game Dealt
SINGLE
DECK

Situation
#25

Amount Bet
$15

Blackjack Pays 3 to 2

Dealer
Chip Tray

Insurance Pays 2 to 1

Discard
Tray

Dealer's Cards

SHOE

**Your
Hand:**

Variable House Rules in Play This Hand:

1. Double Down: 10 or 11 only
2. Double Down After Splitting: Yes
3. Surrender Allowed: Yes
4. Dealer Soft 17s: Must hit

Situation #25

You are playing in a single-deck game, and have been dealt a pair of Jacks for a 20 total. Happily for you, the dealer's up card is a 6, the worst card she can get. Which of the options below represents the correct move?

My Options

    A)   Stand

    B)   Hit

    C)   Double down

    D)   Split

    E)   Surrender

Situation #25 Answer

You won't surrender this powerful hand, nor will you hit or double down in an effort to catch an Ace for 21. That leaves you with the option of standing or splitting. While it wouldn't be the worst play in the world to split a pair of 10s against a 6 because of the high number of times a dealer will break when showing a 6 up, you will lose units in the long run by splitting instead of standing. Rarely will you do anything on a 20 except stand—whether the game is single or multiple deck—and collect your single-unit win the great majority of the time.

Variable House Rules in Play This Hand:

1. Double Down: 10 or 11 only
2. Double Down After Splitting: Yes
3. Surrender Allowed: Yes
4. Dealer Soft 17s: Must stand

Situation #26

You are playing in a single-deck game, and have been dealt a 6 and a 4 for a 10 total. The dealer shows a 10 up card. Which of the options below represents the correct move?

My Options

A) Stand
B) Hit
C) Double down
D) Split
E) Surrender

Situation #26 Answer

You aren't going to stand (obviously), surrender (foolish), or split (can't) this hand. That leaves you with the options of hitting or doubling. The most-powerful hand for doubling down is an 11 followed closely by the 10, which you hold. Doubling down is one of the player's most effective weapons against the dealer in an effort to gain an edge against the house. While the 10 was nice to get, you can't double in this situation because the dealer has a 10 also. If you double, you'll only get one more card (for twice the money), and if you miss catching a 10-count card, you're stuck with your total, which could be a 12, 13, 14, 15, and so on. Well, you get the picture. The dealer, on the other hand, can (must) hit again if she catches a 12, 13, 14, 15, or 16, and could end up making a made hand to beat you. On a 10 versus 10, just hit, whether in a single- or multiple-deck game.

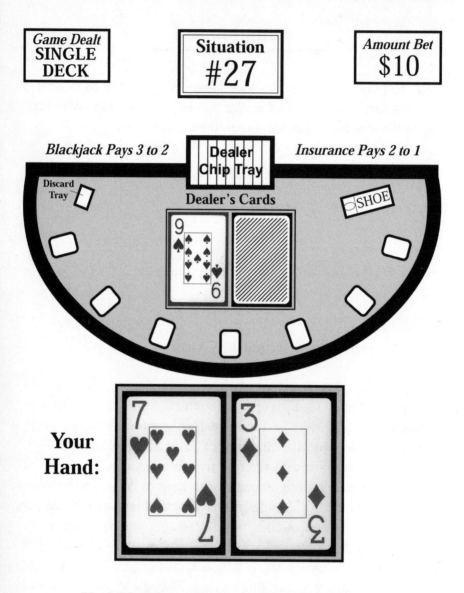

Game Dealt	Situation	Amount Bet
SINGLE DECK	**#27**	**$10**

Blackjack Pays 3 to 2

Insurance Pays 2 to 1

Dealer Chip Tray

Dealer's Cards

Discard Tray

SHOE

Your Hand:

Variable House Rules in Play This Hand:

1. Double Down: Any two cards
2. Double Down After Splitting: Yes
3. Surrender Allowed: Yes
4. Dealer Soft 17s: Must stand

Situation #27

You are playing in a single-deck game, and have been dealt a 7 and a 3 for a 10 total. The dealer shows a 9 up card. Which of the options below represents the correct move?

My Options

    A)   Stand
    B)   Hit
    C)   Double down
    D)   Split
    E)   Surrender

Situation #27 Answer

This situation is very similar to situation #26, but it is different enough to require a different approach. You've learned by now to treat any unseen card as being worth 10. So you can assume the dealer has a 19 and you can assume that the next card to be dealt to you will be a 10, giving you a 20 total. Granted there'll be plenty of occasions when you'll not catch a 10; however, the number of times you win two units instead of one will offset the number of times you lose on this hand. Besides, for every time you don't catch your needed 10 on this hand, the dealer will have the same number of hands in which she doesn't hold a 10 in the hole either. This principle of perfect basic strategy requires that you double down on a 10 against any dealer up card of a 2 through a 9 and just hit it when the dealer shows a 10 or Ace.

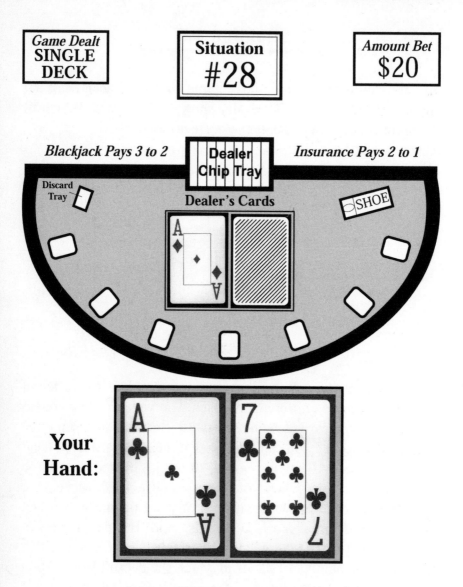

| Game Dealt SINGLE DECK | Situation #28 | Amount Bet $20 |

Blackjack Pays 3 to 2

Insurance Pays 2 to 1

Dealer Chip Tray

Discard Tray

Dealer's Cards

SHOE

Your Hand:

Variable House Rules in Play This Hand:

1. Double Down: Any two cards
2. Double Down After Splitting: Yes
3. Surrender Allowed: Yes
4. Dealer Soft 17s: Must hit

Situation #28

You are playing in a single-deck game, and have been dealt an Ace and a 7 for a soft 18 total. The dealer shows an Ace and does not have a blackjack. Which of the options below represents the correct move?

My Options

A) Stand

B) Hit

C) Double Down

D) Split

E) Surrender

Situation #28 Answer

When a dealer shows an Ace up, she will make a made hand (17 or more) 83 percent of the time in a single-deck game, so you're up against it on this hand. While a soft 18 can be improved, it will take an Ace, 2, or 3 to do so, and the odds are stacked against you. You are more likely to draw a 10 for a hard 18 or worsen your position. Better to leave well enough alone on this hand and stand, hoping either that you can pull off a push or that the dealer will break.

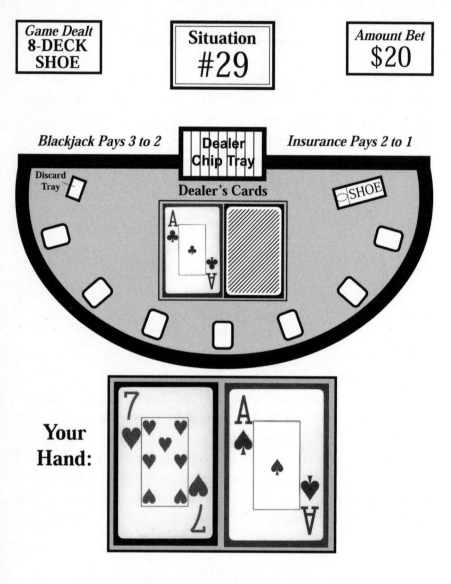

Game Dealt
8-DECK
SHOE

Situation
#29

Amount Bet
$20

Blackjack Pays 3 to 2

Dealer Chip Tray

Insurance Pays 2 to 1

Discard Tray

Dealer's Cards

SHOE

Your Hand:

Variable House Rules in Play This Hand:

1. Double Down: Any two cards
2. Double Down After Splitting: Yes
3. Surrender Allowed: Yes
4. Dealer Soft 17s: Must hit

Situation #29

You are playing in an 8-deck shoe game, and have been dealt a 7 and an Ace for a soft 18 total. The dealer shows an Ace and does not have a blackjack. Which of the options below represents the correct move?

My Options

A) Stand
B) Hit
C) Double down
D) Split
E) Surrender

Situation #29 Answer

This situation is almost identical to situation #28, the only difference being that you are now in an 8-deck shoe game instead of a single-deck game. But wouldn't the play be the same? No, in a multiple-deck game, you would hit this hand instead of stand. The reason? Because in a shoe game there are many more small cards that often come in clumps, and you stand a better chance of catching an Ace, 2, or 3. As mentioned in situation #28, you're up against it on this hand since the dealer will make a made hand more than 80 percent of the time she shows an Ace as her up card. As with standing on a pair of 7s against a 10 in a single-deck game, this hand represents one of the finer points of playing perfect basic strategy and illustrates why you need to memorize and implement the basic strategy shown in the charts included in this book if you want to become a consistent winner.

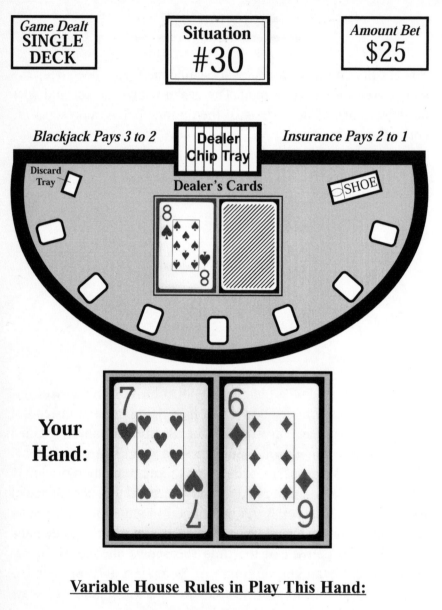

Variable House Rules in Play This Hand:

1. Double Down: Any two cards
2. Double Down After Splitting: Yes
3. Surrender Allowed: No
4. Dealer Soft 17s: Must hit

Situation #30

You are playing in a single-deck game, and have been dealt a 7 and a 6 for a hard 13 total. The dealer's up card is an 8. Of the options listed below, which one is your best move?

My Options

- A) Stand
- B) Hit
- C) Double down
- D) Split
- E) Surrender

Situation #30 Answer

Your hard 13 is a poor hand. With an 8 showing, you have to play the dealer for an 18, a made hand. Standing would be foolish, because a dealer will make a made hand 76 percent of the time when she has an 8 showing. You can't split, you won't double, and surrender isn't allowed in this casino. All you can (and should) do is hit this hand and hope you improve to a made hand (17 or more) without breaking. Again, according to perfect basic strategy, whenever you have a breaking hand (a 12–16) and the dealer has a made hand (7-Ace showing), you have to hit until you get at least 17 or more, or break trying. If, for example, you were to draw a 3 to this hand for a 16 total, you must still hit again and not stop because you successfully caught a small card and think that a big card will likely follow.

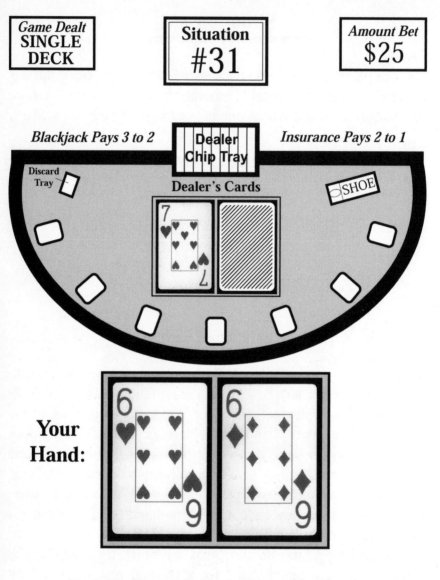

Game Dealt
SINGLE DECK

Situation #31

Amount Bet
$25

Blackjack Pays 3 to 2

Dealer Chip Tray

Insurance Pays 2 to 1

Discard Tray

Dealer's Cards

SHOE

Your Hand:

Variable House Rules in Play This Hand:

1. Double Down: Any two cards
2. Double Down After Splitting: Yes
3. Surrender Allowed: No
4. Dealer Soft 17s: Must hit

Situation #31

You are playing in a single-deck game, and have been dealt a pair of 6s for a hard 12 total. The dealer's up card is a 7. Which of the options listed below represents your best play?

My Options

A) Stand
B) Hit
C) Double down
D) Split
E) Surrender

Situation #31 Answer

When you receive a pair, your first order of business is to consider whether it's beneficial to split them. In this case you have a 12 against a 7 if you don't split them or two 6s against a 7 if you do. Your two 6s should then be looked at as potential 16s since there are more cards worth 10 than any other rank. Since a hard 16 is the worst hand you can hold against a made hand, clearly splitting this hand is the wrong move. You also won't double down because one card (any 10-count card) will cause you to break. Surrender is not an option in this casino, so it's either hit or stand. The dealer will make a made hand 74 percent of the time she shows a 7 up, which means you're going to have to try to make a hand. Hit this hard 12 until you get at least 17 or more, or break trying.

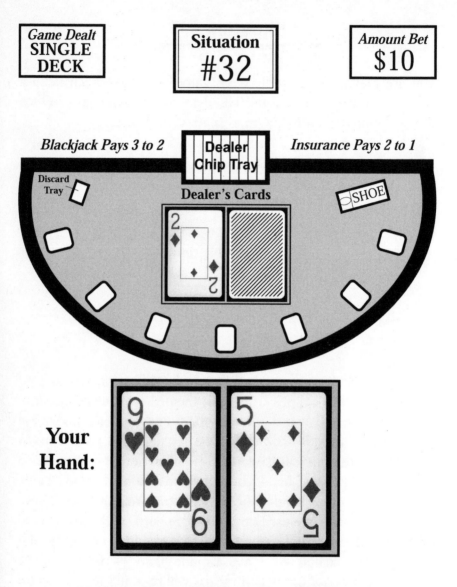

Game Dealt	Situation	Amount Bet
SINGLE DECK	#32	$10

Blackjack Pays 3 to 2

Insurance Pays 2 to 1

Dealer Chip Tray

Discard Tray

Dealer's Cards

SHOE

Your Hand:

Variable House Rules in Play This Hand:

1. Double Down: 10 and 11 only
2. Double Down After Splitting: Yes
3. Surrender Allowed: Yes
4. Dealer Soft 17s: Must hit

Situation #32

You are playing in a single-deck game, and have been dealt a 9 and a 5 for a hard 14 total. The dealer's up card is a 2. Which of the options listed below represents your best play?

My Options

A) Stand
B) Hit
C) Double down
D) Split
E) Surrender

Situation #32 Answer

This situation is one of those unexciting hands that you can't do much about. Because you have a hard 14 total, you have to be aware of breaking if you hit. The dealer technically has a breaking hand as well, although given that she has a 2 up, she'd probably need to have a 10 in the hole and hit another 10 to break to give you a chance. And as unattractive as that sounds, that is your best course of action on this hand. The cardinal principle of playing perfect basic strategy that applies here is this: when both the dealer and you hold breaking hands, you should stand and take your chances on the dealer breaking. Don't expect a lot out of this hand, though, because the dealer will make a made hand 65 percent of the time when showing a 2 up. Still, if you hit this hand as opposed to standing, you'll show a negative win rate in terms of units won over the long haul.

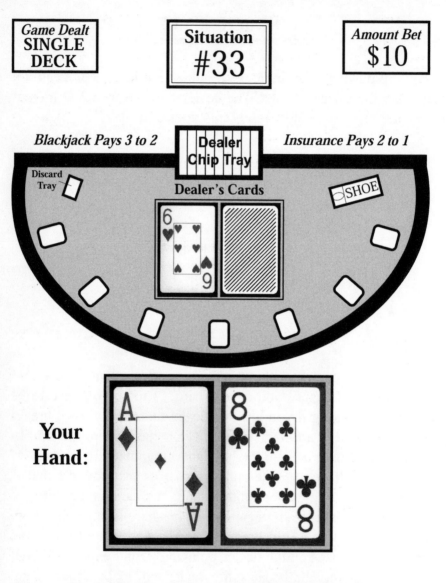

Game Dealt
**SINGLE
DECK**

**Situation
#33**

Amount Bet
$10

Blackjack Pays 3 to 2

**Dealer
Chip Tray**

Insurance Pays 2 to 1

Discard
Tray

Dealer's Cards

SHOE

**Your
Hand:**

Variable House Rules in Play This Hand:

1. Double Down: Any two cards
2. Double Down After Splitting: Yes
3. Surrender Allowed: Yes
4. Dealer Soft 17s: Must hit

Situation #33

You are playing in a single-deck game, and have been dealt an Ace and an 8 for a soft 19 total. The dealer's up card is a 6. Which of the options listed below represents your best play?

My Options

A) Stand

B) Hit

C) Double down

D) Split

E) Surrender

Situation #33 Answer

You're not going to surrender, and you can't split because you don't have a pair. You have 19, so hitting would be pointless. That leaves you with two viable options: standing or doubling. In most cases you would stand on any 19 since it's a solid hand and you have little chance of improving it. In this situation, however, because the dealer has a 6 up—a terrible card for the dealer—you will use her 6 against her by doubling down for an additional $10. No matter what you hit, you can't break. Many of the cards you could draw will be 10s, leaving you with a hard 19. While 7 of the 13 card ranks will lessen your total, 6 will keep it the same or improve it. And again, you're doubling here more because of the dealer up card than your hand. The occasional loss you will suffer by doubling on this hand will be more than made back by your greatly increased number of units won.

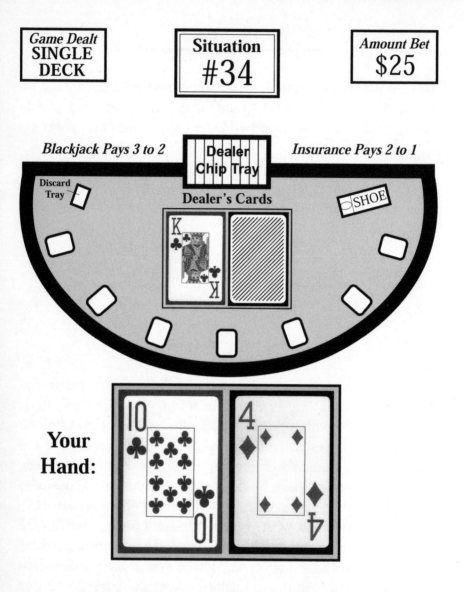

| Game Dealt **SINGLE DECK** | **Situation #34** | *Amount Bet* **$25** |

Blackjack Pays 3 to 2

Insurance Pays 2 to 1

Dealer Chip Tray

Discard Tray

SHOE

Dealer's Cards

Your Hand:

Variable House Rules in Play This Hand:

1. Double Down: Any two cards
2. Double Down After Splitting: Yes
3. Surrender Allowed: Yes
4. Dealer Soft 17s: Must hit

Situation #34

You are playing in a single-deck game, and have been dealt a 10 and a 4 for a hard 14 total. The dealer's up card is a King. When the dealer **peeks** at her hole card to see if she has a blackjack, she puts her hand down and then picks it back up again to take a second peek. Ensured that she does not have a blackjack, she continues with her duties, asking you what you would like to do? Given her actions, what should you do?

My Options

- A) Stand
- B) Hit
- C) Double down
- D) Split
- E) Surrender

Situation #34 Answer

Even though you have a breaking hand against a made hand, you should stand. Why? Because the dealer likely has a 4 in the hole for 14 and could break when it's her turn to draw. How do I know? Experience. Anytime a dealer takes a second look at her hole card to see if she has an Ace, it's because she isn't sure of what she has seen the first time. The only cards you can confuse with a peek-type look are Aces and 4s. Try it yourself. Since she doesn't flip it over for a blackjack after taking the second peek, she likely has a 4.

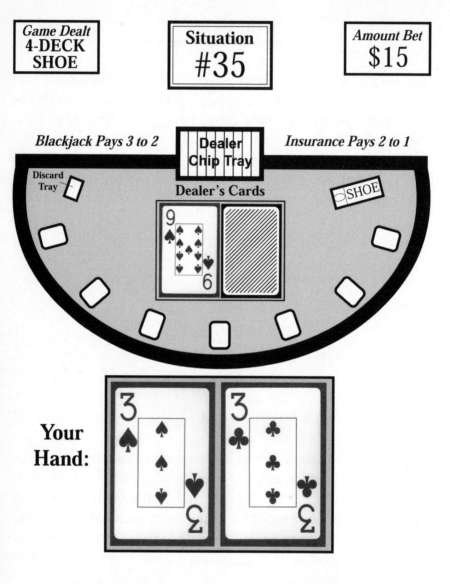

| Game Dealt 4-DECK SHOE | Situation #35 | Amount Bet $15 |

Your Hand:

Variable House Rules in Play This Hand:

1. Double Down: Any two cards
2. Double Down After Splitting: Yes
3. Surrender Allowed: No
4. Dealer Soft 17s: Must hit

Situation #35

You are playing in a 4-deck shoe game, and catch a pair of 3s against the dealer's 9 up. Which of the options listed below represents your best play?

My Options

- A) Stand
- B) Hit
- C) Double down
- D) Split
- E) Surrender

Situation #35 Answer

Well, you've got a real uphill battle on your hands here. The dealer has a nice up card and you've got squat. And if you split them, you've got double squat (two breaking hands instead of one), so splitting is out of the question. Obviously, you won't double, since that would be doubling your exposure to a bad situation. You can't surrender because this casino doesn't allow it. That leaves you with choosing between hitting and standing, and you're certainly not going to stand on a 6. Therefore, by process of elimination, the correct choice is to hit until you have a made hand (17 or more) or die trying (break).

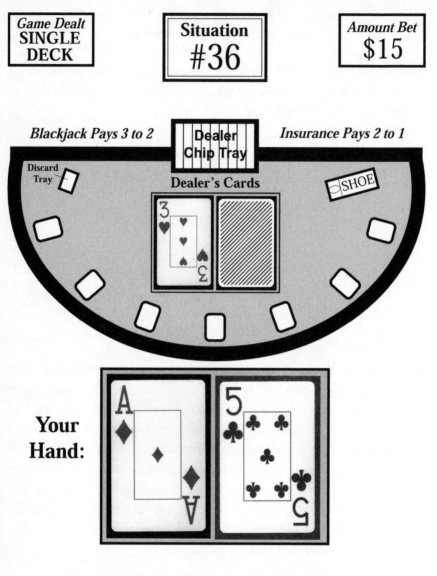

| Game Dealt SINGLE DECK | Situation #36 | Amount Bet $15 |

Blackjack Pays 3 to 2   Insurance Pays 2 to 1

Dealer Chip Tray

Discard Tray

Dealer's Cards

SHOE

Your Hand:

Variable House Rules in Play This Hand:

1. Double Down: Any two cards
2. Double Down After Splitting: Yes
3. Surrender Allowed: Yes
4. Dealer Soft 17s: Must hit

Situation #36

You are playing in a single-deck game, and receive an Ace and a 5 for a soft 16 against the dealer's 3 up. Which of the options listed below is your best move?

My Options

- A) Stand
- B) Hit
- C) Double down
- D) Split
- E) Surrender

Situation #36 Answer

You won't surrender because the dealer has a bad hand and you have a soft total, which can always turn into a good hand. You can't split because you don't have a pair, and you won't stand because your soft total can be improved on without fear of breaking at this point. This leaves you with the options of hitting or doubling down. When a dealer shows a 3 up, she'll make a made hand 62 percent of the time, which means 17 or more. If you double on this hand, you'll make many hard 16s because of the 10-count cards and won't be able to hit again. For this reason, the best move on this hand would be just to hit until you get a hard 13 or more, or a soft 18–21.

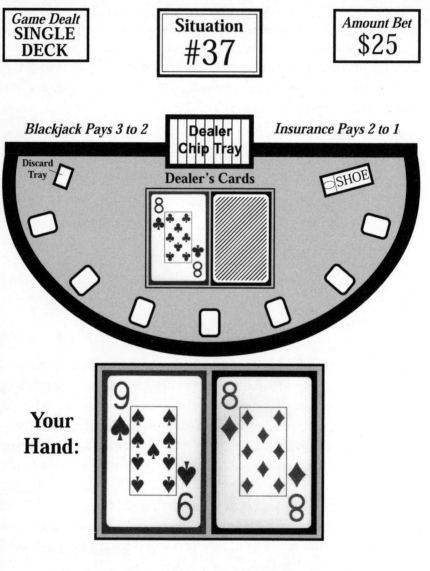

Game Dealt
SINGLE DECK

Situation #37

Amount Bet
$25

Blackjack Pays 3 to 2

Dealer Chip Tray

Insurance Pays 2 to 1

Discard Tray

Dealer's Cards

SHOE

Your Hand:

Variable House Rules in Play This Hand:

1. Double Down: Any two cards
2. Double Down After Splitting: Yes
3. Surrender Allowed: Yes
4. Dealer Soft 17s: Must stand

Situation #37

You are playing in a single-deck game, and have been dealt a 9 and an 8 for a 17 total against the dealer's 8 up. Which of the options listed below is your best move and why?

My Options

    A)   Stand
    B)   Hit
    C)   Double down
    D)   Split
    E)   Surrender

Situation #37 Answer

You can't split because you don't have a pair. You won't surrender because you have a made hand. You won't double down on a 17 because, as you already know, you don't double down on any total higher than an 11 because of the possibility of breaking. This leaves you with the options of hitting or standing. You should stand. But why stand on this hand when you would hit a hard 16 against the 8, a probable 18 hand for the dealer? Because 17 is the magic number in blackjack. Dealers have to hit until they get at least 17, at which point they have to stand. This is why you hit your 16s but not your 17s. And all isn't necessarily lost on this hand. While you do have to figure the dealer for an 18 in terms of strategy because more cards are worth 10 than any other one number, there are more total cards worth something other than 10 (2s–9s). In this situation an Ace down is even worse than a 10 for you.

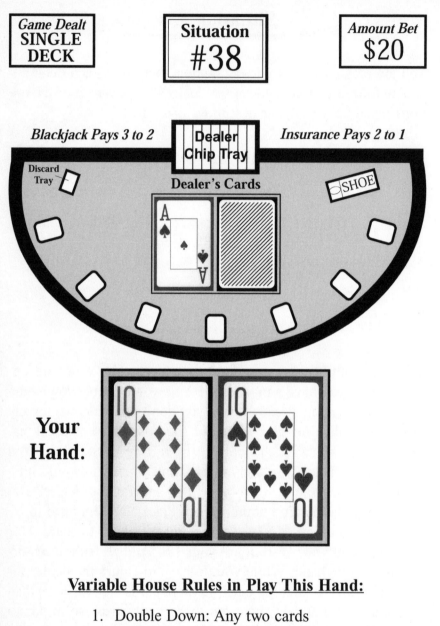

| Game Dealt SINGLE DECK | Situation #38 | Amount Bet $20 |

Blackjack Pays 3 to 2   Insurance Pays 2 to 1

Your Hand:

Variable House Rules in Play This Hand:

1. Double Down: Any two cards
2. Double Down After Splitting: Yes
3. Surrender Allowed: Yes
4. Dealer Soft 17s: Must stand

Situation #38

You are playing in a single-deck game, and have been dealt a pair of 10s against the dealer's Ace up. The dealer asks if you want insurance. Do you?

My Options

    A)   Take insurance.

    B)   Do not take insurance.

Situation #38 Answer

As you learned earlier in this book, insurance is a bad bet unless you are a proficient card counter and utilize it in certain situations with the right count. So you quickly know you are not going to take insurance, *ever*. But just how bad a bet is it in terms of money won or lost? Let's figure it out.

In this single-deck game of 52 cards, there are 16 cards worth 10 (the 10s, Jacks, Queens, and Kings), one of which the dealer will need as her hole card to have the blackjack. There are, then, 36 cards not worth 10. There are three cards on the table, two of which are 10s (your hand). This means there are 35 cards left that are not worth 10, and 14 that are, for a 35-to-14 ratio. Consider if you took out insurance in this situation for 98 hands in a row for $10 each time (the required half of your $20 bet). You'd win the insurance bet 28 times and lose it 70 times. Thus, 28 wins × $20 (your 2-to-1 winning insurance bets) = $560 in wins, and 70 losses × $10 (your losing insurance bets) = $700. That's a loss of $140 for every 98 times you take insurance on this hand. Insurance is always a bad bet. Never, never take insurance.

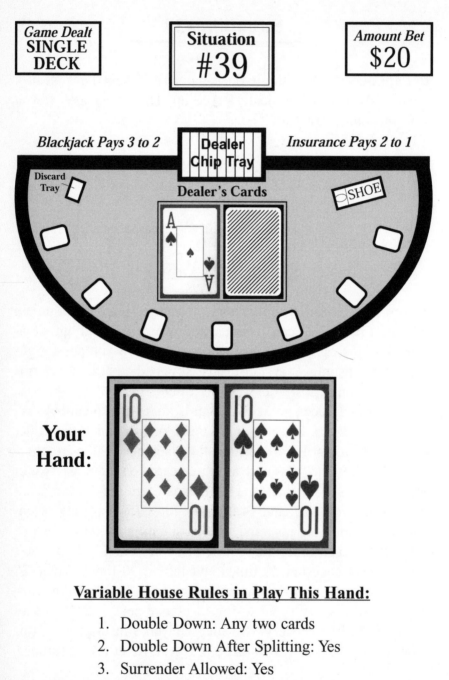

| Game Dealt SINGLE DECK | Situation #39 | Amount Bet $20 |

Variable House Rules in Play This Hand:

1. Double Down: Any two cards
2. Double Down After Splitting: Yes
3. Surrender Allowed: Yes
4. Dealer Soft 17s: Must stand

Situation #39

After you turned down the dealer's offer of insurance on this hand, she did not have the 10-count card in the hole for a blackjack. It is now your turn to act. You have to decide whether to stand on this hand or split the 10s for two hands. Which should you do?

My Options

A) Stand.

B) Split since there is a good ratio of 10-count cards left in the deck, and the dealer positively doesn't have one.

Situation #39 Answer

Are you a card counter? No? Then don't act like one. You'll just get yourself into trouble. Concentrate on playing the best perfect basic strategy you can until the day comes when you are a proficient card counter. Until then, unless you know *for sure* the deck's count and condition, *always* stand on a hard 20. If you go monkeying around by splitting a 20 because you *think* you know a deck's condition—especially against an Ace up—you could easily lose two hands instead of one. Don't get greedy until you're good enough to get greedy.

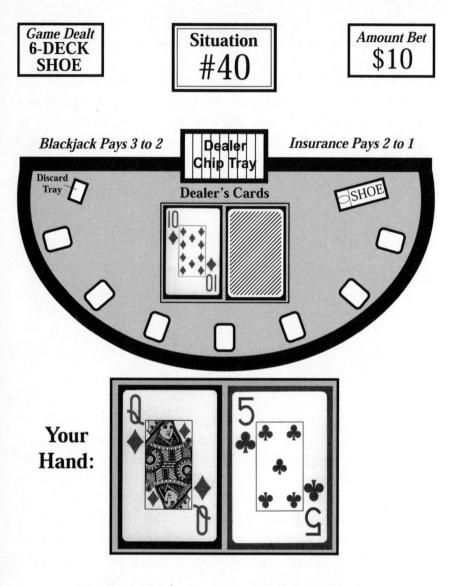

| Game Dealt 6-DECK SHOE | Situation #40 | Amount Bet $10 |

Blackjack Pays 3 to 2   **Dealer Chip Tray**   **Insurance Pays 2 to 1**

Discard Tray

Dealer's Cards

SHOE

Your Hand:

Variable House Rules in Play This Hand:

1. Double Down: Any two cards
2. Double Down After Splitting: Yes
3. Surrender Allowed: Yes
4. Dealer Soft 17s: Must stand

Situation #40

In a 6-deck shoe game, you have received a Queen and a 5 for a hard 15 total against the dealer's 10 up. Which of the below options is your best choice, and why?

My Options

- A) Stand
- B) Hit
- C) Double down
- D) Split
- E) Surrender

Situation #40 Answer

You cannot split this hand because your two cards are not of equal value. You will not double because you could easily break, thereby losing twice as much. That leaves you with the options of hitting, standing, or surrendering. Let's calculate your chances based on playing this exact hand 100 times in a row in each of the three options left to us. If you stand, you will lose 76 percent of the time, winning only when the dealer busts. If you hit, you will lose 71 percent of the time. If you surrender, you will lose half your bet on all 100 hands. In terms of $1,000 put into play ($10 × 100 hands), this is what it translates into for each of the three strategies: by surrendering every time, you will have $500 left; by standing every time, you will have $480 left; by hitting this hand every time, you will have $580 left. While all three propositions are losers, you will lose less money by hitting than either standing or surrendering. Hit this hand every time without thinking about it.

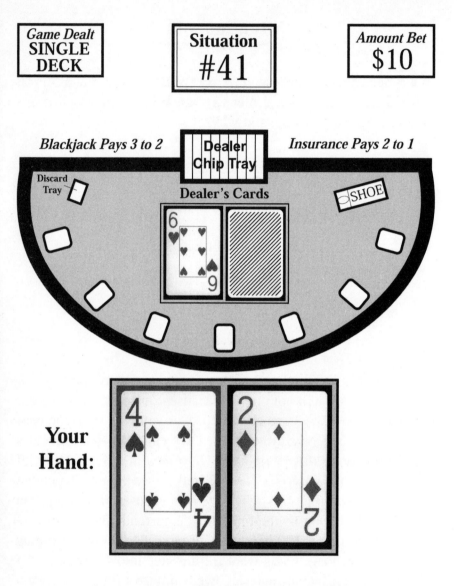

Game Dealt SINGLE DECK	Situation #41	Amount Bet $10

Blackjack Pays 3 to 2

Dealer Chip Tray

Insurance Pays 2 to 1

Discard Tray

Dealer's Cards

SHOE

Your Hand:

Variable House Rules in Play This Hand:

1. Double Down: Any two cards
2. Double Down After Splitting: Yes
3. Surrender Allowed: Yes
4. Dealer Soft 17s: Must stand

Situation #41

In a single-deck game, you have been dealt a 4 and a 2 for a 6 total. The dealer receives a 6 as her up card. Which of the below options is your best choice, and why?

My Options

A) Stand

B) Hit

C) Double down

D) Split

E) Surrender

Situation #41 Answer

You certainly won't stand because you could easily improve your hand by hitting without danger of breaking. You can't split because you don't have a pair, and you won't surrender because the dealer has such a poor up card. Your choices, then, are to either hit or double down. The dealer's up card, in this case, is actually more important to you than your own hand. With a 6 up, she is going to break 42 percent of the time. While you would like to double down here, you just can't because there are too many small cards that could give you a 7, 8, 9, 10, or 11 total, all of which could be improved on by drawing still another card. By doubling down on such a low total as 6, you could easily leave yourself out in the cold with a low three-card total and end up losing twice as much. Another cardinal principle in playing perfect basic strategy says that with a total of 7 or below (assuming you don't hold a pair of 2s or 3s) you only hit. Don't consider doubling until you have a total of at least 8, and even then, it needs to be a 5–3 combination, not 6–2, as you learned earlier in this book (see situation #4).

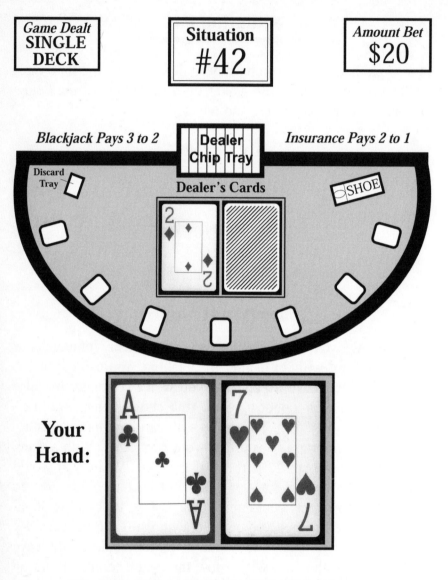

Game Dealt
SINGLE
DECK

Situation
#42

Amount Bet
$20

Blackjack Pays 3 to 2

Dealer
Chip Tray

Insurance Pays 2 to 1

Discard
Tray

Dealer's Cards

SHOE

Your
Hand:

Variable House Rules in Play This Hand:

1. Double Down: Any two cards
2. Double Down After Splitting: Yes
3. Surrender Allowed: Yes
4. Dealer Soft 17s: Must stand

Situation #42

In a single-deck game you have been dealt an Ace and a 7 for a soft 18 total. The dealer receives a 2 as her up card. Which of the below options is your best choice, and why?

My Options

A) Stand
B) Hit
C) Double down
D) Split
E) Surrender

Situation #42 Answer

You won't surrender the hand because you have a good total. You can't split because you don't have a pair. That leaves you with the options of hitting, standing, or doubling down. A 2 is a danger-ous up card for the dealer to have against you. Usually, the only way a dealer will break with a deuce up is for her to have a 10 in the hole and draw another 10-count card. Barring that, the dealer will usually make a made hand. While a soft 18 isn't the best hand in the world, it's not bad against a weak up card like a 2. Computer simulations have shown that if you hit this hand in an effort to improve on your 18, you'll suffer a 7 percent drop in your unit win rate, which is significant in blackjack. Doubling leads to a 0.8 percent drop in your win rate, so the best option for this hand is to stand.

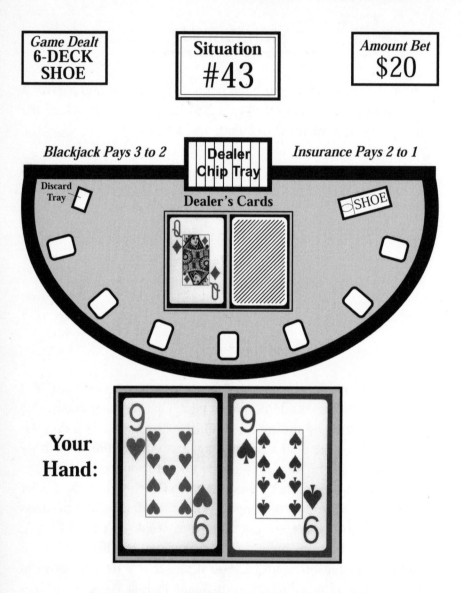

| Game Dealt 6-DECK SHOE | Situation #43 | Amount Bet $20 |

Blackjack Pays 3 to 2

Insurance Pays 2 to 1

Dealer Chip Tray

Discard Tray

Dealer's Cards

SHOE

Your Hand:

Variable House Rules in Play This Hand:

1. Double Down: Any two cards
2. Double Down After Splitting: Yes
3. Surrender Allowed: Yes
4. Dealer Soft 17s: Must stand

Situation #43

In a 6-deck shoe game, you have been dealt a pair of 9s for an 18 total against the dealer's Queen up card. Which of the below options is your best choice, and why?

My Options

A) Stand
B) Hit
C) Double down
D) Split
E) Surrender

Situation #43 Answer

Many beginners have a tendency to split virtually any pair they receive, but—as is the case here—splitting is the wrong move. As it stands, you are at a significant disadvantage with this hand because you have a hard 18 total against a possible 20. But if you split this hand, you will most likely be compounding your problem because you will be well on your way to a pair of 19s, not a good position against a possible 20. Of course, you will not surrender this hand because the dealer could very well have a 2 through a 7, which will give her a lesser-made hand or set her up for breaking. Suck it up on this hand, stand **pat**, and hope the dealer has something other than a 9 or 10 in the hole.

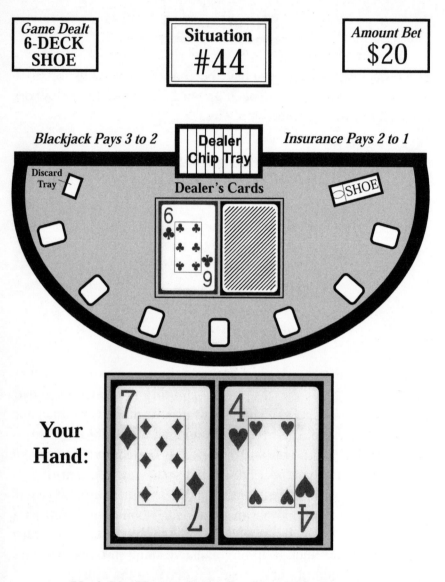

Game Dealt **6-DECK** **SHOE**	**Situation** **#44**	Amount Bet **$20**

Variable House Rules in Play This Hand:

1. Double Down: Any two cards
2. Double Down After Splitting: Yes
3. Surrender Allowed: Yes
4. Dealer Soft 17s: Must stand

Situation #44

In a 6-deck shoe game, you have been dealt a 7 and a 4 for an 11 total against the dealer's 6 up card. Which of the below options is your best choice and why?

My Options

A) Stand

B) Hit

C) Double down

D) Split

E) Surrender

Situation #44 Answer

When it comes to blackjack, this is the kind of hand you live for, an 11 against a 6. Next to a blackjack, this is the hand you'd like to catch every time. Why? First, because the 6 up card represents the best chance you have for the dealer to break. (Actually, a 5 or 6 up for the dealer is about the same, percentage-wise.) Second, because with an 11 total, many of your double downs (which is the correct move on this hand) will turn into 21s, an impossible hand for the dealer to beat and which will only occasionally turn into a push when the dealer makes a 21 as well. And when you're winning on your double downs, you're winning two units instead of one. It's absolutely critical in playing perfect basic strategy to maximize your double down and splitting opportunities because that's how you turn the edge in your favor.

Game Dealt
SINGLE DECK

**Situation
#45**

Amount Bet
$20

Blackjack Pays 3 to 2

Dealer
Chip Tray

Insurance Pays 2 to 1

Discard Tray

Dealer's Cards

SHOE

Your Hand:

Variable House Rules in Play This Hand:

1. Double Down: Any two cards
2. Double Down After Splitting: Yes
3. Surrender Allowed: Yes
4. Dealer Soft 17s: Must stand

Situation #45

In a single-deck game, you have been dealt a 5 and a Jack for a 15 total against the dealer's 5 up card. Which of the below options is your best choice, and why?

My Options

A) Stand
B) Hit
C) Double down
D) Split
E) Surrender

Situation #45 Answer

Obviously, you can't split and won't double down. That leaves you with choosing between standing, hitting, and surrendering, which this casino allows. A hard 15 total such as this hand is a poor one, indeed. What you do have going for you, however, is the fact that the dealer has a 5 up card, one of the two worst up cards she can have. With a 5 up, many times (43 percent, in fact) the dealer will break. While that does mean she'll make a made hand (17 or more) 57 percent of the time to beat you, it's preferable to stand rather than drawing in an effort to improve this dog of a hand. Some players might surrender this hand; however, I wouldn't. The percentages are roughly close enough to even that I wouldn't surrender to a big breaking card like a 5.

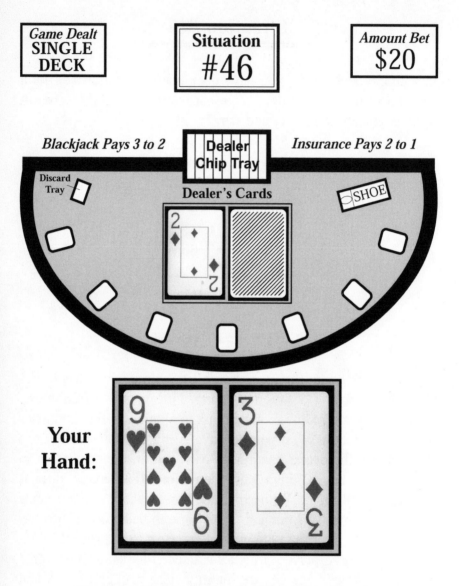

Blackjack Pays 3 to 2

Insurance Pays 2 to 1

Dealer Chip Tray

Discard Tray

Dealer's Cards

SHOE

Your Hand:

Variable House Rules in Play This Hand:

1. Double Down: Any two cards
2. Double Down After Splitting: Yes
3. Surrender Allowed: Yes
4. Dealer Soft 17s: Must stand

Situation #46

In a single-deck game, you have been dealt a 9 and a 3 for a hard 12 total against the dealer's 2 up card. Which of the below options is your best choice, and why?

My Options

A) Stand

B) Hit

C) Double down

D) Split

E) Surrender

Situation #46 Answer

Generally speaking, one of perfect basic strategy's cardinal rules is that you do not hit a breaking hand against a breaking hand. In review, a breaking hand is one that could go over 21 (causing you to break) by hitting one more card. In the case of this hand, if you hit it, you could catch a 10-count card for 22, which means that you break and lose your $20. In the same vein, the dealer has a 2 up. Since we have to play assuming the dealer has a 10-count card in the hole, that gives the dealer a 12 as well, and drawing one more card would give her a 22 as well. *However*, this hand is one of the two exceptions to the rule. When you have a hard 12 against a dealer's 2 up, you should hit the hand. You should also hit if the dealer shows a 3 against your hard 12. Why? Because percentages favor the dealer making a made hand with either a 2 or a 3 showing (65 percent and 62 percent, respectively). You should hit only one card to this hand (or two, if you draw an Ace on the first card), and then stand in an effort to make a made hand.

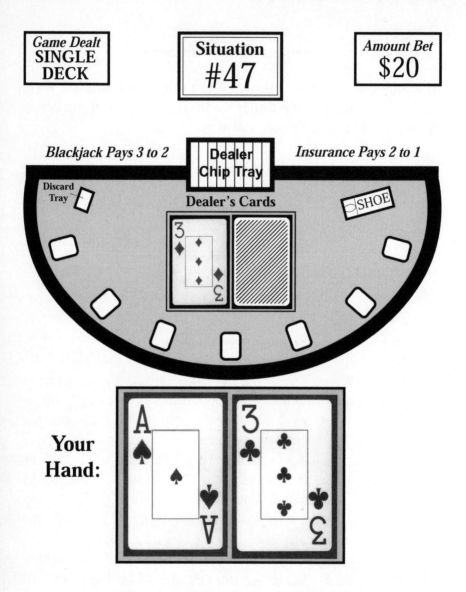

| Game Dealt SINGLE DECK | Situation #47 | Amount Bet $20 |

Blackjack Pays 3 to 2   *Insurance Pays 2 to 1*

Dealer Chip Tray

Discard Tray

Dealer's Cards

SHOE

Your Hand:

Variable House Rules in Play This Hand:

1. Double Down: Any two cards
2. Double Down After Splitting: Yes
3. Surrender Allowed: No
4. Dealer Soft 17s: Must stand

Situation #47

In a single-deck game, you have been dealt an Ace and a 3 for a soft 14 total against the dealer's 3 up card. Which of the below options is your best choice, and why?

My Options

A) Stand
B) Hit
C) Double down
D) Split
E) Surrender

Situation #47 Answer

The dealer is showing a breaking card up, but you have to be careful because she'll still make a made hand (17 or more) 62 percent of the time. Because of that high rate of success on a breaking hand, you can't afford to double down on your soft 14. Too many of the times your soft 14 will turn into a hard 14 on a double down situation, which means that you'll lose twice as many units. Of course, you won't surrender or stand on this hand, nor can you split. That means that your best course of action is to hit this hand in an effort to improve it to a made hand. If, however, you hit and get a 9- or 10-count card, you'll have a hard 13 or 14, in which case you should stand against the 3 up. If you should draw another 3 for a soft 17, then you should hit again.

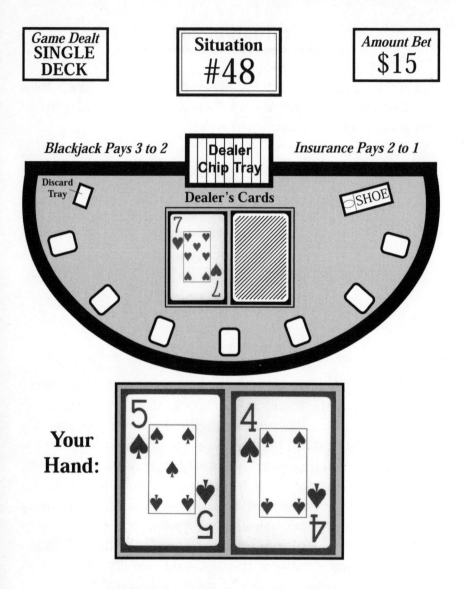

Game Dealt
SINGLE DECK

Situation #48

Amount Bet
$15

Blackjack Pays 3 to 2

Dealer Chip Tray

Insurance Pays 2 to 1

Discard Tray

Dealer's Cards

SHOE

Your Hand:

Variable House Rules in Play This Hand:

1. Double Down: Any two cards
2. Double Down After Splitting: Yes
3. Surrender Allowed: No
4. Dealer Soft 17s: Must stand

Situation #48

In a single-deck game, you have been dealt a 5 and a 4 for a 9 total against the dealer's 7 up card. Which of the below options is your best choice, and why?

My Options

A) Stand
B) Hit
C) Double down
D) Split
E) Surrender

Situation #48 Answer

You're not going to surrender and you can't split this hand. You're not going to stand because you have an excellent chance to improve on your 9. The question, then, is whether to double down or just hit. The optimum hand for doubling on is 11, then 10. After that it's 9, but you're starting to approach the fringe of when it's beneficial against a card like a 7, which could easily represent a made hand. All the dealer has to have is a 10-count card in the hole for a 17, and if you double and catch a 2, 3, 4, 5, 6, or 7, you're toast for $30 instead of $15 (six units instead of three if your units are $5). The best course of action is just to hit this hand because if you draw one of the aforementioned six cards you can still hit it again in an effort to make a made hand.

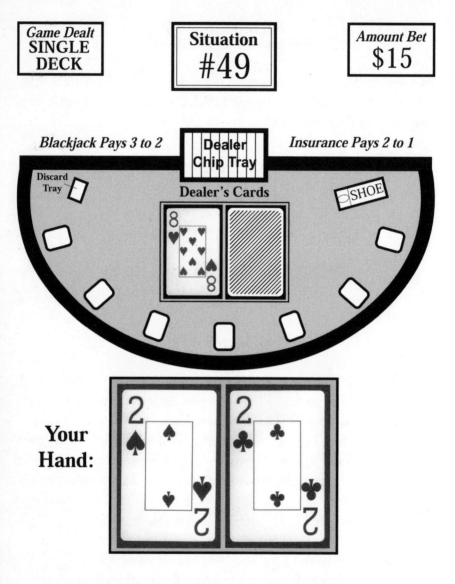

Game Dealt
SINGLE
DECK

Situation
#49

Amount Bet
$15

Blackjack Pays 3 to 2

Dealer Chip Tray

Insurance Pays 2 to 1

Discard Tray

Dealer's Cards

SHOE

Your Hand:

Variable House Rules in Play This Hand:

1. Double Down: Any two cards
2. Double Down After Splitting: Yes
3. Surrender Allowed: Yes
4. Dealer Soft 17s: Must hit

Situation #49

You have been dealt a pair of 2s in a single-deck game. The dealer receives an 8 as her up card. Of all the options listed below, which one represents your best play?

My Options

A) Stand
B) Hit
C) Double down
D) Split
E) Surrender

Situation #49 Answer

As you've learned by now, you have to figure the dealer for an 18 with her 8 up, since more cards in the deck are worth 10 than any other number. So, the question you have to ask yourself is, "Am I better off with a 4 against the dealer's 8 or a couple of 2s against that 8?" As bad as a 4 is against her 8, it's preferable to two hands starting with 2 each. Therefore, splitting is not your best option. Because there are too many ways to make a hand with a 4, you won't surrender, either. A 4 total is far too low to stand on, so that leaves you with either hitting or doubling down. Clearly a 4 total is a poor choice to double on, so the easy and clear choice here is to hit until you get at least a hard 17 or soft 18 total, or bust out trying.

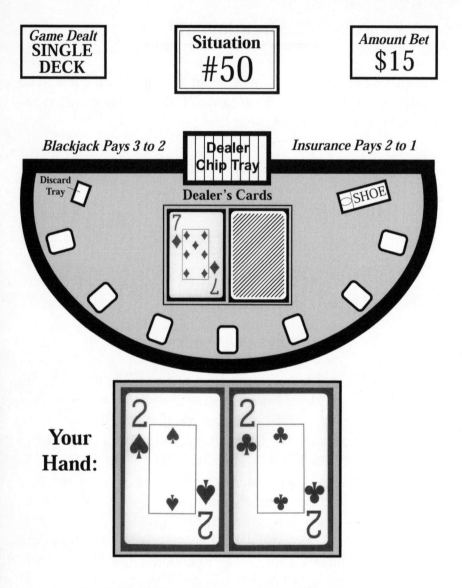

Game Dealt	Situation	Amount Bet
SINGLE DECK	**#50**	**$15**

Blackjack Pays 3 to 2   Dealer Chip Tray   *Insurance Pays 2 to 1*

Discard Tray

Dealer's Cards

SHOE

Your Hand:

Variable House Rules in Play This Hand:

1. Double Down: Any two cards
2. Double Down After Splitting: Yes
3. Surrender Allowed: Yes
4. Dealer Soft 17s: Must hit

Situation #50

You have been dealt a pair of 2s in a single-deck game. The dealer receives a 7 as her up card. Of all the options listed below, which one represents your best play?

My Options

A)   Stand

B)   Hit

C)   Double down

D)   Split

E)   Surrender

Situation #50 Answer

This situation is almost the same as the previous one, except this time the dealer shows a 7 up instead of the 8. Is there any real difference, since both a 7 and an 8 up card represent made hands for the dealer? In this case, yes. Remember earlier when I said that 17 is the magic number in blackjack (see situation #37)? It is because it is the level at which the dealer goes from unmade hand (16) to made hand (17). Think of 17 as the "just made it line" for the dealer. Now, remember back in situation #46 when I told you to hit a 12 against a 2 or a 3 up? Again, think of 12 as the "just made it line" for drawing against a marginal breaking hand. Put these two "just made its" together, and you have a situation whereby two 2s are a better play against a 7 than a 4 against a 7. With a 4 against a 7 (by not splitting the 2s), you have a truly poor hand against a hand that will become made 74 percent of the time. With two 2s against the 7, you have a shot at a win and a loss instead of just a loss, thereby breaking even on the hand. Split this hand.

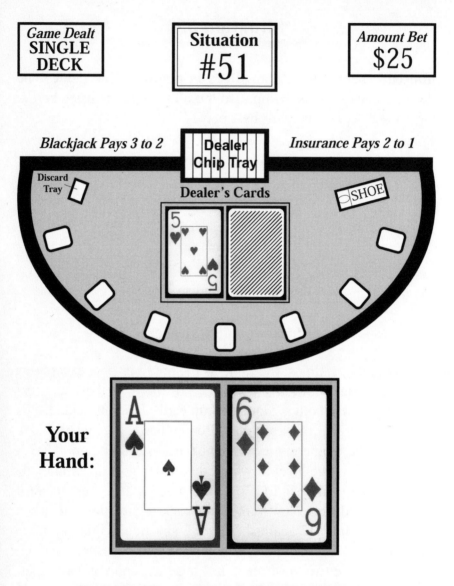

Variable House Rules in Play This Hand:

1. Double Down: Any two cards
2. Double Down After Splitting: Yes
3. Surrender Allowed: Yes
4. Dealer Soft 17s: Must hit

Situation #51

You have been dealt an Ace and a 6 for a soft 17 total in a single-deck game. The dealer receives a 5 as her up card. Of all the options listed below, which one represents your best play?

My Options

    A) Stand
    B) Hit
    C) Double down
    D) Split
    E) Surrender

Situation #51 Answer

The 5 up for the dealer was a nice card for you since the dealer will statistically break about as often with a 5 up as a 6. Your Ace-6 for a soft 17 total is a very favorable total for you since it allows you the option of standing on a made hand (17, albeit a soft 17) or hitting in an effort to improve your hand. Any Ace, 2, 3, or 4 will improve this hand to 18, 19, 20, or 21. Any 10-count card will leave you no worse off than you are now, with 17. Only 5 ranks (5, 6, 7, 8, or 9) will make this a worse hand for you, but even then, you can fall back on the fact that the dealer has a 5 up and stands a fair chance of breaking anyway. So the correct move here is to double down for an additional $25 since you can't break, you stand a good chance of improving your 17 total, and the dealer stands a good chance of breaking. You have a lot going for you on this hand, so make sure you maximize it by doubling.

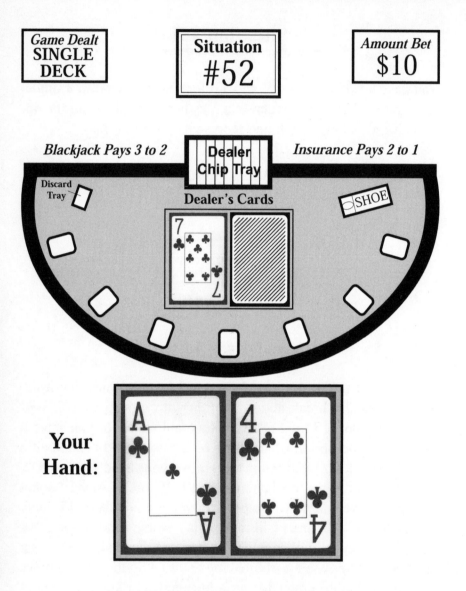

Game Dealt
SINGLE
DECK

Situation
#52

Amount Bet
$10

Blackjack Pays 3 to 2

Dealer
Chip Tray

Insurance Pays 2 to 1

Discard
Tray

Dealer's Cards

SHOE

Your
Hand:

Variable House Rules in Play This Hand:

1. Double Down: Any two cards
2. Double Down After Splitting: Yes
3. Surrender Allowed: Yes
4. Dealer Soft 17s: Must hit

Situation #52

You have been dealt an Ace and a 4 for a soft 15 total in a single-deck game. The dealer receives a 7 as her up card. Of all the options listed below, which one represents your best play?

My Options

A) Stand
B) Hit
C) Double down
D) Split
E) Surrender

Situation #52 Answer

You're not going to surrender because you have too many ways of making a made hand here. You can't split because you don't have a pair. You're not going to stand on a soft 15 (which would be a poor hand to stand on anyway) because you can count your total as 5 and go from there. That leaves hitting or doubling as your viable options. If you double down, you certainly won't break because you have a soft total, but you'll catch a lot of hard 15s if you double, not to mention a fair share of hard 14s (with a 9), hard 13s (with an 8), hard 12s (with a 7), and hard 16s (with an Ace). Sounds like a lot of chances for things to go wrong on a double down with this hand *against a made hand* (dealer has a 7 up). Your best move is to hit this hand in an effort to make a made hand, and if you draw any of the cards mentioned, hit again with the same purpose: hit until you have a hard 17 or better or a soft 18 or better, or break trying.

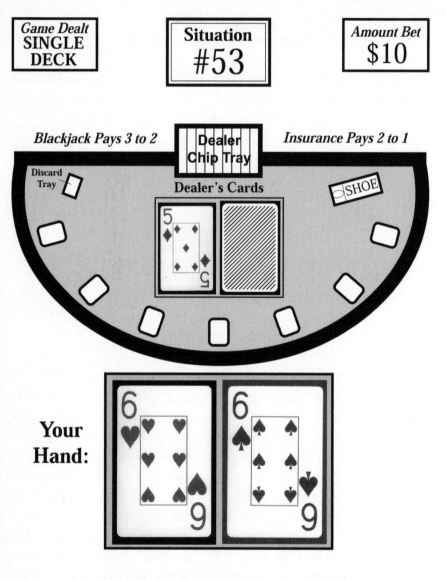

| Game Dealt SINGLE DECK | Situation #53 | Amount Bet $10 |

Blackjack Pays 3 to 2

Insurance Pays 2 to 1

Dealer Chip Tray

Discard Tray

Dealer's Cards

SHOE

Your Hand:

Variable House Rules in Play This Hand:

1. Double Down: Any two cards
2. Double Down After Splitting: Yes
3. Surrender Allowed: Yes
4. Dealer Soft 17s: Must hit

Situation #53

You have been dealt a pair of 6s in a single-deck game. The dealer receives a 5 as her up card. Of all the options listed below, which one represents your best play?

My Options

A) Stand
B) Hit
C) Double down
D) Split
E) Surrender

Situation #53 Answer

Start at the beginning. The dealer shows a 5 up. What hand are you figuring her for? That's right, 15, because you always figure the down card is a 10. Now, would you be better off with one 12 against that 15 or splitting it into two 16s? If you said two 16s, you'd be right. I know, I know, I said 16 was the worst hand you could catch, so why am I recommending that you intentionally set yourself up with two 16s? Because what you're relying on here are two things: first, with a 5 up, the dealer is going to break a fair amount of the time, and you're going to win both hands outright; second, by playing this as two hands, you stand a decent chance of catching a small card first on at least one of the hands and a 10 after that, giving you at least one made hand. And remember, the dealer will break as often with a 5 up as a 6 up. And if you happen to catch two 16s after splitting, you can stand, but the dealer can't. If she catches a 15, she still has to hit.

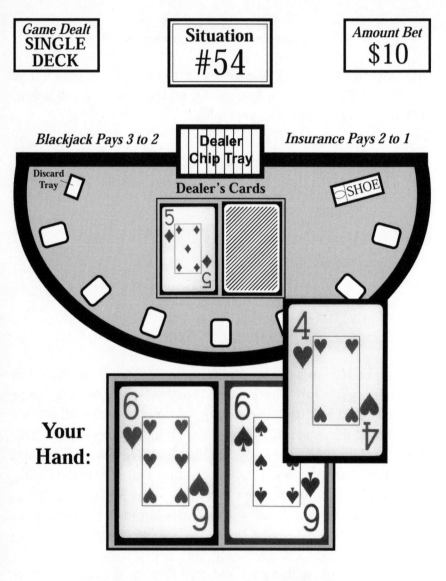

Situation
#54

Amount Bet
$10

Blackjack Pays 3 to 2

Dealer
Chip Tray

Insurance Pays 2 to 1

Discard
Tray

Dealer's Cards

SHOE

Your
Hand:

Variable House Rules in Play This Hand:

1. Double Down: Any two cards
2. Double Down After Splitting: Yes
3. Surrender Allowed: Yes
4. Dealer Soft 17s: Must hit

Situation #54

After splitting your pair of 6s in situation #53, you receive a 4 on your first new hand. Of the options listed below, which is your best play?

My Options

A) Stand

B) Hit

C) Double down

D) Split

E) Surrender

Situation #54 Answer

One option here is clearly the player's best move, and that is to double down. Many beginning players are not aware that it is possible to double down after splitting a pair, and most casinos do not make it easily known that it is an option. Reason? Good players who know what they are doing only split their hands when they have a strong advantage, and, in doing so, take twice as much money from the casino. Call me cynical, but had the up card been a 7 through a 10, many dealers would have been more than happy to remind you that you had the option of splitting your 6s.

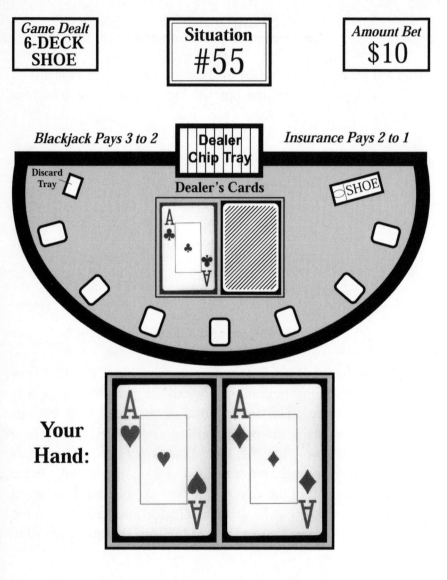

Game Dealt
6-DECK
SHOE

Situation
#55

Amount Bet
$10

Blackjack Pays 3 to 2

Dealer Chip Tray

Insurance Pays 2 to 1

Discard Tray

Dealer's Cards

SHOE

Your Hand:

Variable House Rules in Play This Hand:

1. Double Down: Any two cards
2. Double Down After Splitting: Yes
3. Surrender Allowed: Yes
4. Dealer Soft 17s: Must hit

Situation #55

In a 6-deck shoe game, you receive a pair of Aces against an Ace up for the dealer. The dealer does not have a blackjack, and now it is your turn to act. Which of the options below represents your best course of action?

My Options

A) Stand
B) Hit
C) Double down
D) Split
E) Surrender

Situation #55 Answer

Well, you're certainly not going to stand on a 2 or 12, or surrender a pair of Aces. You're also not going to double down on a 2 or 12. That leaves you with the options of splitting your pair or hitting to improve your hand. Earlier in this book, if you'll remember, I mentioned that one of the cardinal principles of perfect basic strategy dictates that you always split Aces and 8s (see situation #6). But even against an Ace up? Yes. But even when the rules say that we only get one card on each of our Aces while the dealer can draw until she gets a made hand if she happens to turn over a poor hand and later draws a poor hand? Yes. Always split Aces and 8s, no exceptions. Do it without thinking.

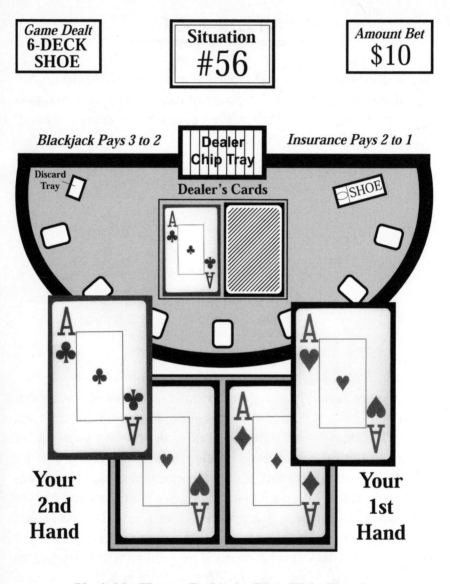

| Game Dealt 6-DECK SHOE | Situation #56 | Amount Bet $10 |

Blackjack Pays 3 to 2

Insurance Pays 2 to 1

Dealer Chip Tray

Discard Tray

Dealer's Cards

SHOE

Your 2nd Hand

Your 1st Hand

Variable House Rules in Play This Hand:

1. Double Down: Any two cards
2. Double Down After Splitting: Yes
3. Surrender Allowed: Yes
4. Dealer Soft 17s: Must hit

Situation #56

After splitting your Aces in situation #55 in this 6-deck shoe game, you receive your allowed one card for each hand, and it is an Ace in both cases. Now what do you do?

My Options

A) Stand

B) Hit

C) Double down

D) Split

E) Surrender

Situation #56 Answer

Boy, this hand sure turned into the north end of a skunk walking south. Okay, what to do: First of all, you can't hit again because blackjack rules are universal in that if you split Aces, you get only one card for each Ace. Second, you can't double down for the same reason. Third, in about 99.99 percent of the world's casinos, you're not allowed to split your Aces again. Other ranks, yes. Aces, no. Do you see a distinct *casino-advantage* pattern here? Other than standing, what can you do? You can surrender, which is what I recommend on both hands. With an Ace as an up card, the dealer is going to make a made hand nearly 90 percent of the time in a multiple-deck game. Given those huge odds, if you surrender half of each of your bets, you'll in effect end up losing only one unit on a hand that looks almost certain to lose two units if played out.

Game Dealt
**6-DECK
SHOE**

**Situation
#57**

Amount Bet
$20

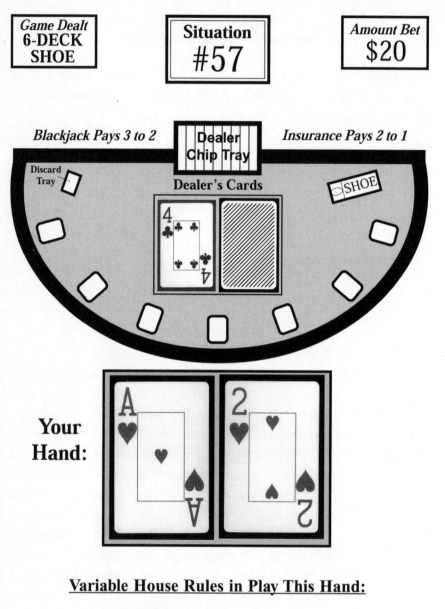

Blackjack Pays 3 to 2   *Insurance Pays 2 to 1*

Dealer
Chip Tray

Discard
Tray

Dealer's Cards

SHOE

**Your
Hand:**

Variable House Rules in Play This Hand:

1. Double Down: Any two cards
2. Double Down After Splitting: Yes
3. Surrender Allowed: Yes
4. Dealer Soft 17s: Must hit

Situation #57

In a 6-deck shoe game, you receive an Ace and a 2 for a soft 13 against a 4 up for the dealer. Which of the options below represents your best course of action?

My Options

A)   Stand
B)   Hit
C)   Double down
D)   Split
E)   Surrender

Situation #57 Answer

You can't split and you're not going to surrender against a poor dealer up card. You also aren't going to stand on a soft 13 because there are too many ways to improve this hand. That leaves you with the choices of hitting or doubling down. The dealer has a very weak hand with the 4 up, which lends itself to a possible 14 and then 24 for a bust. In a single-deck game, this hand would be worth doubling on, but in a 6-deck shoe game with its many more small cards (which often come in clumps), you have to play it a bit more carefully. In a multiple-deck game such as this one, you should only hit this hand and not double since the dealer tends to make a made hand a bit more often than in a single-deck game.

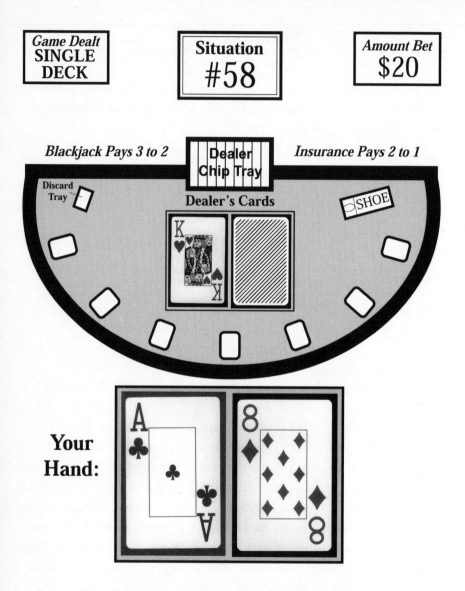

| Game Dealt SINGLE DECK | Situation #58 | Amount Bet $20 |

Blackjack Pays 3 to 2   Dealer Chip Tray   **Insurance Pays 2 to 1**

Discard Tray

Dealer's Cards

SHOE

Your Hand:

Variable House Rules in Play This Hand:

1. Double Down: Any two cards
2. Double Down After Splitting: Yes
3. Surrender Allowed: Yes
4. Dealer Soft 17s: Must hit

Situation #58

In a single-deck game, you receive an Ace and an 8 for a soft 19 against a King up for the dealer. Of all the options listed below, which is your best play?

My Options

A) Stand

B) Hit

C) Double down

D) Split

E) Surrender

Situation #58 Answer

You're up against it on this hand with a soft 19 against a 10-count card up and possible 10-count card in the hole for a dealer's 20. You won't surrender this solid hand, and you can't split it. To double down would be downright foolish since only an Ace or 2 would help you. The question, then, is whether to hit or stand, and it's not too tough a choice. Hitting would be about as foolish as doubling, just for half the money. With only an Ace or 2 as a probable savior for this hand and the other 11 of the 13 ranks hurting you, just stand and hope the dealer has something other than a 10 in the hole.

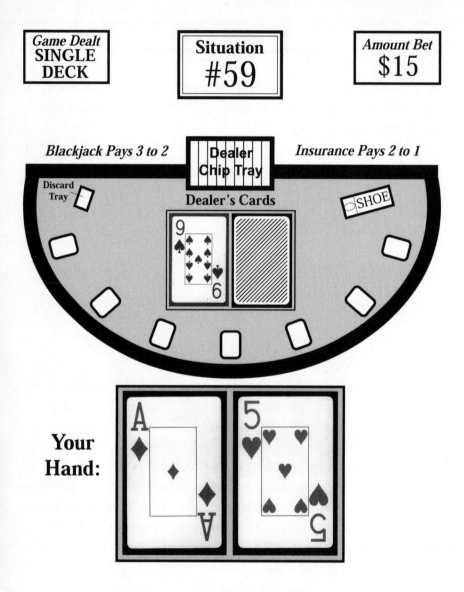

Game Dealt
SINGLE DECK

Situation #59

Amount Bet
$15

Blackjack Pays 3 to 2

Insurance Pays 2 to 1

Dealer Chip Tray

Discard Tray

Dealer's Cards

SHOE

Your Hand:

Variable House Rules in Play This Hand:

1. Double Down: Any two cards
2. Double Down After Splitting: Yes
3. Surrender Allowed: Yes
4. Dealer Soft 17s: Must hit

Situation #59

In a single-deck game, you receive an Ace and a 5 for a soft 16 against a 9 up for the dealer. Of all the options listed below, which is your best play?

My Options

A) Stand

B) Hit

C) Double down

D) Split

E) Surrender

Situation #59 Answer

Your hand is a 6 or 16, your choice. The dealer has a 9 showing, meaning that you have to figure her for a 19 under the tenets of playing perfect basic strategy. So, obviously, you can't stand on either total. Nor can you split since you don't have a pair. You won't surrender this hand because soft totals can easily be made into playable made hands. Again, the question comes down to one of hitting or doubling down. You're in a weak position against a strong up card, so you're not going to double down. You want to hit this hand and hope for a 3, 4, or 5. You'll also stand on a 2, but anything else, you'll have to hit again in an effort to make a made hand, even if you bust trying.

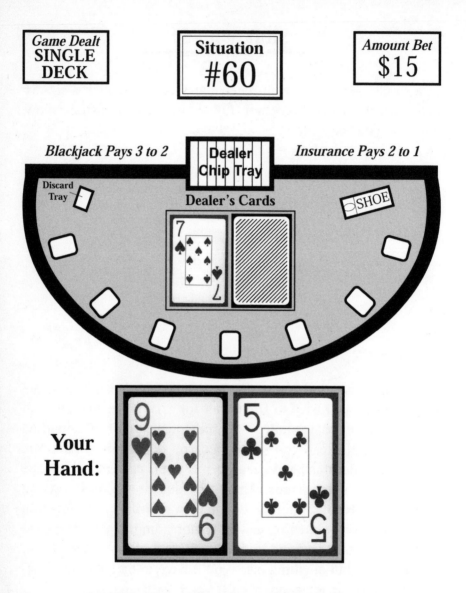

Game Dealt
SINGLE
DECK

Situation
#60

Amount Bet
$15

Blackjack Pays 3 to 2

Dealer Chip Tray

Insurance Pays 2 to 1

Discard Tray

Dealer's Cards

SHOE

Your Hand:

Variable House Rules in Play This Hand:

1. Double Down: 10 and 11 only
2. Double Down After Splitting: Yes
3. Surrender Allowed: No
4. Dealer Soft 17s: Must hit

Situation #60

In a single-deck game, you have been dealt a 9 and a 5 for a hard 14 total against a 7 up for the dealer. Of all the options listed below, which is your best play?

My Options

- A) Stand
- B) Hit
- C) Double down
- D) Split
- E) Surrender

Situation #60 Answer

You can't split since you don't have a pair. Surrender isn't allowed in this casino. To double down would be ill-advised since you would bust if you hit an 8, 9, 10, Jack, Queen, or King and would have a hard 16 with an Ace. Hitting isn't a much better option than doubling except that you'll only lose one bet instead of two. So you're faced with either standing or hitting. If you stand, you'll likely lose since the dealer will make a made hand three times out of the four (74 percent of the time) she shows a 7 up. As unattractive as it is, your best option is to hit this hand until you have at least a 17 or break trying.

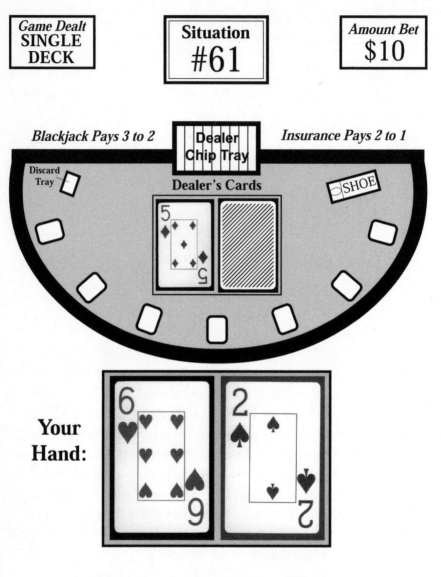

| Game Dealt SINGLE DECK | Situation #61 | Amount Bet $10 |

Variable House Rules in Play This Hand:

1. Double Down: Any two cards
2. Double Down After Splitting: Yes
3. Surrender Allowed: Yes
4. Dealer Soft 17s: Must hit

Situation #61

In a single-deck game, you have been dealt a 6 and a 2 for an 8 total against a 5 up for the dealer. Of all the options listed below, which is your best play?

My Options

A) Stand

B) Hit

C) Double down

D) Split

E) Surrender

Situation #61 Answer

By now you should have learned to deduce quickly that the dealer has a lousy up card since she has a good shot at having a 15, which means a good shot at breaking. Consequently, you aren't going to surrender. You can't split the hand because it isn't a pair. Since you only have an 8 total, you won't be standing, either. So, do you to hit or double? You've also learned by now that a 5 up card is every bit as bad for the dealer as a 6 up card in terms of breaking. So do you double down? No. If you'll remember way back in situation #4, I gave you the 5-3/6-2 age analogy in which 5-3 was better than 6-2 because age 53 is better than 62. This is how I remember that 5-3 is okay to double down on against a breaking hand like this while 6-2 is not. In fact, you never double down on 6-2 against any hand, whether the game is single or multiple deck. Just hit this hand until you get 12 or more and then stand.

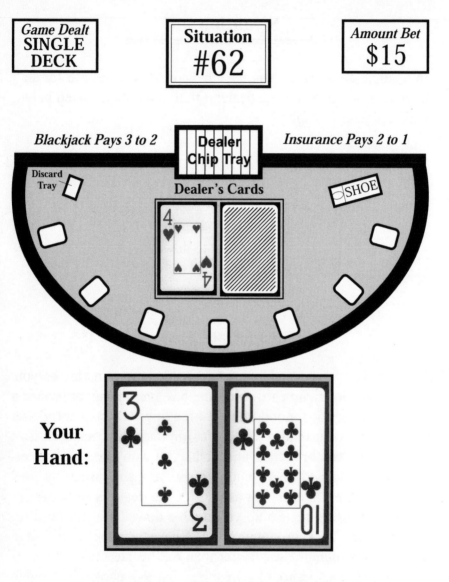

| Game Dealt SINGLE DECK | Situation #62 | Amount Bet $15 |

Blackjack Pays 3 to 2

Insurance Pays 2 to 1

Dealer Chip Tray

Discard Tray

Dealer's Cards

SHOE

Your Hand:

Variable House Rules in Play This Hand:

1. Double Down: Any two cards
2. Double Down After Splitting: Yes
3. Surrender Allowed: Yes
4. Dealer Soft 17s: Must hit

Situation #62

In a single-deck game, you have been dealt a 3 and a 10 for a 13 total against a 4 up for the dealer. Of all the options listed below, which is your best play?

My Options

A) Stand
B) Hit
C) Double down
D) Split
E) Surrender

Situation #62 Answer

By now plays such as this one should be second nature to you. First, look at your hand to see if you have something that you can potentially split or double down on. You don't in either case. Next, consider the dealer's up card and potential hand. In this case, a 4 up means that you figure her for a 14 in terms of plotting your strategy. You now know that a 4 up is considered a breaking hand because one more card could potentially break her if she indeed has the 10 in the hole. You definitely have a breaking hand, as a 9 or any 10-count card will put you over 21. This leaves you with the cardinal principle of perfect basic strategy, which says you (almost) never hit a breaking hand against a breaking hand. The only exception is a 12 against a 2 or 3. Stand on this hand and hope the dealer breaks.

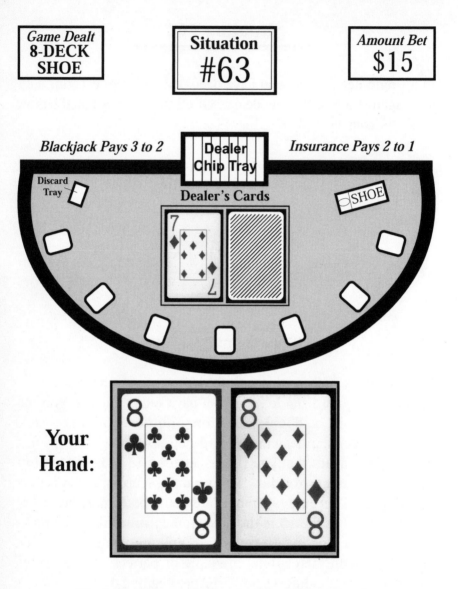

| Game Dealt 8-DECK SHOE | Situation #63 | Amount Bet $15 |

Blackjack Pays 3 to 2   Insurance Pays 2 to 1

Dealer Chip Tray

Discard Tray

Dealer's Cards

SHOE

Your Hand:

Variable House Rules in Play This Hand:

1. Double Down: Any two cards
2. Double Down After Splitting: Yes
3. Surrender Allowed: Yes
4. Dealer Soft 17s: Must hit

Situation #63

While seated in the third-base position at the table, you have been dealt a pair of 8s in an 8-deck shoe game against the dealer's 7 up card. You notice that of the 12 cards dealt to the other six players before you at the table, 10 of them are 10-count cards and all six players have a made hand. Given the apparent likelihood that you stand little chance of drawing a 10 to each of your 8s if you split them, what is your best option?

My Options

A) Stand

B) Hit

C) Double down

D) Split

E) Surrender

Situation #63 Answer

You do what you're always supposed to do when you catch a pair of 8s, you split them. Just because ten 10-count cards came right before you doesn't mean you won't catch some as well. Remember, this is an 8-deck shoe game containing more than 400 cards, which often come clumped together because of the nature of shuffling and how cards get played. If this were a single-deck game and this same situation occurred, you'd have a case for making an exception to a very strong rule even if you weren't a counter because ten 10s out of 16 on one hand leaves few left for you. Go ahead and split the 8s because you don't want to stand on a 16 against a 7 and you don't want to hit it either.

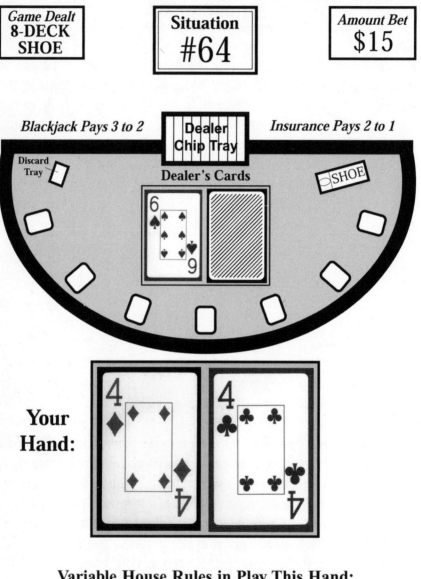

| Game Dealt 8-DECK SHOE | Situation #64 | Amount Bet $15 |

Your Hand:

Variable House Rules in Play This Hand:

1. Double Down: Any two cards
2. Double Down After Splitting: Yes
3. Surrender Allowed: Yes
4. Dealer Soft 17s: Must hit

Situation #64

You have been dealt a pair of 4s in an 8-deck shoe game against the dealer's 6 up card. Of the options listed below, which is your best play and why?

My Options

- A) Stand
- B) Hit
- C) Double down
- D) Split
- E) Surrender

Situation #64 Answer

You won't surrender, of course, because you have a good hand and the dealer has the worst card she could catch, a 6. You won't stand because hitting or doubling won't break you. That leaves hitting, doubling, or splitting. Another cardinal principle of playing perfect basic strategy dictates that you *never* split a pair of 4s, so that option is out. (Two hands starting with 4 are much, much worse than starting with one hand of 8.) So, should you double down or just hit? In a single-deck game, you would double down because the cards run more true to their percentages. In an 8-deck shoe game like this, however, small cards can easily run in clumps, and you don't want to double your bet with the potential for a clump of small cards to hurt you. So just hit this hand. This is another of the fine point distinctions between playing perfect basic strategy in a single-deck game and a multiple-deck game.

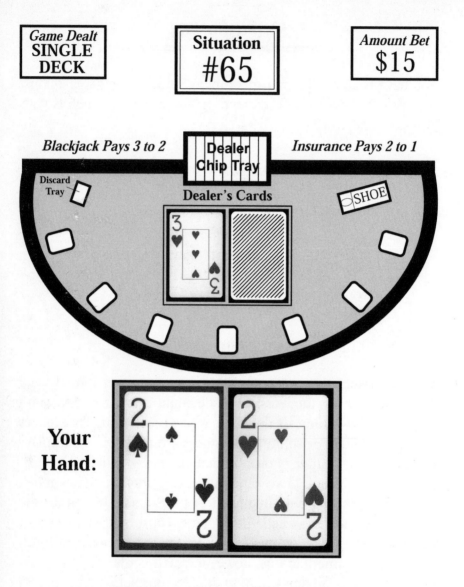

| Game Dealt **SINGLE DECK** | Situation **#65** | Amount Bet **$15** |

Blackjack Pays 3 to 2   *Insurance Pays 2 to 1*

Dealer Chip Tray

Discard Tray

Dealer's Cards

SHOE

Your Hand:

Variable House Rules in Play This Hand:

1. Double Down: Any two cards
2. Double Down After Splitting: Yes
3. Surrender Allowed: Yes
4. Dealer Soft 17s: Must hit

Situation #65

You have been dealt a pair of 2s in a single-deck game against the dealer's 3 up card. Of the options listed below, which is your best play and why?

My Options

- A) Stand
- B) Hit
- C) Double down
- D) Split
- E) Surrender

Situation #65 Answer

You won't stand on your 4 total because you can't bust no matter what card comes next. You won't surrender because of the dealer's poor up card. You won't double down because you know that you never double down on any total less than 9 with but two exceptions (5-3 against a 5 or 6 in a single-deck game). That leaves you with choosing between hitting and splitting. Earlier in the book you had this same hand in a shoe game (see situation #21). Is the strategy different in a single-deck game? Yes. In the shoe game, you were told to hit this hand. In a single-deck game, you should split this into two hands, and I'll bet you're getting to the point where you can tell me why. Because in a single-deck game, the cards run truer and a 3 up is a decent breaking card for the dealer. In a shoe game, many more small cards often come clumped together, making the dealer's 3 less damaging to her than in a single-deck game.

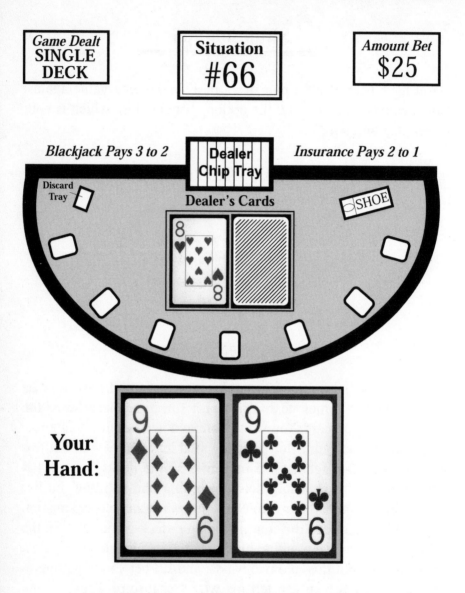

Game Dealt
SINGLE DECK

Situation #66

Amount Bet $25

Blackjack Pays 3 to 2

Dealer Chip Tray

Insurance Pays 2 to 1

Discard Tray

Dealer's Cards

SHOE

Your Hand:

Variable House Rules in Play This Hand:

1. Double Down: Any two cards
2. Double Down After Splitting: Yes
3. Surrender Allowed: Yes
4. Dealer Soft 17s: Must hit

Situation #66

You have been dealt a pair of 9s in a single-deck game against the dealer's 8 up card. Of the options listed below, which is your best play and why?

My Options

A) Stand
B) Hit
C) Double down
D) Split
E) Surrender

Situation #66 Answer

Obviously, you aren't going to surrender this solid hand. You'd be an idiot to hit a hard 18 and insane to double down since both moves have a high probability of busting the hand. So that leaves you with either standing or splitting. If you stand, you have a certain 18 against a possible 18, which would result in a push. If you split this hand, you'll have two possible 19s against a possible 18, meaning two potential winners. Your correct move, then, is to split this hand, setting yourself up for two potential 19s against the dealer's possible 18.

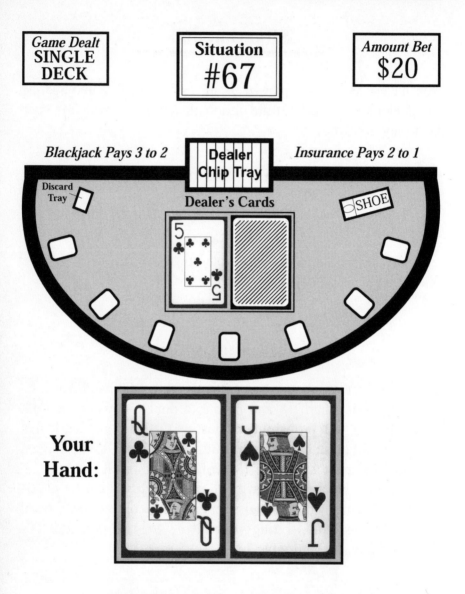

| Game Dealt SINGLE DECK | Situation #67 | Amount Bet $20 |

Blackjack Pays 3 to 2   *Insurance Pays 2 to 1*

Dealer Chip Tray

Discard Tray

Dealer's Cards

SHOE

Your Hand:

Variable House Rules in Play This Hand:

1. Double Down: Any two cards
2. Double Down After Splitting: Yes
3. Surrender Allowed: Yes
4. Dealer Soft 17s: Must hit

Situation #67

In the first hand dealt in a single-deck game, you have received a Queen and a Jack for a 20 total. The dealer has dealt herself a 5 up. Collectively, the first three players in front of you have received only one 10-count card in the 9 cards they drew. It is now your turn to act. Given the extreme shortage of 10s dealt out so far in the hand, do you split this hand or stand?

My Options

A) Stand

B) Split

Situation #67 Answer

In the grand scheme of life we call blackjack, there are certain things you can count on, and a pair of 10s for a 20 total is one of them. Of all the winning and losing combinations possible in this game, only two combinations show a consistent winning percentage over the long haul regardless of the dealer's up card. One is a blackjack—naturally—and the other is a 20. No other two-card combination can make such a claim. While this hand has seen a sudden increase in 10s (providing a **ten-rich deck**), you still should just stand on this hand and not try to split it into two hands, even though the dealer shows a breaking card. About twenty-five years ago, on one of my treks from the Midwest to Las Vegas, I happened to pass through Texas. For those who aren't aware of it, the great state of Texas posts signs at each point of entry telling visitors, "Don't Mess With Texas." In the same vein, "Don't Mess With a 20." (Implication of both: You'll get hurt.)

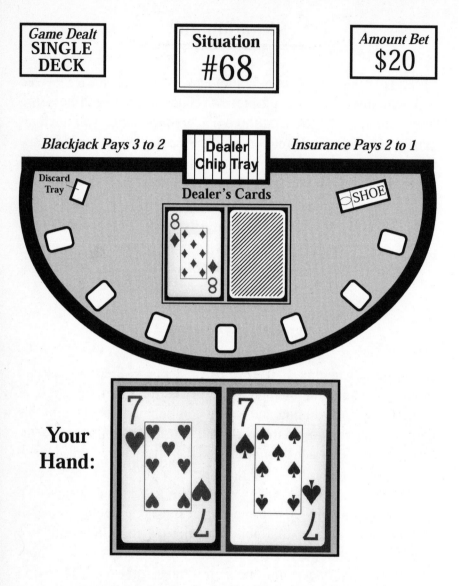

Your Hand:

Variable House Rules in Play This Hand:

1. Double Down: Any two cards
2. Double Down After Splitting: Yes
3. Surrender Allowed: No
4. Dealer Soft 17s: Must stand

Situation #68

You have received a pair of 7s in a single-deck game against the dealer's 8 up card. Of the options listed below, which is your best?

My Options

A) Stand

B) Hit

C) Double down

D) Split

E) Surrender

Situation #68 Answer

Before you exercise a knee-jerk reaction to split this hand, you have to use perfect basic blackjack strategy to figure out whether you're better off with one 14 against an 8 or two potential 17s against an 8. If you figure the dealer for a potential 18 (which you have to do since more cards in the deck are worth 10 than any other number), then you don't want to play two potential losers instead of one, so splitting is out. Surrender is out because this casino doesn't allow it. You won't double down because it would be foolish to risk twice the money on a breaking hand against a made hand. Unfortunately, your only option is to hit this poor hand because standing on a 14 against an 8 will cause you to lose 76 percent of the time, the rate a dealer will make a made hand when showing an 8. Hit this hand until you have 17 or more, or break in your attempt.

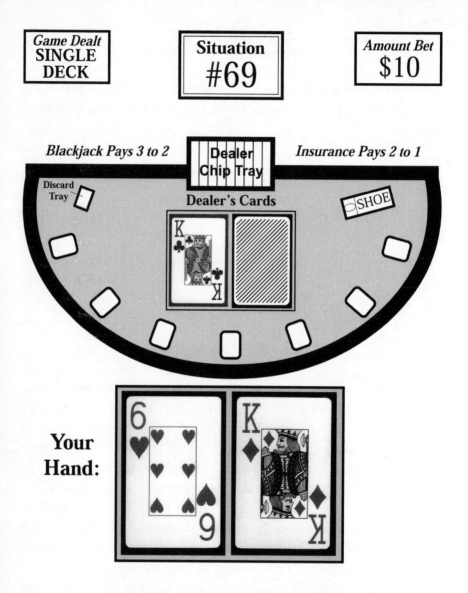

Game Dealt
SINGLE DECK

Situation #69

Amount Bet
$10

Blackjack Pays 3 to 2

Dealer Chip Tray

Insurance Pays 2 to 1

Discard Tray

Dealer's Cards

SHOE

Your Hand:

Variable House Rules in Play This Hand:

1. Double Down: Any two cards
2. Double Down After Splitting: Yes
3. Surrender Allowed: No
4. Dealer Soft 17s: Must stand

Situation #69

In the first hand dealt in a single-deck game, you have received a 6 and a King for a hard 16 total against the dealer's King up. Before it is your turn to act, you notice that all four of the deck's 5s came out to the other players before you. Given that all four of the cards you need to beat the dealer's possible 20 are now gone, should you still hit this hand as perfect basic strategy dictates, or should you stand?

My Options

A) Stand
B) Hit

Situation #69 Answer

If you actually noticed this phenomenon, then kudos to you. You don't have to be a card counter to notice something occasionally that is beneficial to the situation at hand. Earlier in the book I presented a hand in which the player has a pair of 7s against a 10-count up card (see situation #24). In that instance, the correct move is to stand since two of the four cards needed to beat the dealer's possible 20 are already gone (in the player's hand). In this situation, you know that all four of the potential winning cards are gone, and if you hit this hand—as you would normally—you'd only hit one card anyway before stopping. Stand this time instead of hitting and hope the dealer has a small card in the hole that leads her to breaking.

Game Dealt
SINGLE DECK

Situation #70

Amount Bet $20

Blackjack Pays 3 to 2   *Insurance Pays 2 to 1*

Dealer Chip Tray

Discard Tray

Dealer's Cards

SHOE

Your Hand:

Variable House Rules in Play This Hand:

1. Double Down: 10 and 11 only
2. Double Down After Splitting: Yes
3. Surrender Allowed: No
4. Dealer Soft 17s: Must stand

Situation #70

You have received a pair of 5s in a single-deck game against the dealer's 6 up card. Realizing that a 6 up card is bad for the dealer, and in a desire to maximize your winnings on this hand that holds great potential, should you split this hand and hope to catch another small card that will then allow you to double down after splitting, which this casino allows (thereby making three or four times your original bet)?

My Options

A)   Yes, split it to try to win more.

B)   No, do not split the hand.

Situation #70 Answer

So, has the element of getting greedy entered your mind-set? Well, forget it. The dealer has a poor up card and you don't really have a pair of 5s; you need to think of this hand as a 10. Next to an 11, a 10 is the best hand on which to double down. Besides, one of the cardinal principles of playing perfect basic blackjack strategy dictates that you *never* split 5s, especially in an attempt to win more than what you'll get if you win the hand by doubling down. Such moves make the evil spirits come out of casino rafters. You know, those evil spirits who dole out Karma in large instructional doses to foolish gamblers in order to even things out. Don't split this hand. Be content with a double down win the great majority of the time and ward off the evil spirits.

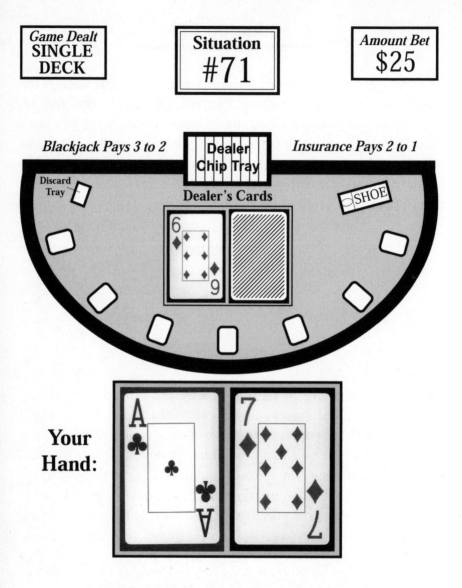

Game Dealt SINGLE DECK

Situation #71

Amount Bet $25

Blackjack Pays 3 to 2

Insurance Pays 2 to 1

Dealer Chip Tray

Discard Tray

Dealer's Cards

SHOE

Your Hand:

Variable House Rules in Play This Hand:

1. Double Down: Any two cards
2. Double Down After Splitting: Yes
3. Surrender Allowed: Yes
4. Dealer Soft 17s: Must stand

Situation #71

You have been dealt an Ace and a 7 for a soft 18 total against the dealer's 6 up card in a single-deck game. Of the options listed below, which is your best play?

My Options

    A) Stand

    B) Hit

    C) Double down

    D) Split

    E) Surrender

Situation #71 Answer

Naturally, you aren't going to surrender this strong hand against a 6. You can't split because it's not a pair. Hitting would be not only completely pointless but probably hazardous to your hand's health since you already have an 18 and your chances of improving the hand by catching another Ace, 2, or 3 are slight. That leaves you with the realistic options of doubling down or standing. Because your 18 is a soft 18 (meaning that you can't break by taking another card) and because the dealer's up card is a 6 (meaning that she stands a good chance of breaking and losing regardless of what you do with your hand), the best option here is to double down to maximize your winnings.

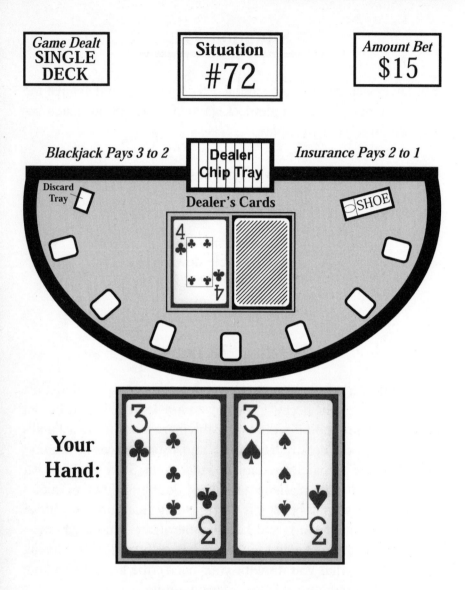

Game Dealt
SINGLE
DECK

Situation
#72

Amount Bet
$15

Blackjack Pays 3 to 2

Dealer
Chip Tray

Insurance Pays 2 to 1

Discard
Tray

Dealer's Cards

SHOE

Your
Hand:

Variable House Rules in Play This Hand:

1. Double Down: Any two cards
2. Double Down After Splitting: Yes
3. Surrender Allowed: Yes
4. Dealer Soft 17s: Must stand

Situation #72

In a single-deck game, you have been dealt a pair of 3s against the dealer's 4. Of the options listed below, which is your best play?

My Options

A) Stand
B) Hit
C) Double down
D) Split
E) Surrender

Situation #72 Answer

The first thing to do when receiving a pair is to decide whether it's a pair worth splitting, that is, you always split Aces and 8s and never split 5s or 10-count cards. Since 3s can be split, the question becomes, "Does it make sense to split them against a 4?" If you split the 3s, you have two potential 13s, and if you do indeed draw a 10 to each 3 for 13, you'll have to stand against the dealer's breaking hand. So, is it worth it? Yes. A 4 is the third worst up card a dealer can catch after a 6 and 5, and the percentages favor your splitting this hand. You might catch a 10 on each 3, but you might also catch a favorable card first (such as a 4 through an 8 or an Ace), all of which will allow you to hit again in an attempt to make a made hand.

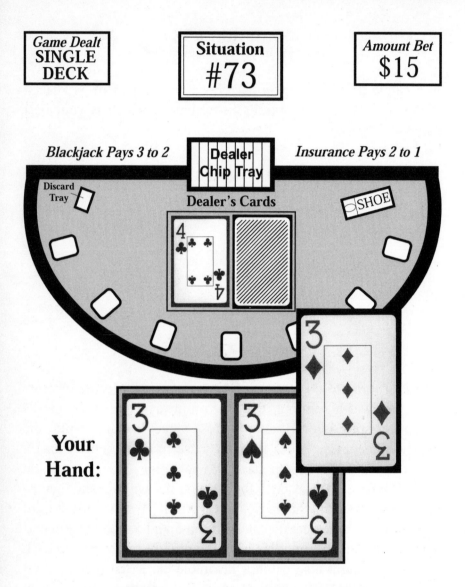

Game Dealt	Situation	Amount Bet
SINGLE DECK	**#73**	**$15**

Blackjack Pays 3 to 2   **Dealer Chip Tray**   *Insurance Pays 2 to 1*

Discard Tray

Dealer's Cards

SHOE

Your Hand:

Variable House Rules in Play This Hand:

1. Double Down: Any two cards
2. Double Down After Splitting: Yes
3. Surrender Allowed: Yes
4. Dealer Soft 17s: Must stand

Situation #73

After splitting the 3s in situation #72, you receive another 3 as the first card to your new first hand. Of the options listed below, which is your best play?

My Options

A) Stand
B) Hit
C) Double down
D) Split
E) Surrender

Situation #73 Answer

Many beginning blackjack players are not aware that they can split again after the first split. If the original split was your best move at the time, then by all means put another $15 out there and split this into a third hand.

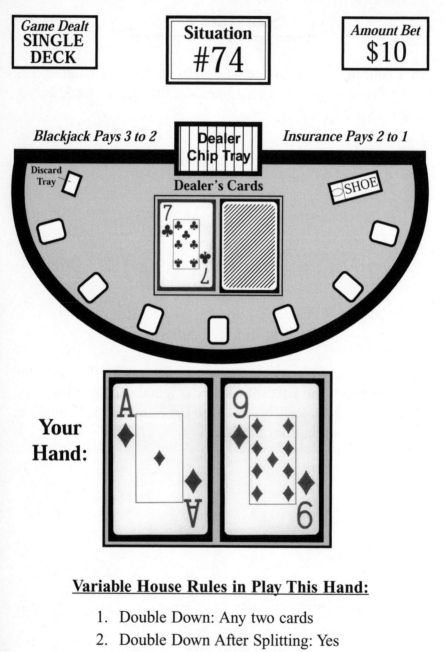

| Game Dealt SINGLE DECK | Situation #74 | Amount Bet $10 |

Blackjack Pays 3 to 2   **Dealer Chip Tray**   Insurance Pays 2 to 1

Discard Tray

Dealer's Cards

SHOE

Your Hand:

Variable House Rules in Play This Hand:

1. Double Down: Any two cards
2. Double Down After Splitting: Yes
3. Surrender Allowed: Yes
4. Dealer Soft 17s: Must stand

Situation #74

You're sitting in the third-base position of a single-deck game when, on the first hand dealt, you catch a soft 20 against the dealer's 7. The guy to your right (who tells you he's a professional blackjack player) is playing three hands at $100 a hand. On one of his hands he has a hard 12, yet he stands, remarking, "Normally I'd hit this, but the deck is so super ten rich that odds are I'll break." He then looks at your hand and says, "Geez, if I had that hand this time, I'd double down because the deck is so heavy with 10s." Given this player's opinions, which of the options below is your best choice?

My Options

A)   Stand

B)   Hit

C)   Double Down

D)   Split

E)   Surrender

Situation #74 Answer

First of all, no professional player is going to stand on a 12 against a 7 on the first hand dealt in any game, single or multiple deck. Second, no professional player is brazenly going to advertise that fact—with either his big bets or his big mouth—especially at the table while the game is going on. Third, don't let anyone convince you to make a stupid play. Stand on all 20s.

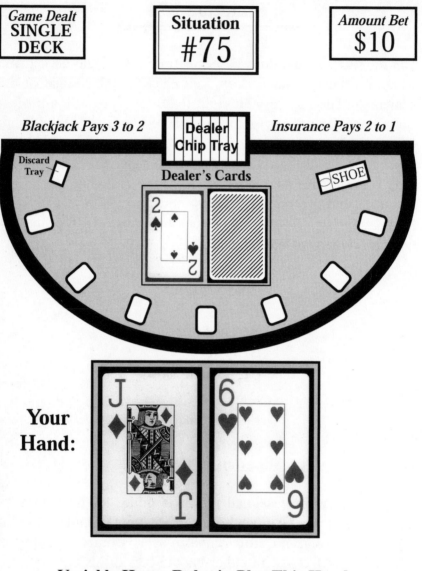

Situation
#75

Amount Bet
$10

Blackjack Pays 3 to 2

Dealer
Chip Tray

Insurance Pays 2 to 1

Discard
Tray

Dealer's Cards

SHOE

Your
Hand:

Variable House Rules in Play This Hand:

1. Double Down: Any two cards
2. Double Down After Splitting: Yes
3. Surrender Allowed: Yes
4. Dealer Soft 17s: Must stand

THE 150 PRACTICE SITUATIONS

Situation #75

In a single-deck game, you have received a Jack and a 6 for a 16 total. The dealer's up card is a 2. Of the options listed below, which is your best play?

My Options

A) Stand

B) Hit

C) Double down

D) Split

E) Surrender

Situation #75 Answer

You can't split because you don't have a pair. You don't want to surrender, even though this casino allows it because the dealer is showing a breaking card. You have a lousy hand, to be sure, but there's some saving grace here in that the dealer is showing a breaking card. If she has a 10-count card in the hole and draws another one, she'll have 22 and lose. Therefore, the only real move you have is to stand on this hand and hope the dealer busts.

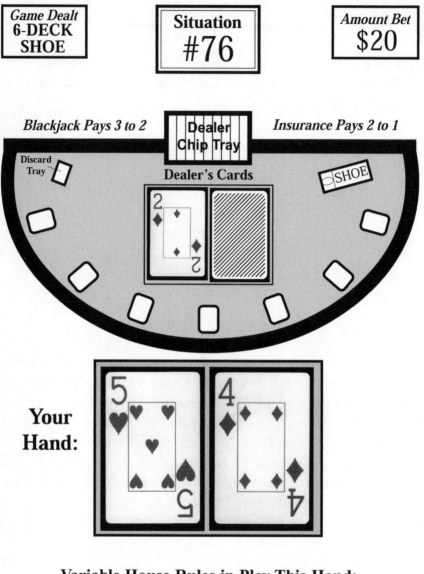

| Game Dealt 6-DECK SHOE | Situation #76 | Amount Bet $20 |

Variable House Rules in Play This Hand:

1. Double Down: Any two cards
2. Double Down After Splitting: Yes
3. Surrender Allowed: Yes
4. Dealer Soft 17s: Must stand

Situation #76

In a 6-deck shoe game, you have received a 5 and a 4 for a 9 total. The dealer's up card is a 2. Of the options listed below, which is your best play?

My Options

A) Stand

B) Hit

C) Double down

D) Split

E) Surrender

Situation #76 Answer

By now you should be starting to settle into the routine of quickly analyzing your options. Since you don't have a pair, you won't be splitting this hand. Because you have a good total and the dealer has a poor total, you won't be surrendering either. Also, since your total is under 11, you won't be standing since you can improve your hand without breaking. That leaves you with the options of hitting or doubling down. In a single-deck game where the cards run more true to form in relation to what's been dealt out, you would double on this hand, figuring that a 10-count card in the hole and another one from the deck will oftentimes break the dealer. In this multiple-deck game, however, you can't count on the cards running truer to form. Consequently, you should just hit a 9 against a deuce in a multiple-deck game and double down against a deuce in a single-deck game.

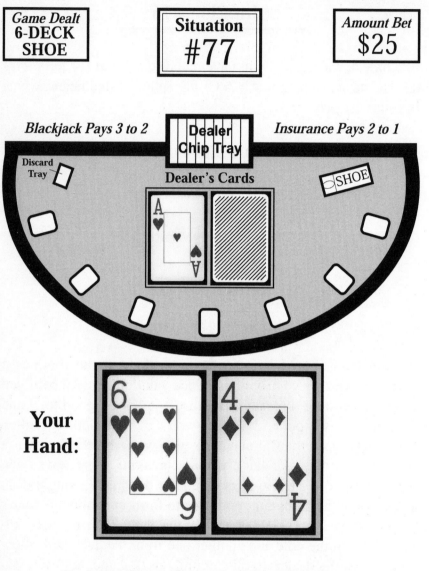

Game Dealt
6-DECK SHOE

Situation #77

Amount Bet
$25

Blackjack Pays 3 to 2

Dealer Chip Tray

Insurance Pays 2 to 1

Discard Tray

Dealer's Cards

SHOE

Your Hand:

Variable House Rules in Play This Hand:

1. Double Down: Any two cards
2. Double Down After Splitting: Yes
3. Surrender Allowed: Yes
4. Dealer Soft 17s: Must stand

Situation #77

In a 6-deck shoe game, you have received a 6 and a 4 for a 10 total. The dealer's up card is an Ace and she didn't have a blackjack. Of the options listed below, which is your best play?

My Options

A) Stand
B) Hit
C) Double down
D) Split
E) Surrender

Situation #77 Answer

Obviously, you shouldn't surrender or stand, and you can't split this hand. As you should know by now, a 10 total is the second best total to double down on next to an 11. Even if the dealer doesn't have a 10 in the hole for a blackjack, the Ace up is a powerful card since it makes for a soft total that can be hit again if the hole card doesn't give the dealer a made hand. Also, in a multiple-deck game such as this, you can't count on the 10-count cards coming with the degree of confidence that you can in a single-deck game. Therefore, on a 10 against an Ace, you should just hit and not double.

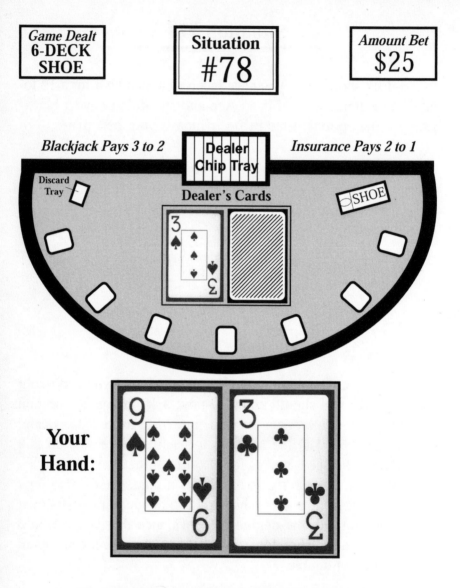

Game Dealt
6-DECK SHOE

Situation #78

Amount Bet $25

Blackjack Pays 3 to 2   *Insurance Pays 2 to 1*

Dealer Chip Tray

Discard Tray

Dealer's Cards

SHOE

Your Hand:

Variable House Rules in Play This Hand:

1. Double Down: Any two cards
2. Double Down After Splitting: Yes
3. Surrender Allowed: Yes
4. Dealer Soft 17s: Must stand

Situation #78

In a 6-deck shoe game, you have received a 9 and a 3 for a 12 total. The dealer's up card is a 3, giving her a breaking hand. Of the options listed below, which is your best play?

My Options

A) Stand
B) Hit
C) Double down
D) Split
E) Surrender

Situation #78 Answer

You won't double down, of course, because you have a breaking hand as well. You can't split because you don't have a pair. You won't surrender because the dealer has a very poor up card and potentially bad hand. The question, then, becomes one of hitting or standing. In the vast majority of cases, you won't hit a breaking hand against a breaking hand, as is the situation here. However, there are two exceptions, whether in a single-deck game or a multiple-deck game such as this one. And those two exceptions are the times that you have a hand of 12 against the dealer's 2 or 3 up card. The combination of your 12 against the dealer's 3 up is not advantageous enough for you just to stand. Hit this hand and memorize it as one of the exceptions to the basic rule of breaking hand versus breaking hand (see situation #46).

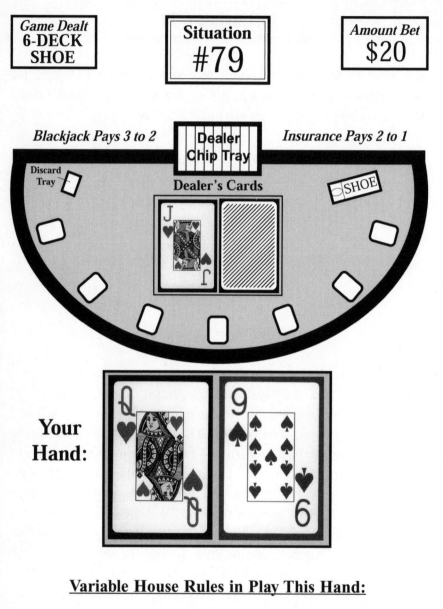

| Game Dealt 6-DECK SHOE | Situation #79 | Amount Bet $20 |

Blackjack Pays 3 to 2

Insurance Pays 2 to 1

Dealer Chip Tray

Discard Tray

Dealer's Cards

SHOE

Your Hand:

Variable House Rules in Play This Hand:

1. Double Down: Any two cards
2. Double Down After Splitting: Yes
3. Surrender Allowed: Yes
4. Dealer Soft 17s: Must stand

Situation #79

In a shoe game being dealt by a rookie dealer and being watched over by her **pit boss**, you have received a 19 total. The dealer, with a Jack up, checks to see if she has an Ace in the hole and accidentally **flashes** her hole card to you in the third-base position. You know for certain it is a **face card** for a 20 total. What should you do?

My Options

A) Stand like I normally would have had I not seen the hole card.
B) Hit since I know I'm beat.
C) Surrender and lose only $10 of my $20 wager.

Situation #79 Answer

A sticky wicket, this one. If you stand, you positively lose. If you hit, odds are 12 to 1 against you winning and 12 to 1 against pushing, although both longshots are better than no shot. Surrender is an interesting alternative on this hand; however, there's another greater issue at play here. If you hit or surrender, especially with a pit boss watching, you're making an *extremely radical play* and one that will guarantee you increased scrutiny by the house. Who would make such a radical play? Counters (they'll assume), cheaters (they'll assume), or dealer confederates (they'll assume), none of which are good for you, especially if you someday hope to be a professional card counter. For me, I stand here, take the loss, and don't get the undesired attention or my picture plastered on every casino's blackjack *watch list.*

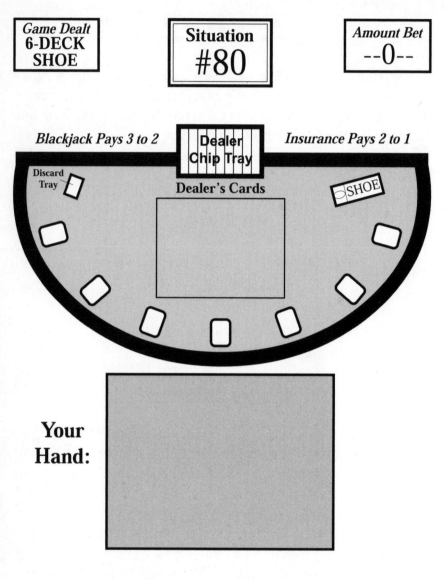

| Game Dealt 6-DECK SHOE | Situation #80 | Amount Bet --0-- |

Blackjack Pays 3 to 2   Insurance Pays 2 to 1

Dealer Chip Tray

Discard Tray

Dealer's Cards

SHOE

Your Hand:

Variable House Rules in Play This Hand:

1. Double Down: Any two cards
2. Double Down After Splitting: Yes
3. Surrender Allowed: Yes
4. Dealer Soft 17s: Must stand

Situation #80

The dealer has asked for everyone's bets before dealing the cards. You have lost five hands in a row for $5, $10, $20, $40, and $80, respectively, in your attempt to keep doubling your bet until you win a hand. Your system of continuing to double your bet until you win is a good one, you think, but you are getting nervous about how big the bets are getting. What should your betting strategy be now?

My Options

A) Bet $5, the minimum allowed until you catch a winner.

B) Bet $160, the amount your system calls for on this hand since you will eventually hit a winning hand.

C) Bet somewhere between the two amounts.

Situation #80 Answer

This system is known as the **Martingale system.** In theory, a person just doubles up the amount of his previous bet until he wins and then starts over reverting to wagering the smallest unit again. The problems: limited player money and table limits, the latter of which is implemented by casinos to prevent just such a betting system from being employed. As for thinking you'll eventually win a hand and recoup all your losses, I once lost 23 straight hands for $25 per hand before I won, and I was a professional. How much money would I have needed to use the Martingale system starting with a $25 bet? My 24th bet (and first winning one in the streak) would have needed to be $209,715,200, with a required bankroll of over $419 million. How much do you like this system now? It's junk. Don't use it.

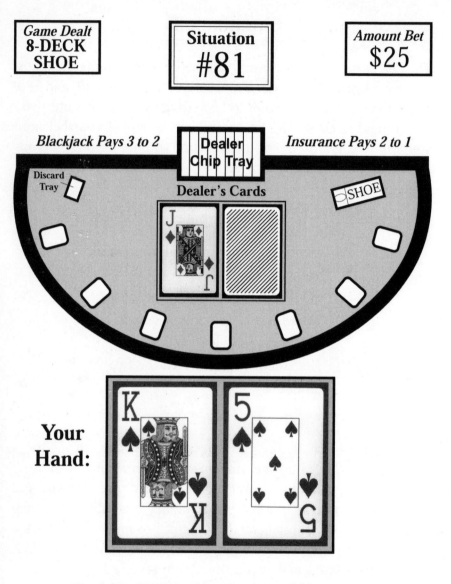

Game Dealt	Situation	Amount Bet
8-DECK SHOE	**#81**	**$25**

Blackjack Pays 3 to 2   Insurance Pays 2 to 1

Dealer Chip Tray

Discard Tray

Dealer's Cards

SHOE

Your Hand:

Variable House Rules in Play This Hand:

1. Double Down: 10 and 11 only
2. Double Down After Splitting: No
3. Surrender Allowed: Yes (early)
4. Dealer Soft 17s: Must hit

Situation #81

In an 8-deck shoe game, you have received a King and a 5 for a 15 total. The dealer's up card is a Jack, and she asks the players if anyone would like to surrender before she checks her hole card. Should you surrender or not?

My Options

    A)   Surrender.

    B)   Do not surrender.

Situation #81 Answer

There are two kinds of surrender, early and late. In this instance, you are being offered early surrender, meaning the chance to surrender *before* the dealer checks her hole card. While you should surrender this hand, practically speaking there are not very many casinos in the world today that offer early surrender anymore because it is a decided player advantage. If they do, they typically have many other rules in effect that negate this advantage, three of which you will notice in the Variable House Rules on the opposite page. Your opportunities to double down are restricted to only 10 and 11. You are not permitted to double down after splitting. And the dealer must hit soft 17s instead of standing. For the record, anytime you catch a 15 or 16 against a 10-count card or an Ace, you should always take early surrender in the rare instances it is offered.

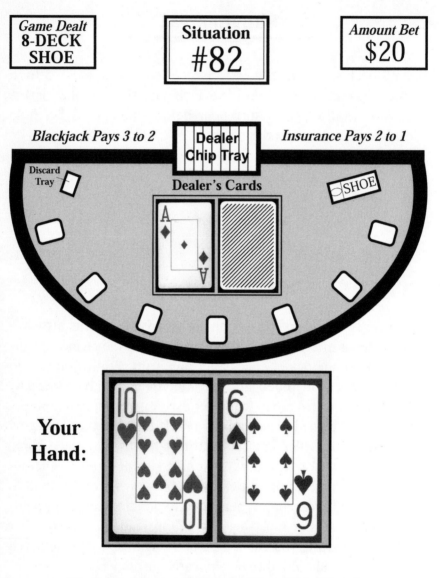

Game Dealt
8-DECK SHOE

Situation
#82

Amount Bet
$20

Blackjack Pays 3 to 2

Dealer Chip Tray

Insurance Pays 2 to 1

Discard Tray

Dealer's Cards

SHOE

Your Hand:

Variable House Rules in Play This Hand:

1. Double Down: 10 and 11 only
2. Double Down After Splitting: No
3. Surrender Allowed: Yes (late)
4. Dealer Soft 17s: Must hit

Situation #82

In an 8-deck shoe game, you have received a 10 and a 6 for a 16 total. The dealer's up card is an Ace, and she does not have a blackjack. Of the options listed below, which is your best play?

My Options

A) Stand

B) Hit

C) Double down

D) Split

E) Surrender

Situation #82 Answer

The dealer has a very powerful up card, so you have to be careful. Of course, you can't split this hand because it's not a pair. You won't double down because you have a poor hand that you could easily break on and because you don't want to lose twice as much. That leaves you with standing, hitting, or surrendering. The dealer will make a made hand (17 or more) 83 percent of the time she shows an Ace up, therefore standing isn't a viable option. If you hit this hand, you'll break more than half the time. Therefore, when it's your turn to play, you should say "Surrender" and forfeit $10 of your $20 wager (representing just a 50 percent loss), the best proposition for you in this horrible situation. Again, late surrender isn't worth worrying about most of the time, but in this example in which the dealer holds the best possible card for her and you hold the worst possible hand for you, it's worth taking.

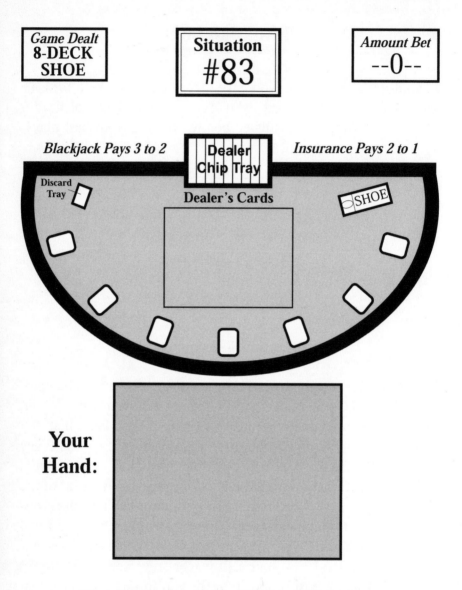

Variable House Rules in Play This Hand:

1. Double Down: 10 and 11 only
2. Double Down After Splitting: Yes
3. Surrender Allowed: No
4. Dealer Soft 17s: Must hit

Situation #83

You've experienced a string of incredible luck. Betting mostly $5 a hand (and never more than $10) for more than two hours, you find yourself up $1,500. Whatever you've done (splitting, doubling, etc.) has worked with almost frightening regularity. You're considering raising your betting level but aren't sure you should mess with success. In regard to your betting strategy, what should you do?

My Options

- A) Keep betting $5 a hand.
- B) Raise your bets just to $10 a hand.
- C) **Press** (raise) your bets to at least $25 a hand.
- D) Bet really big, about $200–$300 per hand.

Situation #83 Answer

This exact situation happened to me in 1977 at Harvey's Club in Lake Tahoe the first time I ever played blackjack! I was almost dizzy from my success. But I made a critical mistake. I didn't press my bets the whole session. Had I started increasing my bets to $10 once I was up a couple hundred, then to $25 once I was up $500, or so, and then to a higher level when I got up even more, I would've (and should've) walked out of that place with $25,000. Moral: when you're up a bunch—playing on their money—increase your betting level proportionately. In thirty years since, I've not had a streak of luck even close to this one. As for option D, no way. Lady luck can turn quickly, and to bet so disproportionately out of your bankroll would be foolish. Remember, all your earnings could vanish in a few hands.

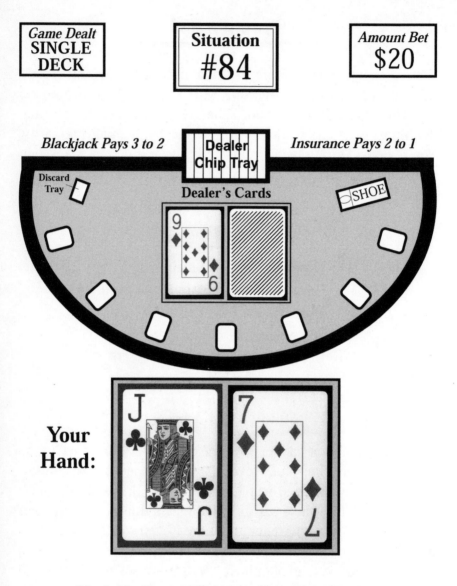

| Game Dealt SINGLE DECK | Situation #84 | Amount Bet $20 |

Blackjack Pays 3 to 2

Insurance Pays 2 to 1

Dealer Chip Tray

Discard Tray

Dealer's Cards

SHOE

Your Hand:

Variable House Rules in Play This Hand:

1. Double Down: 10 and 11 only
2. Double Down After Splitting: No
3. Surrender Allowed: Yes (late)
4. Dealer Soft 17s: Must hit

Situation #84

In a single-deck game, you have received a Jack and a 7 for a 17 total. The dealer's up card is a 9. You notice that the other three players at the table—collectively—receive five 10-count cards between them. You know that normally you should stand on a 17 versus a 9, but in lieu of all the big cards that have fallen, including the dealer's 9, you are considering hitting this hand. What should you do?

My Options

A) Stand, as dictated by perfect basic strategy.

B) Hit, since so many large cards have fallen.

C) Surrender, since it's allowed and you're probably already beaten.

Situation #84 Answer

First of all, you're not going to surrender a made hand. As for hitting this hand because so many large cards have fallen, forget it. You'll break if you draw a 5, 6, 7, 8, 9, 10, Jack, Queen, or King. That's 9 of the 13 ranks. Even with the large (i.e., breaking) cards that are already on the table, there are still 29 cards left in the deck that'll break your hand. Hitting a 17 is silly. Don't do it. Stand, and if you're beat, you're beat. A certain number of hands are going to be losers in blackjack, no matter what you try to do. Just accept it. A 17 against a 9 is one of those hands when you clearly have the short end of the stick. Stand, accept the outcome, and move on to the next hand.

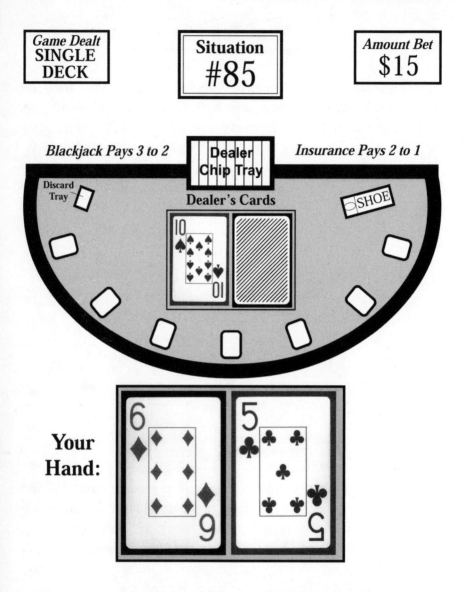

Variable House Rules in Play This Hand:

1. Double Down: 10 and 11 only
2. Double Down After Splitting: No
3. Surrender Allowed: No
4. Dealer Soft 17s: Must hit

Situation #85

In a single-deck game, you have received a 6 and a 5 for an 11 total. The dealer's up card is a 10 and she does not have a blackjack. Of the options listed below, which is your best play?

My Options

A) Stand
B) Hit
C) Double down
D) Split
E) Surrender

Situation #85 Answer

By now you should be quickly identifying certain hands that are either favorable or unfavorable to you. Other than a blackjack, one of the most favorable hands to a player is an 11 because it allows you the chance to double down on most occasions, thereby increasing your winnings. But is an 11 against a 10 a favorable opportunity? Yes. Granted, it's not as good as when the dealer's up card is a 6, but 11 against a 10 is still a positive play for doubling down. Yes, there will be times when the dealer will have a 7, 8, 9, or 10 in the hole for a made hand and you'll receive an Ace through a 5 for an unmade hand; then you'll lose two bets instead of one, but there will be more times when you'll win two bets. Whether in a single-deck game or shoe game, it's to your advantage always to double down on an 11 against a 10.

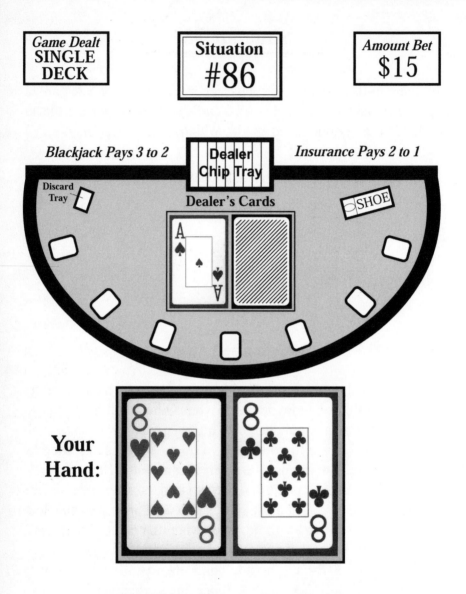

Variable House Rules in Play This Hand:

1. Double Down: 10 and 11 only
2. Double Down After Splitting: No
3. Surrender Allowed: Yes (early/late)
4. Dealer Soft 17s: Must hit

Situation #86

In a single-deck game, you have received a pair of 8s against the dealer's Ace up. Given the Variable House Rules listed on the opposite page, which of the options below is your best play?

My Options

A) Stand
B) Hit
C) Double down
D) Split
E) Surrender

Situation #86 Answer

If you said surrender, congratulations. There are many reasons why surrendering this hand for the $7.50 loss (half of your wager) makes sense. First, the dealer could have a blackjack, which means that you don't even get a chance to beat her. Second, if she doesn't have a blackjack, you're at a strategic disadvantage because you can't double after splitting (in case you hit a 3 to either hand), and the dealer must hit a soft 17 (to her advantage if she has a 6 in the hole). Take the early surrender on this hand since this casino allows it.

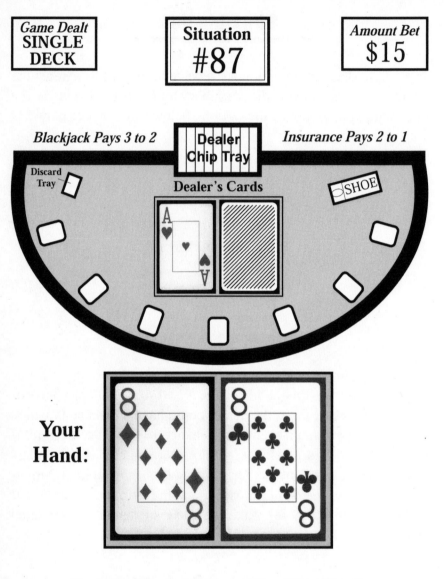

| Game Dealt SINGLE DECK | Situation #87 | Amount Bet $15 |

Blackjack Pays 3 to 2

Insurance Pays 2 to 1

Dealer Chip Tray

Discard Tray

Dealer's Cards

SHOE

Your Hand:

Variable House Rules in Play This Hand:

1. Double Down: 10 and 11 only
2. Double Down After Splitting: No
3. Surrender Allowed: Yes (late)
4. Dealer Soft 17s: Must hit

Situation #87

Now, same hand as situation #86, but with different house rules. In a single-deck game, you have received a pair of 8s against the dealer's Ace up and she does not have a blackjack. Given the Variable House Rules listed on the opposite page, which of the below options is your best play?

My Options

A) Stand

B) Hit

C) Double down

D) Split

E) Surrender

Situation #87 Answer

Okay, the dealer doesn't have a blackjack, so play continues on the hand. Now it's your turn. What do you do? If you said split, since we always split Aces and 8s, you'd be . . . wrong. What? Yes, you'd be wrong. Reason being, always splitting Aces and 8s is a principle of *basic strategy*, but when surrender is allowed (even if it's just late surrender), a principle of *perfect* basic strategy dictates that you surrender a pair of 8s against an Ace. Basic strategy works under the assumption that surrender isn't allowed because, practically speaking, it's not allowed in very many casinos in today's world. In the few casinos you'll find surrender allowed, as mentioned earlier in this book, you'll find other rules in play that are not player friendly, such as allowing double downs on 10 and 11 only, and no doubling after splitting.

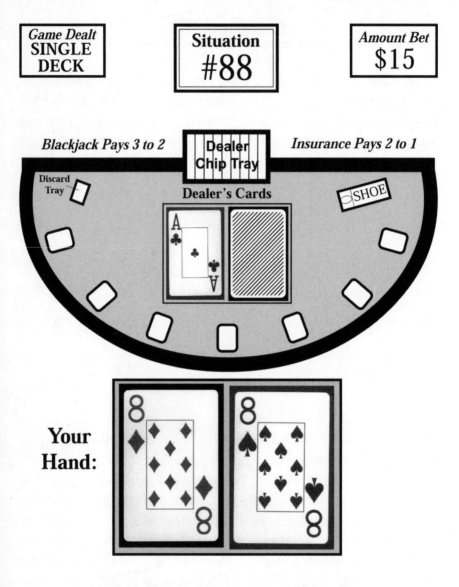

Variable House Rules in Play This Hand:

1. Double Down: Any two cards
2. Double Down After Splitting: Yes
3. Surrender Allowed: Yes (late)
4. Dealer Soft 17s: Must stand

Situation #88

Okay, let's try it again, same hand as situations #86 and #87 but once more with different house rules. In a single-deck game, you have received a pair of 8s against the dealer's Ace up and she does not have a blackjack. Given the Variable House Rules listed on the opposite page, which of the below options is your best play?

My Options

    A)   Stand

    B)   Hit

    C)   Double down

    D)   Split

    E)   Surrender

Situation #88 Answer

Finally, you're in a player's casino. These house rules are much more favorable to the player, and as such, you should split the 8s. When the original computer simulations were run many years ago, it was determined that the best move for a pair of 8s against an Ace was to split, not because it gave the player a winning rate of return, but because *it allowed the player to lose fewer units in the long run than by hitting or standing*. Add to that the fact that you can double down after splitting in this casino (which you would do if you hit a 3 to your 8), and the winning percentages increase a bit in the player's favor. So, always split 8s against an Ace *unless* you're allowed *early* surrender. Late surrender, as this casino offers, doesn't represent enough of a player advantage to take it.

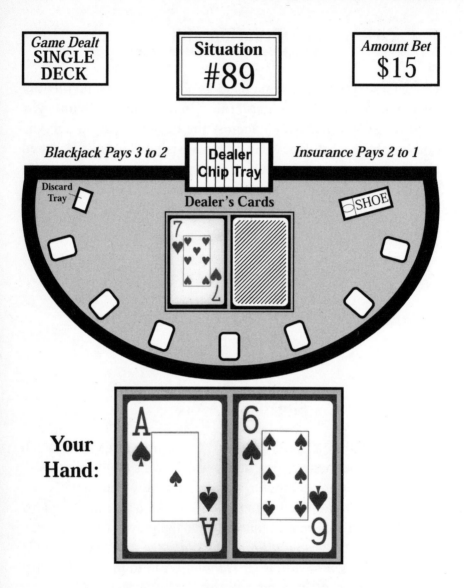

| Game Dealt SINGLE DECK | Situation #89 | Amount Bet $15 |

Blackjack Pays 3 to 2 — Dealer Chip Tray — *Insurance Pays 2 to 1*

Discard Tray

Dealer's Cards

SHOE

Your Hand:

Variable House Rules in Play This Hand:

1. Double Down: Any two cards
2. Double Down After Splitting: Yes
3. Surrender Allowed: No
4. Dealer Soft 17s: Must stand

Situation #89

In a single-deck game, you have received an Ace and a 6 for a soft 17 total. The dealer has received a 7 as her up card. Of the options listed below, which is your best play?

My Options

A) Stand

B) Hit

C) Double down

D) Split

E) Surrender

Situation #89 Answer

You can't surrender this hand because the casino doesn't allow it, nor should you if it did. You can't split this hand because it isn't a pair. If you stand, you have a 17. The dealer has a 7 up, so you have to play her for a 17, which means a push. However, if she has an Ace in the hole, she beats you. If she has a 2, 3, or 4, she's set up for a 19, 20, or 21 if a 10-count card comes, all of which beat your soft 17. You're in a bit of a bad situation if you just stand, so you must either hit or double. As already mentioned, if the dealer catches any of 8 of the 13 ranks, you'll either lose or push, so doubling your bet wouldn't be wise. So, the best move for you is to hit this hand and hope for an Ace, 2, 3, or 4, or at least a 10-count card so that you're no worse off than you are now.

| Game Dealt SINGLE DECK | Situation #90 | Amount Bet $10 |

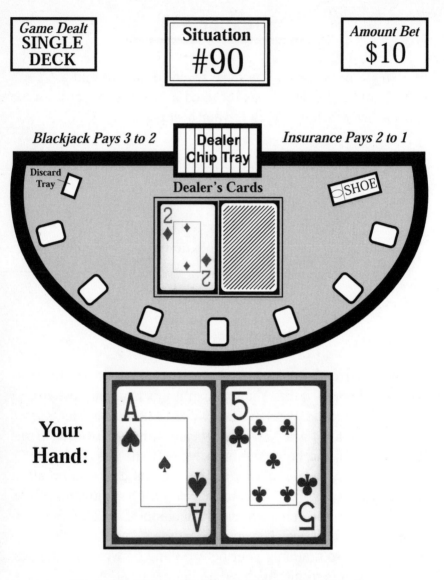

Blackjack Pays 3 to 2   Dealer Chip Tray   Insurance Pays 2 to 1

Discard Tray

Dealer's Cards

SHOE

Your Hand:

Variable House Rules in Play This Hand:

1. Double Down: Any two cards
2. Double Down After Splitting: Yes
3. Surrender Allowed: No
4. Dealer Soft 17s: Must hit

Situation #90

In a single-deck game, you have received an Ace and a 5 for a soft 16 total. The dealer has received a 2 as her up card. Of the options listed below, which is your best play?

My Options

A) Stand

B) Hit

C) Double down

D) Split

E) Surrender

Situation #90 Answer

Surrender isn't allowed and you don't have a pair, so those two options are out. You're not going to stand on a soft 16 since there are so many ways to improve your hand without breaking. That leaves you with hitting or doubling down as your realistic options. While the dealer's 2 is a breaking card and you're in no danger of breaking if you double down, it's disadvantageous to do so since the dealer will make a made hand 65 percent of the time when she shows a 2. The best move here is to hit until you get a hard 17 or more, or a soft 18 or more.

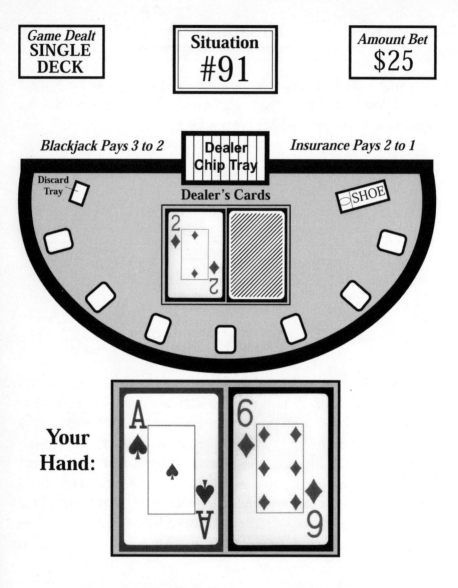

Variable House Rules in Play This Hand:

1. Double Down: Any two cards
2. Double Down After Splitting: Yes
3. Surrender Allowed: No
4. Dealer Soft 17s: Must stand

Situation #91

In a slight departure from situation #90, but still in a single-deck game, you have received an Ace and a 6 for a soft 17 total. The dealer has again received a 2 as her up card. Of the options listed below, which is your best play?

My Options

A) Stand

B) Hit

C) Double down

D) Split

E) Surrender

Situation #91 Answer

Did things change that much from situation #90 to this one by catching a soft 17 instead of a soft 16 against the dealer's 2? Yes. You're still not going to surrender, split, or stand. This time, however, you should double down instead of just hitting. Why? Because when you held the soft 16 in situation #90, the main reason you didn't double down is because of the high number of times you would've drawn a 10-count card for a hard 16, an *unmade* hand, and any dealer *made* hand would beat you *for twice as much money*. In this situation, any 10-count card you draw (and there are plenty of them still in the deck) will give you a hard 17, a *made* hand. Therefore, on an Ace-6 versus a dealer's 2, it is now in your best interest to double down instead of just hitting.

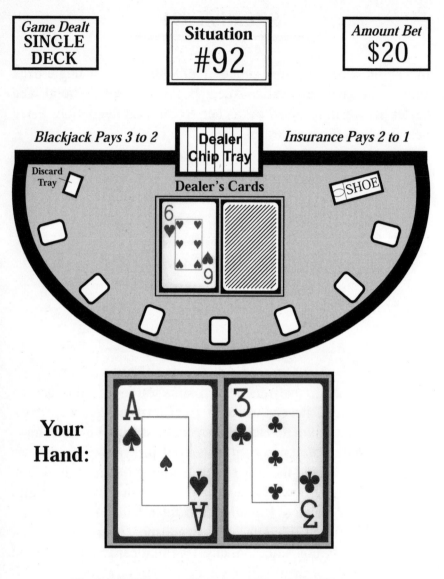

Game Dealt
SINGLE DECK

Situation #92

Amount Bet $20

Blackjack Pays 3 to 2   *Insurance Pays 2 to 1*

Dealer Chip Tray

Discard Tray

Dealer's Cards

SHOE

Your Hand:

Variable House Rules in Play This Hand:

1. Double Down: Any two cards
2. Double Down After Splitting: Yes
3. Surrender Allowed: Yes
4. Dealer Soft 17s: Must stand

Situation #92

In a single-deck game, you have received an Ace and a 3 for a soft 14 total against the dealer's 6 up card. Of the options listed below, which is your best play?

My Options

A) Stand
B) Hit
C) Double down
D) Split
E) Surrender

Situation #92 Answer

Obviously, you will not surrender because of the dealer's poor up card. You cannot split because you do not have a pair. You are also not going to stand on a soft 14 because there is no way to break, no matter what card you hit. Therefore, you will either hit or double down. In this instance, you are playing as much on the dealer's up card as your own hand, since the dealer will break quite often with a 6 up. So, since there is no chance of you breaking, with an excellent chance of the dealer breaking, and many cards will actually improve your hand to a made hand (3, 4, 5, 6, or 7), you should double down in an effort to maximize your winnings.

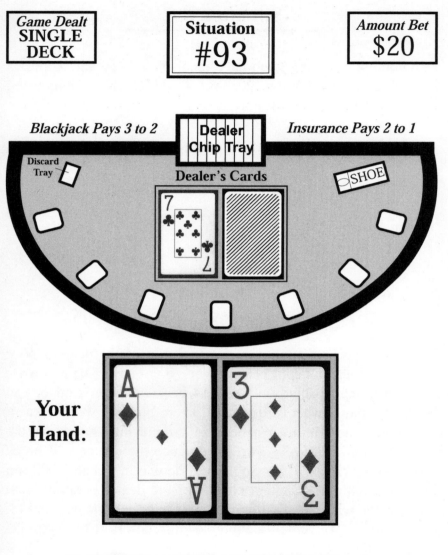

| Game Dealt SINGLE DECK | Situation #93 | Amount Bet $20 |

Blackjack Pays 3 to 2   Insurance Pays 2 to 1

Dealer Chip Tray

Discard Tray

Dealer's Cards

SHOE

Your Hand:

Variable House Rules in Play This Hand:

1. Double Down: Any two cards
2. Double Down After Splitting: Yes
3. Surrender Allowed: Yes
4. Dealer Soft 17s: Must stand

Situation #93

In a slight variance from situation #92, you have received an Ace and a 3 for a soft 14 total against the dealer's 7 up card in a single-deck game. Of the options listed below, which is your best play?

My Options

A) Stand
B) Hit
C) Double down
D) Split
E) Surrender

Situation #93 Answer

As in situation #92, you won't be splitting, surrendering, or standing. The question again is one of hitting or doubling down. Is there really that much difference in the two situations? Yes. In situation #92 you were working against a 6 up, from the player's standpoint a great card for the dealer to have since she will break so often. This time, however, your Ace-3 is opposing a 7, a card that isn't conducive to breaking. This makes all the difference in the world. If you'll remember, much earlier in this book I told you that 17 was the magic number in blackjack because it represents the line between made hands and breaking hands, particularly for the dealer (see situation #37). In this situation, you should just hit the hand instead of doubling because doubling could get you an Ace, 2, 8, 9, 10, Jack, Queen, or King, all of which give you an unmade hand and set you up for a $40 loss instead of a $20 loss if you double down.

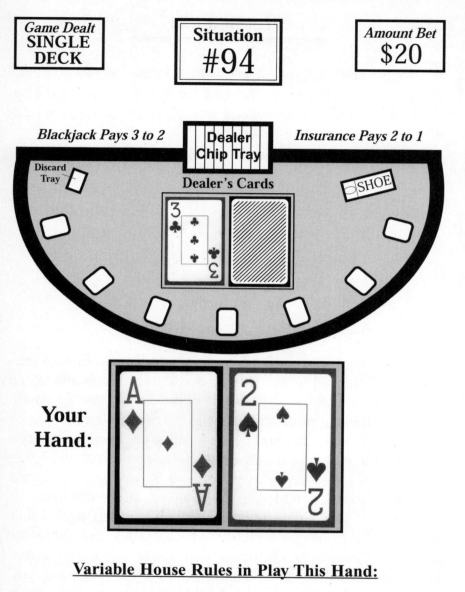

| Game Dealt SINGLE DECK | Situation #94 | Amount Bet $20 |

Blackjack Pays 3 to 2   **Insurance Pays 2 to 1**

Dealer Chip Tray

Discard Tray

Dealer's Cards

SHOE

Your Hand:

Variable House Rules in Play This Hand:

1. Double Down: Any two cards
2. Double Down After Splitting: Yes
3. Surrender Allowed: Yes
4. Dealer Soft 17s: Must stand

Situation #94

In a single-deck game, you have been dealt an Ace and a 2 for a soft 13 total against the dealer's 3. Of the options listed below, which is your best play?

My Options

A)   Stand
B)   Hit
C)   Double down
D)   Split
E)   Surrender

Situation #94 Answer

You won't surrender the hand because you can still make something out of this soft total and because the dealer has a breaking card up. You can't split because you don't have a pair. You won't stand because there are too many ways to improve your hand without breaking. That leaves you with the options of hitting or doubling down. Many times you'll double down against a breaking card, but not this time. Reason being that a 3 up card isn't enough of a disadvantage to the dealer to make it worth your while to risk two bets instead of one. The dealer will make a made hand 62 percent of the time when showing a 3. There are just too many card combinations that'll leave you with an unmade hand when you double down (Ace, 2, 3, 9, 10, Jack, Queen, and King). Since 8 of the 13 ranks work against you on a double-down move, your best play here is to hit the hand, and if you catch something poor such as an Ace, 2, 3, or 4, you can still hit your hand again in an effort to improve it.

Variable House Rules in Play This Hand:

1. Double Down: Any two cards
2. Double Down After Splitting: Yes
3. Surrender Allowed: Yes
4. Dealer Soft 17s: Must stand

Situation #95

In a slight variance from situation #94, you have been dealt an Ace and a 2 for a soft 13 total against the dealer's 4. Of the options listed below, which is your best play?

My Options

A) Stand
B) Hit
C) Double down
D) Split
E) Surrender

Situation #95 Answer

Once again, you won't be surrendering, splitting, or standing, so the issue comes down to hitting or doubling down for two bets. In this case, it's better to double down than just to hit. There is enough of a difference in dealer performance between a 3 and a 4 to warrant your doubling down against the 4 but not the 3 when holding a soft 13. One of the things you should keep in mind is that—in general—the worst card a dealer can show is a 6, followed by a 5, and then a 4. On many double-down situations, the line separating *do* from *don't* is the line between the 3 and the 4.

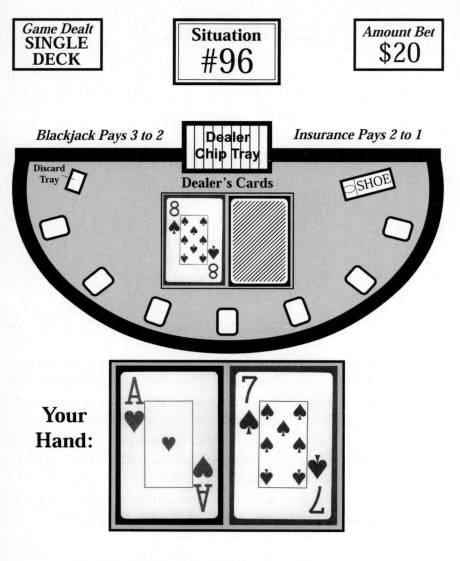

Game Dealt
SINGLE DECK

Situation #96

Amount Bet $20

Blackjack Pays 3 to 2

Dealer Chip Tray

Insurance Pays 2 to 1

Discard Tray

Dealer's Cards

SHOE

Your Hand:

Variable House Rules in Play This Hand:

1. Double Down: Any two cards
2. Double Down After Splitting: Yes
3. Surrender Allowed: Yes
4. Dealer Soft 17s: Must stand

Situation #96

In a single-deck game, you have received an Ace and a 7 for a soft 18 total against the dealer's 8 up. Of the options listed below, which represents your best move?

My Options

- A) Stand
- B) Hit
- C) Double down
- D) Split
- E) Surrender

Situation #96 Answer

You won't be surrendering this hand because you have a good total. You can't split because you don't have a pair. That leaves you with the options of standing, hitting, or doubling. With a soft 18 against the 8, you have to figure the dealer for an 18 (a 10-count card in the hole). By standing, you're essentially accepting a push. If you hit the hand, in an effort to beat an 18 by the dealer, the only way you improve your hand is to catch an Ace, 2, or 3 for 19, 20, or 21, respectively. That's only three ranks that improve your hand. Of the other ten ranks, four (10, Jack, Queen, and King) leave you right where you are with an 18 total. That means that six ranks (4, 5, 6, 7, 8, and 9) leave you worse off than before, especially given the likelihood that the dealer is holding an 18. Since hitting this hand is a poor move, doubling down would be even worse since you'd be risking twice the money. Your best move, then, is to stand and hope the dealer doesn't have an Ace in the hole and accept the possible push.

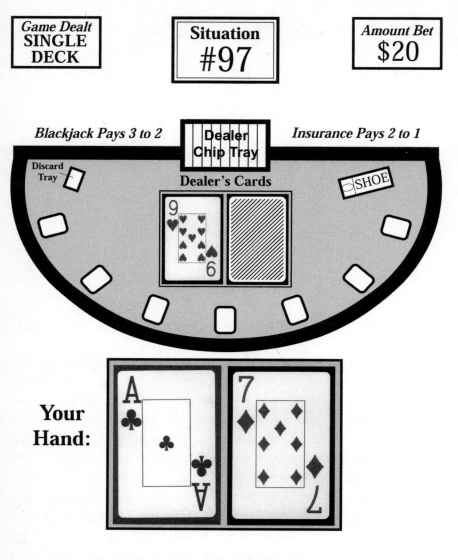

Game Dealt SINGLE DECK

Situation #97

Amount Bet $20

Blackjack Pays 3 to 2

Dealer Chip Tray

Insurance Pays 2 to 1

Discard Tray

Dealer's Cards

SHOE

Your Hand:

Variable House Rules in Play This Hand:

1. Double Down: Any two cards
2. Double Down After Splitting: Yes
3. Surrender Allowed: Yes
4. Dealer Soft 17s: Must stand

Situation #97

In a slight variance from situation #96, you have received an Ace and a 7 for a soft 18 total against the dealer's 9 up. Of the options listed below, which represents your best move?

My Options

A)   Stand

B)   Hit

C)   Double down

D)   Split

E)   Surrender

Situation #97 Answer

Figuring the dealer for a 19, you can't like your hand of soft 18. Now, what to do. You won't surrender because there's still hope for your soft hand. You can't split because you don't have a pair. If this were a hard 18, you would stand, but since it is a soft 18, you have options. Doubling down, however, isn't one of them because you'd just be putting twice as much money at risk in a precarious position. That leaves you with hitting or standing. As I mentioned earlier, if this were a hard 18 you'd stand because the odds of improving your hand (hitting an Ace, 2, or 3) are slim. But with a soft 18, you at least have the option of trying for one of the three small cards, knowing that if you hit a 10-count card you'll still be at 18 and no worse off than you are now. And if you hit something such as a 4 through an 8, you can still hit again in an effort to try to win a hand in which the odds are already against you.

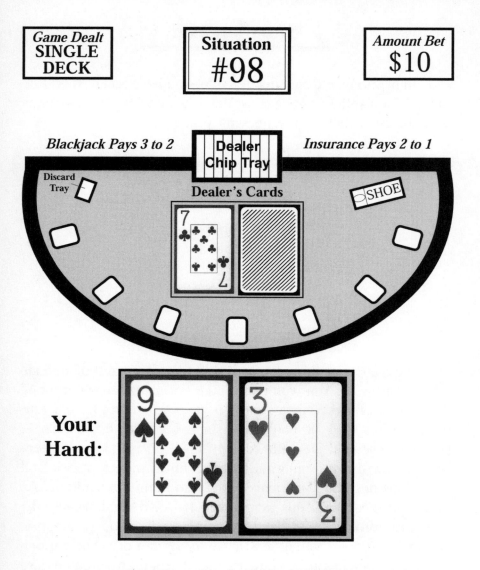

| Game Dealt SINGLE DECK | Situation #98 | Amount Bet $10 |

Blackjack Pays 3 to 2   Dealer Chip Tray   **Insurance Pays 2 to 1**

Discard Tray

Dealer's Cards

SHOE

Your Hand:

Variable House Rules in Play This Hand:

1. Double Down: Any two cards
2. Double Down After Splitting: Yes
3. Surrender Allowed: No
4. Dealer Soft 17s: Must stand

Situation #98

In a single-deck game, you have been dealt a 9 and a 3 for a 12 total against the dealer's 7. Of the options below, which is your best play?

My Options

A) Stand
B) Hit
C) Double down
D) Split
E) Surrender

Situation #98 Answer

Many of the plays you make in blackjack will be simple and automatic. This is one of them. You have to figure the dealer for 17 since she's showing a 7 and all unseen cards (such as her hole card) have to be figured as being worth 10. Since you have a 12 and the dealer a possible 17, you have to hit this hand until you, too, have at least a 17 or bust trying. One unalterable tenet of playing perfect basic strategy dictates that whenever the dealer has a made hand (7-Ace showing), you must hit until you, too, have a made hand (17 or more). The percentages are against you, but that will be the case much of the time. It's because so many of the hands you play will be like this one that you must maximize your splitting and double down opportunities when they come along.

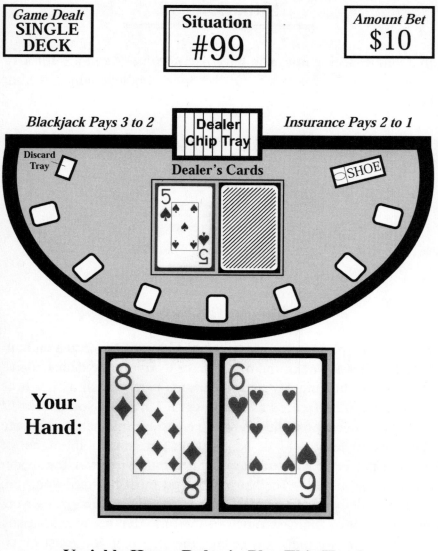

| Game Dealt SINGLE DECK | Situation #99 | Amount Bet $10 |

Blackjack Pays 3 to 2

Dealer Chip Tray

Insurance Pays 2 to 1

Discard Tray

Dealer's Cards

SHOE

Your Hand:

Variable House Rules in Play This Hand:

1. Double Down: Any two cards
2. Double Down After Splitting: Yes
3. Surrender Allowed: No
4. Dealer Soft 17s: Must stand

Situation #99

In a single-deck game, you have been dealt an 8 and a 6 for a 14 total against the dealer's 5. Of the options below, which is your best play?

My Options

A) Stand
B) Hit
C) Double down
D) Split
E) Surrender

Situation #99 Answer

Similar to situation #98, this is another type of hand that will come your way often and requires no deep thought or analysis about what to do. Another principle of playing perfect basic strategy dictates that whenever you have a hard 14 and the dealer shows a breaking hand (2–6 as her up card), you stand. You are relying (hoping for statistical probabilities to come through for you over the long run, in essence) on the dealer breaking rather than trying to make a made hand of your own.

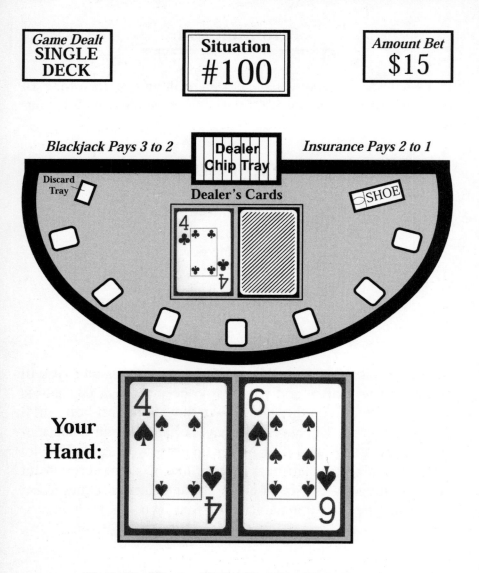

Game Dealt
SINGLE DECK

Situation
#100

Amount Bet
$15

Blackjack Pays 3 to 2

Dealer Chip Tray

Insurance Pays 2 to 1

Discard Tray

Dealer's Cards

SHOE

Your Hand:

<u>Variable House Rules in Play This Hand:</u>

1. Double Down: Any two cards
2. Double Down After Splitting: Yes
3. Surrender Allowed: No
4. Dealer Soft 17s: Must stand

Situation #100

In a single-deck game, you have been dealt a 4 and a 6 for a 10 total against the dealer's 4. Of the options below, which is your best play?

My Options

A) Stand
B) Hit
C) Double down
D) Split
E) Surrender

Situation #100 Answer

As in situations #98 and #99, this is another no-brainer type of hand that will come often. When you get your hand, you should first decide if it presents an opportunity for splitting (this hand doesn't) or doubling down (this hand does because it is a 10 total, a great doubling hand). The next thing you need to do is decide—based on the dealer's up card—if you actually want to follow through with your splitting or double-down opportunity. In this case, we do want to double down because the dealer is showing a weak up card, a 4, and one with which she will often break. This is where the real money is made in blackjack, doubling down and splitting pairs against poor dealer up cards. Make the most of these opportunities.

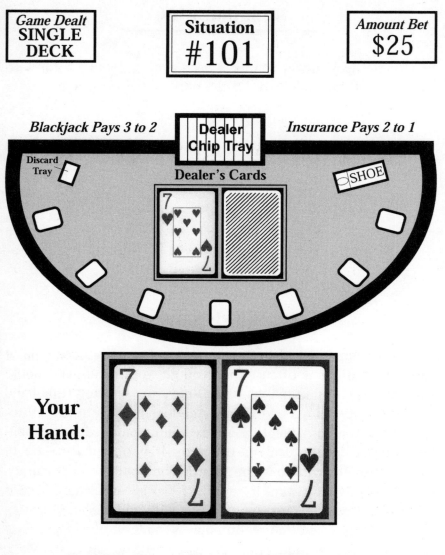

Game Dealt	Situation	Amount Bet
SINGLE DECK	**#101**	**$25**

Blackjack Pays 3 to 2   Dealer Chip Tray   Insurance Pays 2 to 1

Discard Tray

Dealer's Cards

SHOE

Your Hand:

Variable House Rules in Play This Hand:

1. Double Down: Any two cards
2. Double Down After Splitting: Yes
3. Surrender Allowed: No
4. Dealer Soft 17s: Must stand

Situation #101

In a single-deck game, you have been dealt a pair of 7s for a 14 total against the dealer's 7. Of the options below, which is your best play?

My Options

    A)   Stand
    B)   Hit
    C)   Double down
    D)   Split
    E)   Surrender

Situation #101 Answer

Surrender is not allowed, so that option is out. You won't stand on a 14 against a 7 because the dealer has a made hand while you have a breaking hand. Doubling down on a 14 against a made hand would be plain foolish. That leaves you with the options of hitting or splitting. Hitting a breaking hand against a made hand is always undesirable. In this situation you have one out, and that is to split this pair. Instead of one hand of 14, you'll have two hands of possible 17, a more preferable position to be in. Also, this casino allows you to double down after you split, so hopefully, you'll catch a 3 or a 4 on at least one of your 7s so that you can exercise another player-advantage option.

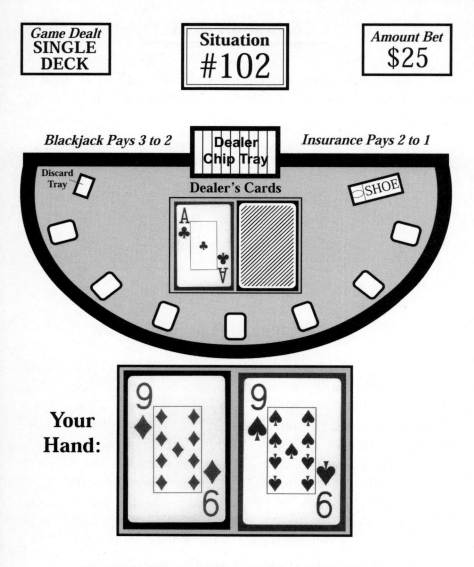

Game Dealt	Situation	Amount Bet
SINGLE DECK	**#102**	**$25**

Blackjack Pays 3 to 2   *Insurance Pays 2 to 1*

Your Hand:

Variable House Rules in Play This Hand:

1. Double Down: Any two cards
2. Double Down After Splitting: Yes
3. Surrender Allowed: Yes (early/late)
4. Dealer Soft 17s: Must stand

Situation #102

In a single-deck game at an extremely liberal casino, you have been dealt a pair of 9s for an 18 total against the dealer's Ace. This casino offers both early and late surrender. The dealer asks if you would like to take early surrender before she checks her hole card. Should you?

My Options

A) Yes

B) No

Situation #102 Answer

This is a rare casino that is offering you early surrender. Statistically, there are 49 remaining unseen cards in the deck, 16 of which are worth 10 and will give the dealer a blackjack. That means that there are 33 cards that will not give her a blackjack. This 33-to-16 ratio is slightly in favor of her not having a blackjack, so I would refuse it. As a reminder of what I mentioned earlier in the book, if you aren't a proficient card counter, the taking of both insurance and surrender isn't worth your while in most cases. If your hand were a terrible hard total, such as 14, 15, or 16, I would surrender in that case, but since you already have a decent made hand, if you can escape a dealer blackjack here, you have a reasonable shot at winning this hand.

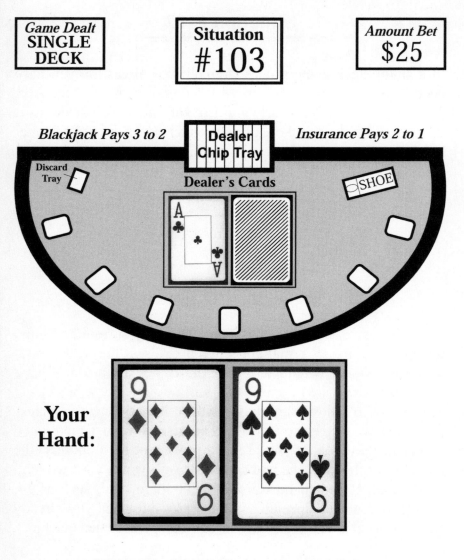

Game Dealt	Situation	Amount Bet
SINGLE DECK	#103	$25

Blackjack Pays 3 to 2   Insurance Pays 2 to 1

Dealer Chip Tray

Discard Tray

Dealer's Cards

SHOE

Your Hand:

Variable House Rules in Play This Hand:

1. Double Down: Any two cards
2. Double Down After Splitting: Yes
3. Surrender Allowed: Yes (early/late)
4. Dealer Soft 17s: Must stand

Situation #103

In a continuation of the same hand from situation #102, the dealer does not have a blackjack. It is now your turn to act. Of the options listed below, which is your best move?

My Options

A) Stand
B) Hit
C) Double down
D) Split
E) Surrender

Situation #103 Answer

You escaped the dealer blackjack, so now you have a reasonable shot at winning this hand. That means, of course, that you won't be taking late surrender. You also won't, naturally, double down on an 18 total. You also won't hit this hand. That leaves your decision between standing and splitting. Any time the dealer shows an Ace up, she'll make a made hand 83 percent of the time over the long haul, so you know you have to make a made hand here. If you stand, you have a made hand of 18. If you split, you could potentially make two 19s, but odds are you'll hit one 10-count card and one small card, improving one hand and worsening the other. Your best move here is to stand pat on your one 18 and not split it in an effort to make two better hands. Just because you have a pair, doesn't mean you have to split it.

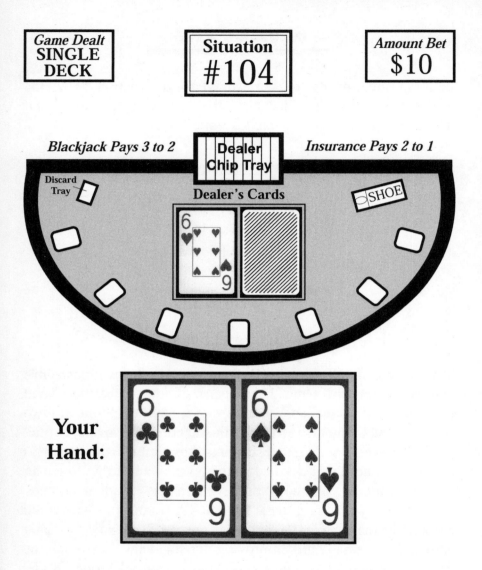

Game Dealt
SINGLE DECK

Situation #104

Amount Bet
$10

Blackjack Pays 3 to 2

Dealer Chip Tray

Insurance Pays 2 to 1

Discard Tray

Dealer's Cards

SHOE

Your Hand:

Variable House Rules in Play This Hand:

1. Double Down: Any two cards
2. Double Down After Splitting: Yes
3. Surrender Allowed: No
4. Dealer Soft 17s: Must hit

Situation #104

In a single-deck game, you have been dealt a pair of 6s against the dealer's 6. Of the options listed below, which is your best move?

My Options

A) Stand
B) Hit
C) Double down
D) Split
E) Surrender

Situation #104 Answer

The dealer's 6 was nice to see, but your pair of 6s were not. Still, we can make a profit on this hand. You can't surrender this hand, nor would you if the rules allowed. Some beginning players naively double down on a hand like this because they know the 6 up is bad for the dealer and only the four ranks valued at 10 (10, Jack, Queen, and King) will break them while the other nine (Ace–9) will not. You should never double down on a 12 in blackjack. If you want to double your money on this hand, the way to do it is to split it into two hands. You might even make more than double your money because this particular casino allows you to double down after you split, a *valuable* player option. If you happen to catch an Ace, 3, 4, or 5 after you split, you can double down again and increase your winning units even more of the time.

Variable House Rules in Play This Hand:

1. Double Down: Any two cards
2. Double Down After Splitting: Yes
3. Surrender Allowed: Yes
4. Dealer Soft 17s: Must hit

Situation #105

In a single-deck game, you have been dealt a pair of 4s against the dealer's 7. Of the options listed below, which is your best move?

My Options

A) Stand
B) Hit
C) Double down
D) Split
E) Surrender

Situation #105 Answer

You won't surrender this hand because you have something good to work with. You won't stand because you only have an 8, and you can't possibly break by drawing. You need to improve to a made hand since the dealer has one. That leaves you with hitting, splitting, or doubling down. An 8 against a 7 isn't enough of an advantage for the player when it comes to doubling down. If the dealer has a 10 in the hole for a 17 (which is what you have to play her for), then only a 10-count card or an Ace (just 5 of the 13 ranks) will win this hand for you if you double, leaving you with 8 ranks that'll lose you two bets. That brings it down to hitting or splitting. If you split this hand, you'll have two poor hands (two possible 14s) against a made hand. Ugh. Your best move is just to hit this hand until you have a made hand (17 or more) or break trying to get there.

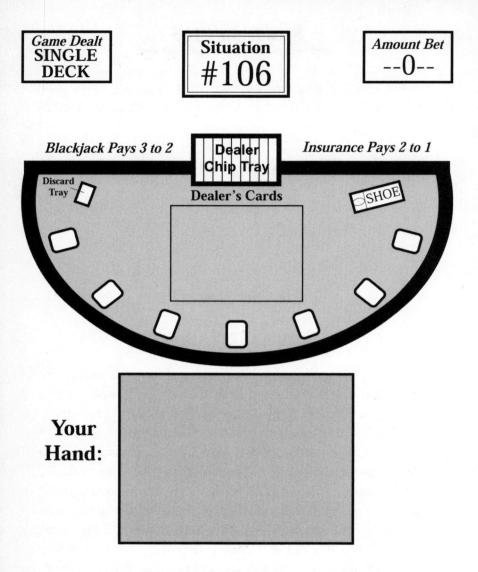

Game Dealt
SINGLE DECK

Situation #106

Amount Bet
--0--

Blackjack Pays 3 to 2

Dealer Chip Tray

Insurance Pays 2 to 1

Discard Tray

Dealer's Cards

SHOE

Your Hand:

Variable House Rules in Play This Hand:

1. Double Down: Any two cards
2. Double Down After Splitting: Yes
3. Surrender Allowed: Yes
4. Dealer Soft 17s: Must hit

Situation #106

For two hours you played at the same table and did quite well, getting $700 ahead playing mostly $10 hands. Then, over the last 30 minutes, you dropped $250 of it back, all since the arrival of a rude, irritating, mouthy drunk who has gotten under your skin. Even though he is an obviously poor player, he has won a small fortune with his high-roller bets, which irritates you even more. What should you do?

My Options

A) Continue to grind it out, hoping for a comeback.

B) Make larger wagers like the **high roller**.

C) Get mouthy back and be rude to him, hoping he'll leave.

D) Punch him out because he obviously deserves it.

E) Sit out for a while and try to collect your thoughts and regain your cool, but don't leave that **hot** table.

F) Leave and play at another table.

G) Call it a night and go home or back to your hotel room, but either way, *stop gambling*.

Situation #106 Answer

Any of the last three choices would be acceptable, so long as you get out of your funk and can maintain a positive mind-set with the total concentration playing blackjack for money requires. If you can't get your act together either at that table or at another one, call it quits for the night. Playing when irritated or angry is one of the fastest ways to lose your entire bankroll.

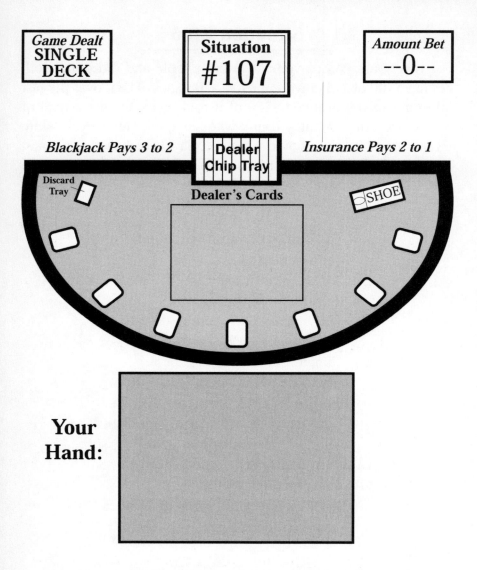

Variable House Rules in Play This Hand:

1. Double Down: Any two cards
2. Double Down After Splitting: Yes
3. Surrender Allowed: Yes
4. Dealer Soft 17s: Must hit

Situation #107

You have just arrived at the casino for what you hope will be a long, productive night of playing and are just sitting down to the blackjack table when the cocktail waitress arrives and asks you what you would like to drink. Of the options below, which would be your choice?

My Options

A) Coffee, since it's obviously going to be a long night.

B) Your favorite soft drink or bottled water.

C) Your favorite beer or mixed drink, whichever will put you the most at ease for your long night ahead.

D) Nothing. All eating and drinking should be done away from the blackjack table.

Situation #107 Answer

First of all, you should never approach a blackjack session with the mind-set that it's going to be a long night. It should be as long (or as short) as it needs to be, depending on how you're doing. Any gambling system (and playing perfect basic strategy *is* a system of sorts) no matter how sound, won't win every time, just most of the time. If you set out planning on a long night and lose a lot very quickly, it won't be prudent to pull more money out of your bankroll and keep playing just because you had a certain time frame in your head when you walked in. As for which drink you should choose, any of them except C would be fine. Whatever sets you at ease and puts you in a proper frame of mind should be your choice, except alcohol. Even a few alcoholic drinks can cloud the mind, a mind that needs to stay clear for the proper analysis of every play you are asked to make.

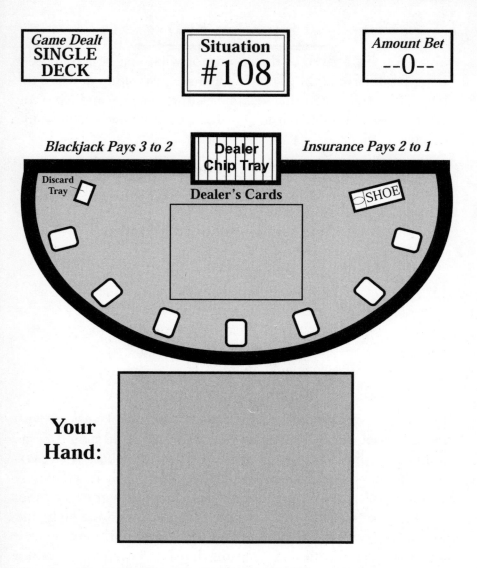

| Game Dealt SINGLE DECK | Situation #108 | Amount Bet --0-- |

Blackjack Pays 3 to 2

Insurance Pays 2 to 1

Dealer Chip Tray

Discard Tray

SHOE

Dealer's Cards

Your Hand:

Variable House Rules in Play This Hand:

1. Double Down: Any two cards
2. Double Down After Splitting: Yes
3. Surrender Allowed: Yes
4. Dealer Soft 17s: Must hit

Situation #108

You're walking around the blackjack area trying to decide which table to play at. All the tables are nearly full except one, a $50 minimum table, which has only one player, a truly beautiful woman in a low-cut dress who is seated in the third-base spot. When she sees you considering whether to sit down, she smiles, makes strong eye contact, and invites you to sit down at the table. Your normal betting limits—based on your bankroll—are in the $10–$20 range. What do you do?

My Options

A) Sit down and play, even with the disproportionate limits.
B) Sit at one of the other tables, even if not at third base.
C) Wait for third base to open up at one of the other tables.
D) Go to another casino, if that option is possible.

Situation #108 Answer

Option D, if possible, option C if not. Avoid women like this. Strange women who act like this are either hookers or **shills**. Since I'm sure you know what a hooker is, let me explain what a house shill is. It's a person who is hired by the house (and who uses house money to gamble with) to attract men to the higher-limit tables. Women like this who easily come on to a strange man are pros at what they do, which is make men bet more than they should and in a more reckless manner than is prudent. Avoid them. Furthermore, in some shadier establishments, house shills are trained to lead men to the tables with crooked dealers.

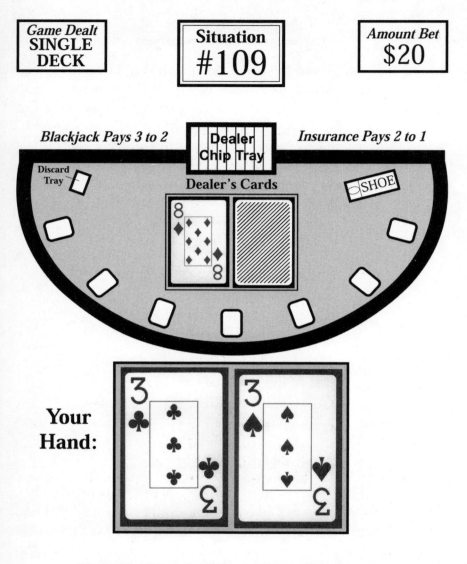

| Game Dealt SINGLE DECK | Situation #109 | Amount Bet $20 |

Blackjack Pays 3 to 2

Dealer Chip Tray

Insurance Pays 2 to 1

Discard Tray

Dealer's Cards

SHOE

Your Hand:

Variable House Rules in Play This Hand:

1. Double Down: Any two cards
2. Double Down After Splitting: Yes
3. Surrender Allowed: No
4. Dealer Soft 17s: Must stand

Situation #109

In a single-deck game, you have been dealt a pair of 3s against the dealer's 8. Of the options listed below, which is your best play?

My Options

A) Stand
B) Hit
C) Double down
D) Split
E) Surrender

Situation #109 Answer

With a 6 total, you obviously won't be standing because you can hit this hand without breaking. You won't be doubling down because the best you could hope for is a soft 17, not good enough against an 8 up card and possible 18 dealer hand. You can't surrender because this casino doesn't allow it, nor would you if it did. That leaves you with either splitting or hitting. If you split, you'll have to put another $20 out, giving you two possible 13s against a possible 18. Not a good plan. Thus, your best play here is to hit this hand until you have at least a soft 18 or a hard 17.

| Game Dealt SINGLE DECK | Situation #110 | Amount Bet $10 |

Blackjack Pays 3 to 2

Insurance Pays 2 to 1

Your Hand:

Variable House Rules in Play This Hand:

1. Double Down: Any two cards
2. Double Down After Splitting: Yes
3. Surrender Allowed: Yes
4. Dealer Soft 17s: Must stand

Situation #110

In a single-deck game, you have been dealt a 5 and a 3 against the dealer's 7. Of the options listed below, which is your best play?

My Options

- A) Stand
- B) Hit
- C) Double down
- D) Split
- E) Surrender

Situation #110 Answer

Naturally, you aren't going to stand on this hand since you only have an 8 total and can't break no matter what card you draw next. You can't split it because you don't have a pair. Even though this casino allows surrender, you won't be exercising that option because you have a good, workable total against a lesser-made hand. That leaves you with either hitting or doubling down. While your 8 total is a bit of an advantage over the dealer's 7, it isn't enough to risk two bets for just one more card. Your best move on this hand is to hit until you get a made hand (17 or more) or break trying.

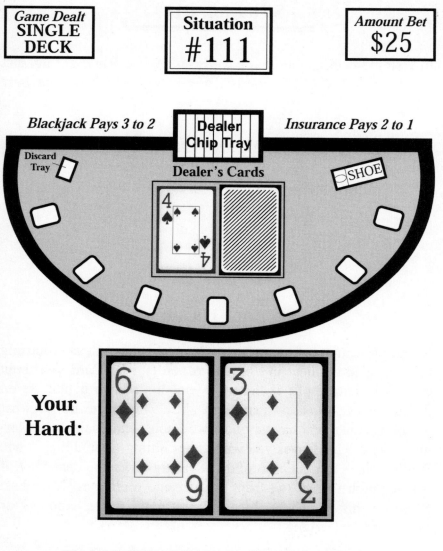

Variable House Rules in Play This Hand:

1. Double Down: Any two cards
2. Double Down After Splitting: Yes
3. Surrender Allowed: Yes
4. Dealer Soft 17s: Must stand

Situation #111

In a single-deck game, you have been dealt a 6 and a 3 against the dealer's 4. Of the options listed below, which is your best play?

My Options

    A)   Stand
    B)   Hit
    C)   Double down
    D)   Split
    E)   Surrender

Situation #111 Answer

Surrendering isn't an option because you have a good starting hand against the dealer's 4, a break card for her. You can't split because you don't have a pair. You won't be standing because you could still improve on this hand. That leaves you with the options of doubling down or hitting. Because the dealer is showing a 4 (the third worst up card she can have) and because you have a hand that can easily be made into a 19, you should slide another $25 chip into the betting circle and double down. As a blackjack player, these are the opportunities you relish because this hand is one of the ones you'll win much more than you'll lose and because you'll be winning two bets instead of one, which helps to erase the built-in house advantage.

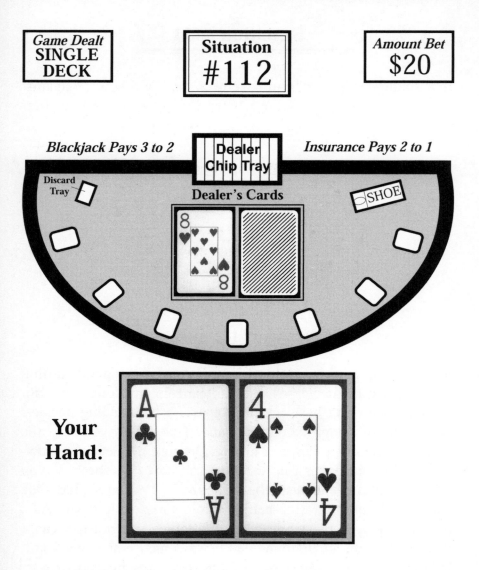

Game Dealt
SINGLE DECK

Situation
#112

Amount Bet
$20

Blackjack Pays 3 to 2   *Insurance Pays 2 to 1*

Dealer Chip Tray

Discard Tray

SHOE

Dealer's Cards

Your Hand:

Variable House Rules in Play This Hand:

1. Double Down: Any two cards
2. Double Down After Splitting: Yes
3. Surrender Allowed: No
4. Dealer Soft 17s: Must hit

Situation #112

In a single-deck game, you have been dealt an Ace and a 4 against the dealer's 8. Of the options listed below, which is your best play?

My Options

A) Stand
B) Hit
C) Double down
D) Split
E) Surrender

Situation #112 Answer

You have a 15, but it's a soft 15, so there's hope against this solid dealer up card. Since you have to figure the dealer for an 18, you have to do something other than stand. Surrender isn't allowed, nor would you take it if it were. You can't split this hand because it's not a pair. That leaves you with choosing between hitting and doubling down. If you double down for another $20, you'll be risking $40 on a hand that could easily turn from a soft 15 into a hard 15 by catching a 10-count card. And besides all the 10s that will hurt you if you double, the 7, 8, 9, or Ace will likely doom you as well. Thus, doubling down is clearly out of the picture. Your only option is to hit this hand until you get at least a hard 17 or break trying. Since the dealer has an 8 showing, you have to assume she has or will have a made hand and you need the same.

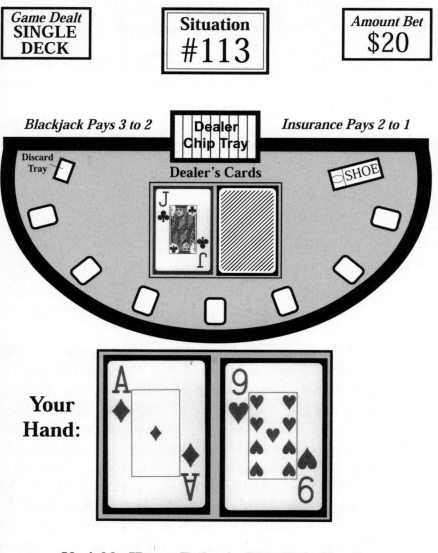

Game Dealt
SINGLE DECK

Situation #113

Amount Bet
$20

Blackjack Pays 3 to 2

Dealer Chip Tray

Insurance Pays 2 to 1

Discard Tray

Dealer's Cards

SHOE

Your Hand:

Variable House Rules in Play This Hand:

1. Double Down: Any two cards
2. Double Down After Splitting: Yes
3. Surrender Allowed: Yes
4. Dealer Soft 17s: Must hit

Situation #113

In a single-deck game, you have been dealt an Ace and a 9 against the dealer's Jack. Of the options listed below, which is your best play?

My Options

A) Stand
B) Hit
C) Double down
D) Split
E) Surrender

Situation #113 Answer

You won't surrender a 20 and you can't split the hand because it's not a pair. Hitting would be almost pointless because only an Ace would improve your hand (giving you a 21). For the same reason you wouldn't double down, especially since the dealer has a powerful up card. All you can really do here is stand on your soft 20 and hope the dealer has something other than a 10-count card down so that you don't end up pushing on your powerful hand.

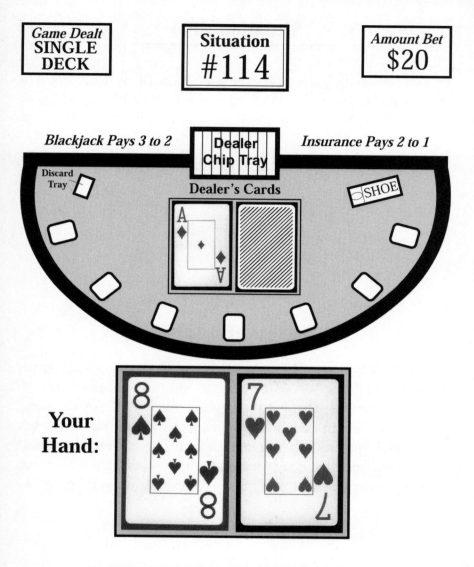

Game Dealt
SINGLE DECK

Situation #114

Amount Bet $20

Blackjack Pays 3 to 2

Dealer Chip Tray

Insurance Pays 2 to 1

Discard Tray

Dealer's Cards

SHOE

A

Your Hand:

8 ♠

7 ♥

Variable House Rules in Play This Hand:

1. Double Down: Any two cards
2. Double Down After Splitting: Yes
3. Surrender Allowed: No
4. Dealer Soft 17s: Must hit

Situation #114

In a single-deck game, you have been dealt an 8 and a 7 for a 15 total against the dealer's Ace and the dealer does not have a blackjack. Of the options listed below, which is your best play?

My Options

- A) Stand
- B) Hit
- C) Double Down
- D) Split
- E) Surrender

Situation #114 Answer

This situation is one of the very few hands you would surrender while playing perfect basic strategy blackjack if the rules allowed, but since this casino doesn't allow it, you have to try something else. You can't split this hand because it's not a pair. You won't be doubling down because you have a breaking hand against a powerful up card. You can't stand because a dealer will make a made hand more than 80 percent of the time when showing an Ace up and you don't have a made hand yet. So, your only real option is to hit until you make 17 or more, or break trying. Don't get discouraged by such hands because a fair amount of them will be just like this—a busting hand against a made hand—and you just have to be automatic in your approach. Hit a breaking hand against a made hand.

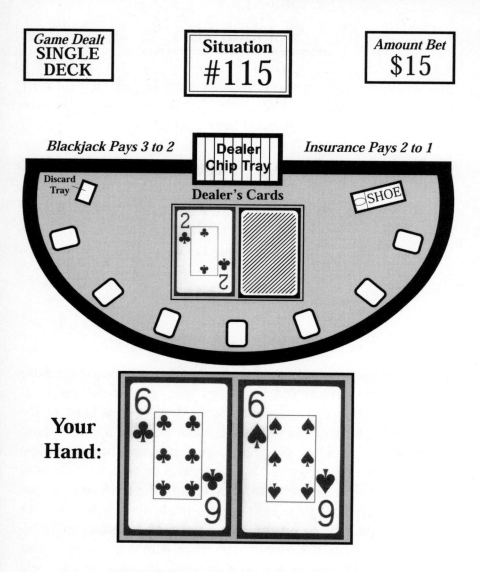

Variable House Rules in Play This Hand:

1. Double Down: Any two cards
2. Double Down After Splitting: Yes
3. Surrender Allowed: Yes
4. Dealer Soft 17s: Must hit

Situation #115

In a single-deck game, you have been dealt a pair of 6s against the dealer's 2. Of the options listed below, which is your best play?

My Options

A)   Stand
B)   Hit
C)   Double down
D)   Split
E)   Surrender

Situation #115 Answer

You're not going to surrender because the dealer has a breaking hand and you have ways to improve yours. You're not going to double down because you'd be risking $30 instead of $15 with a chance of breaking if you drew a 10-count card. That leaves you with the options of hitting, splitting, or standing. This is a unique situation in that it's one of the few hands where it doesn't make a lot of difference which of the three options you choose, at least percentage-wise. If you just hit the hand, you'll gain about four units in each 1,000 times you play this hand as opposed to standing. If you split, you'll also gain four units over standing. However, in this particular casino, you have the option of doubling after splitting, so if you catch a 3, 4, or 5, you can double down on your 9, 10, or 11 and gain even more units. Therefore, I would split this hand in a single-deck game.

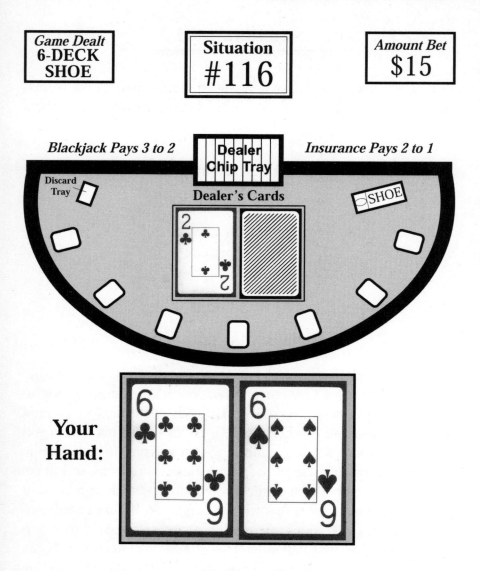

Game Dealt
6-DECK SHOE

Situation #116

Amount Bet
$15

Blackjack Pays 3 to 2

Dealer Chip Tray

Insurance Pays 2 to 1

Discard Tray

Dealer's Cards

SHOE

Your Hand:

Variable House Rules in Play This Hand:

1. Double Down: Any two cards
2. Double Down After Splitting: Yes
3. Surrender Allowed: Yes
4. Dealer Soft 17s: Must hit

Situation #116

In a slight variation from situation #115, you have caught the same hand against the same dealer up card but in a 6-deck shoe game instead of a single-deck game. Of the options listed below, which is your best play?

My Options

A) Stand
B) Hit
C) Double down
D) Split
E) Surrender

Situation #116 Answer

Was the last line of situation #115's answer a giveaway? It was supposed to be. So, if it was correct to split this hand in a single-deck game, does the giveaway mean that it's not correct to split it in a shoe game? That's right. Because so many small cards can come out in clumps, when you get this hand in a shoe game, you should just hit it instead of splitting it into two hands like you do in a single-deck game. Again, in a single-deck game, the cards tend to run truer than in a shoe game and it'll be a bit easier for the dealer to break on a 2.

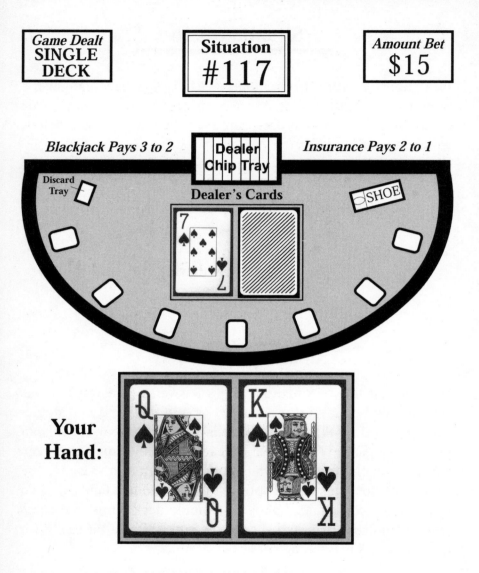

| Game Dealt SINGLE DECK | Situation #117 | Amount Bet $15 |

Blackjack Pays 3 to 2   *Insurance Pays 2 to 1*

Your Hand:

Variable House Rules in Play This Hand:

1. Double Down: Any two cards
2. Double Down After Splitting: Yes
3. Surrender Allowed: Yes
4. Dealer Soft 17s: Must hit

Situation #117

In a single-deck game, you receive a Queen and a King for a 20 total. The dealer receives a 7. You notice that neither of the other two players receive a 10-count card in the combined six cards they were dealt. Given the obvious number of 10s left in the deck, should you split this hand in an attempt to win twice as much against the dealer's lesser card?

My Options

A)   Stand
B)   Hit
C)   Double down
D)   Split
E)   Surrender

Situation #117 Answer

While a Queen and a King aren't technically a pair, in blackjack they count as a pair since they are both worth 10. You won't be splitting them, however, because . . . why? That's right, you don't mess with 20s. It doesn't matter what the dealer's up card is and it doesn't matter what cards have been dealt (or not been dealt). *You just don't mess with 20s*. Period. It's better to take an almost sure one win rather than take a chance on two maybe wins.

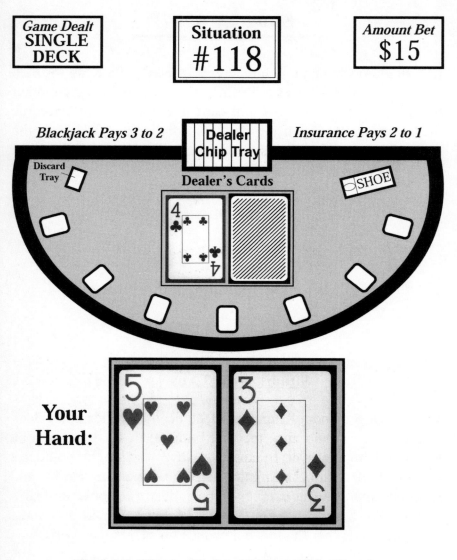

Variable House Rules in Play This Hand:

1. Double Down: Any two cards
2. Double Down After Splitting: Yes
3. Surrender Allowed: Yes
4. Dealer Soft 17s: Must hit

Situation #118

In a single-deck game, you are dealt a 5 and a 3 for an 8 total against the dealer's 4. Of the options listed below, which is your best play?

My Options

    A)   Stand
    B)   Hit
    C)   Double down
    D)   Split
    E)   Surrender

Situation #118 Answer

Surrender is out of the question because you have a good starting total against a breaking hand for the dealer. You can't split because you don't have a pair. You won't be standing on this hand because you can improve it with no risk of breaking. That leaves you with hitting or doubling down. On this particular hand there is a fine line between the benefit of hitting and doubling, so it won't be the end of the world whichever way you choose to go, but technically it will be a very slight advantage to you just to hit this hand and not double.

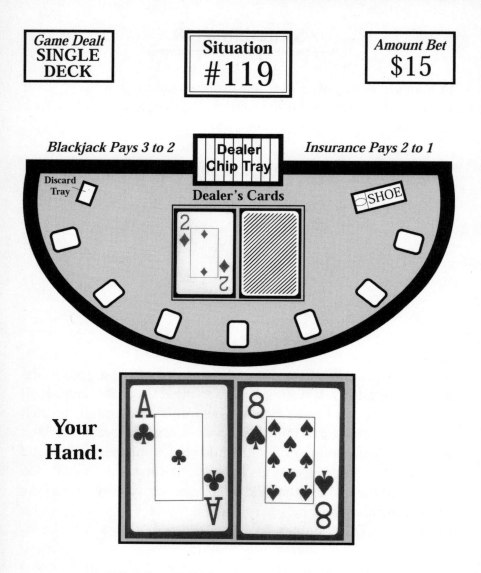

Situation
#119

Amount Bet
$15

Blackjack Pays 3 to 2

Dealer
Chip Tray

Insurance Pays 2 to 1

Discard
Tray

Dealer's Cards

SHOE

**Your
Hand:**

Variable House Rules in Play This Hand:

1. Double Down: Any two cards
2. Double Down After Splitting: Yes
3. Surrender Allowed: Yes
4. Dealer Soft 17s: Must hit

Situation #119

In a single-deck game, you are dealt an Ace and an 8 for a soft 19 total against the dealer's 2. Of the options listed below, which is your best play?

My Options

A)   Stand
B)   Hit
C)   Double down
D)   Split
E)   Surrender

Situation #119 Answer

You won't surrender because you have a good hand against the dealer's break card. You won't split this hand because you don't have a pair. There's really no point in hitting because the only cards that can improve your hand are an Ace or a 2, and one of each are already on the board. That leaves you with the realistic possibilities of standing or doubling down. While hitting would be pointless, doubling gives you the added aspect of making twice as much money. You always have to take a close look at any soft total for the possibility of doubling down. In this instance, however, the dealer's 2 is not enough of a disadvantage to her to make it worth your while to double down. She's going to make a made hand of 17 or more 65 percent of the time and 19 or more 38 percent of the time. You don't want to risk twice the money against those odds. Just stand with this hand.

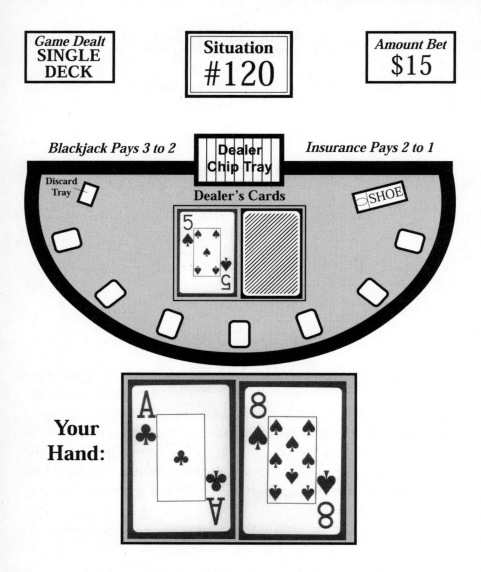

Game Dealt
SINGLE DECK

Situation
#120

Amount Bet
$15

Blackjack Pays 3 to 2

Insurance Pays 2 to 1

Dealer Chip Tray

Discard Tray

Dealer's Cards

SHOE

Your Hand:

Variable House Rules in Play This Hand:

1. Double Down: Any two cards
2. Double Down After Splitting: Yes
3. Surrender Allowed: Yes
4. Dealer Soft 17s: Must hit

Situation #120

In a minor variation from situation #119, you have received the same hand as before, but this time the dealer catches a 5 instead of a 2. Of the options listed below, which is your best play?

My Options

A) Stand
B) Hit
C) Double down
D) Split
E) Surrender

Situation #120 Answer

So, does it make any difference that the dealer has a 5 instead of a 2, being that the 5 is one of the worst cards a dealer can show? No, it makes no difference on this hand. It's not so much that you should or shouldn't consider doubling down because of the weaker card the dealer receives, the main point here is that—with one exception—you don't mess with 19s any more than 20s. The only exception is when your soft 19 is going up against a 6. It wouldn't be a tragedy if you doubled on this hand, but there's a slight statistical advantage to standing.

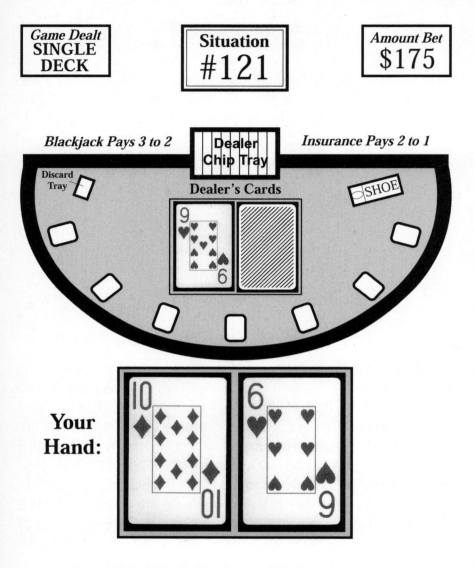

Game Dealt
SINGLE DECK

Situation
#121

Amount Bet
$175

Blackjack Pays 3 to 2

Dealer Chip Tray

Insurance Pays 2 to 1

Discard Tray

Dealer's Cards

SHOE

Your Hand:

Variable House Rules in Play This Hand:

1. Double Down: Any two cards
2. Double Down After Splitting: Yes
3. Surrender Allowed: No
4. Dealer Soft 17s: Must hit

Situation #121

After a productive two-hour session in which you win $175 playing $10–$20 per hand, you decide to bet one more hand before quitting. You also decide that since you are playing on house money, you will bet the entire $175 you are ahead on one last hand, win or lose. In this single-deck game, you receive a 10 and a 6 for a 16 total against the dealer's 9. Of the options below, which is your best play?

My Options

    A)   Stand because the bet is so large.
    B)   Stand because it's the right move.
    C)   Hit and hope for a winner.
    D)   Split.
    E)   Surrender.

Situation #121 Answer

Can you identify the cardinal rule you violated here? You bet *way* out of proportion to your bankroll, and now you've caught a horrible hand against a powerful up card. Even though hitting this hand is a losing proposition, you've got to do it because standing is an even more losing proposition. Many players get weak-kneed when they catch a poor hand against a good up card with a large bet on the table. Remember, if it's the right move, it's the right move, no matter how much money is on the line. Next time, don't foolishly put all your winnings at risk on one hand. In gambling, anything can happen at any time and—unfortunately—usually does. Play smart.

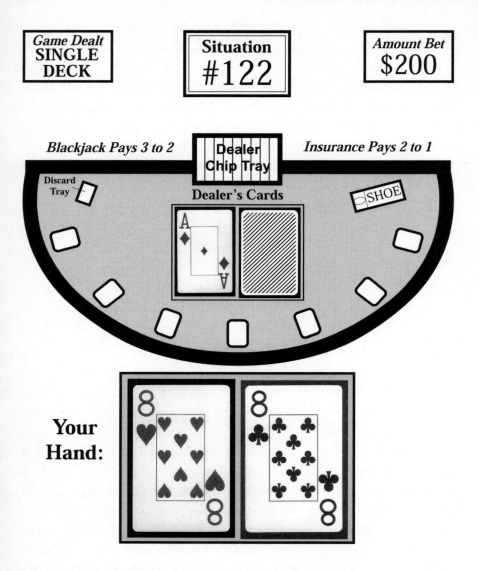

| Game Dealt SINGLE DECK | Situation #122 | Amount Bet $200 |

Blackjack Pays 3 to 2   Dealer Chip Tray   **Insurance Pays 2 to 1**

Discard Tray   SHOE

Dealer's Cards

Your Hand:

Variable House Rules in Play This Hand:

1. Double Down: Any two cards
2. Double Down After Splitting: No
3. Surrender Allowed: No
4. Dealer Soft 17s: Must hit

Situation #122

Similar to situation #121, you have a productive two-hour session in which you win $200 playing mostly $10 hands. Once again you decide to bet all your winnings on one last hand. This time, however, you catch a pair of 8s against the dealer's Ace. She asks if you want to take insurance on the hand. Do you?

My Options

A) Take insurance because of the size of the bet.

B) Do not take insurance, in spite of the size of the bet.

Situation #122 Answer

Well, you did it again. You made a huge bet way out of proportion to your bankroll, getting caught in a compromising situation. After building up a nice pile of chips, you're now in a position to lose it all on one hand. If you take the insurance, it will cost you $100, or half of your bet. If you take it and the dealer doesn't have the blackjack, you've just lost half your winnings. If the dealer does have the blackjack, you break even and risked all your winnings to do so. Pretty poor situation either way for you. As I mentioned earlier in the book, insurance is a losing proposition. What you need to do here is decline the insurance, hold your breath, and hope the dealer doesn't have a blackjack. If you survive, pinch yourself and promise you won't bet out of proportion to your bankroll again.

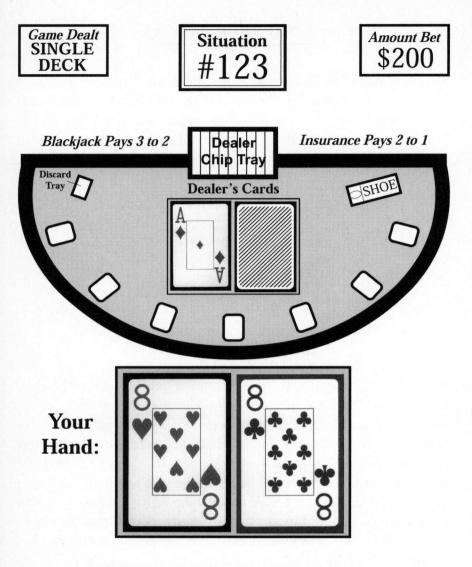

| Game Dealt **SINGLE DECK** | Situation **#123** | Amount Bet **$200** |

Blackjack Pays 3 to 2   **Insurance Pays 2 to 1**

Dealer Chip Tray

Discard Tray

Dealer's Cards

SHOE

Your Hand:

Variable House Rules in Play This Hand:

1. Double Down: Any two cards
2. Double Down After Splitting: No
3. Surrender Allowed: No
4. Dealer Soft 17s: Must hit

Situation #123

In a continuation of the same hand that began in situation #122, you decline the insurance and the dealer does not have a black-jack. It is now your turn to act. Of the options listed below, which is your best play?

My Options

    A)   Stand
    B)   Hit
    C)   Double down
    D)   Split
    E)   Surrender

Situation #123 Answer

Imagine if you could surrender (this casino doesn't allow it), you'd lose $100 and almost consider it your best option. Naturally, you won't double down since you'd be risking twice the money with many chances to break on your 16. If you stand, the dealer will make a made hand well over 80 percent of the time, and you don't have a made hand yet. That leaves you with hitting or splitting. If you hit, you're playing one 16 against an Ace. If you split, you're playing two possible 18s against the Ace. As you learned earlier, you should always split Aces and 8s. The problem you have here, though, is that you're going to have to put another $200 out to split the hand, and if you lose both hands, you're going back to your room a loser after doing a nice job of building up your winnings in the previous two hours. Still, split the hand.

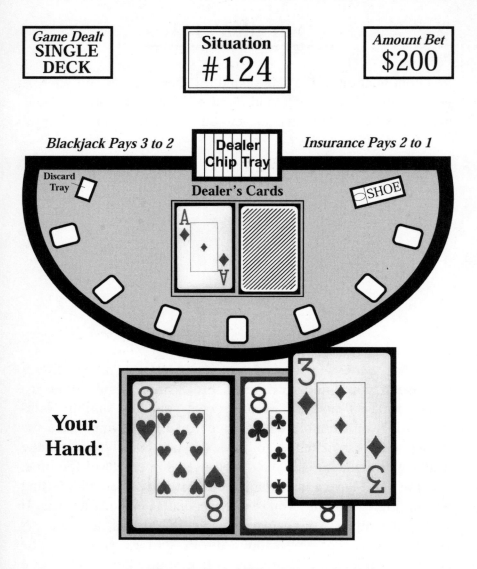

| Game Dealt SINGLE DECK | Situation #124 | Amount Bet $200 |

Blackjack Pays 3 to 2   **Insurance Pays 2 to 1**

Dealer Chip Tray

Discard Tray

SHOE

Dealer's Cards

Your Hand:

Variable House Rules in Play This Hand:

1. Double Down: Any two cards
2. Double Down After Splitting: No
3. Surrender Allowed: No
4. Dealer Soft 17s: Must hit

Situation #124

In a continuation of the same hand, #123, after splitting your 8s you catch a 3 to your first hand. Of the options listed below, which is your best play?

My Options

A) Stand
B) Hit
C) Double down
D) Split
E) Surrender

Situation #124 Answer

The 3 has to make your heart leap, if for no other reason than if you double down—as you should on this hand—you're going to have to push *another* $200 out onto the table, now putting $600 at risk. And to think, just a hand ago you were playing for a comfortable $10 a pop. As dizzying as this hand has gotten, as long as you have the money to double down, you should, because with this 11 total you might have found the only light in a hand that started as a black hole.

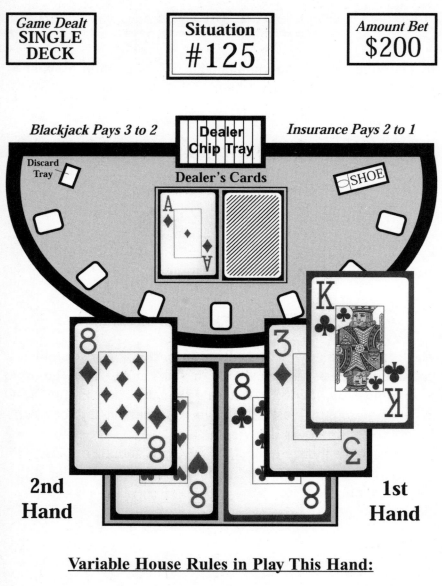

| Game Dealt SINGLE DECK | Situation #125 | Amount Bet $200 |

Blackjack Pays 3 to 2   Insurance Pays 2 to 1

Dealer Chip Tray

Discard Tray

Dealer's Cards

SHOE

2nd Hand

1st Hand

Variable House Rules in Play This Hand:

1. Double Down: Any two cards
2. Double Down After Splitting: No
3. Surrender Allowed: No
4. Dealer Soft 17s: Must hit

Situation #125

In a continuation of the same hand, #124, after doubling down on 11 on your first hand, you receive a King for a 21 total. The dealer then deals you another 8, giving you a pair of 8s on your second hand. Of the options listed below, which is your best play?

My Options

A) Stand
B) Hit
C) Double down
D) Split
E) Surrender

Situation #125 Answer

Basic strategy dictates that you always split Aces and 8s, and when you split them the first time, you end up with a nice 21, an almost sure winner. But let's think about this a minute. After looking into the jaws of a $200 loss when the hand started, you've turned things around with an almost sure $400 winner on your first hand. Even if you lose the second hand for $200, you'll still be up $200 on the hand (and $400 for the session), better than when you started all this silliness by betting stupidly. If you now restrict yourself to losing no more than $200 on this second hand, you'll stave off disaster. This will be a strategic exception to the normal basic strategy rule—brought about by your large bet—but instead of splitting this time, just hit the hand and try to make a made hand. You might luck out and win three bets instead of one, and even if you break in your efforts, you'll still avoid the disaster you foolishly set yourself up for.

| Game Dealt SINGLE DECK | Situation #126 | Amount Bet $15 |

Blackjack Pays 3 to 2   **Dealer Chip Tray**   **Insurance Pays 2 to 1**

Discard Tray

Dealer's Cards

SHOE

Your Hand:

Variable House Rules in Play This Hand:

1. Double Down: Any two cards
2. Double Down After Splitting: No
3. Surrender Allowed: Yes
4. Dealer Soft 17s: Must hit

Situation #126

In a single-deck game, you have been dealt an Ace and a 2 for a soft 13 total against the dealer's 9. Of the options listed below, which is your best move?

My Options

A) Stand
B) Hit
C) Double down
D) Split
E) Surrender

Situation #126 Answer

You won't surrender this hand even though the dealer has a strong up card because your soft total can be improved on without breaking. You can't split because you don't have a pair. You won't stand because you have a definite possibility of improving this hand without breaking. That leaves you with the options of hitting and doubling down. By now you should've learned that doubling down on a soft breaking hand against a dealer's made hand wouldn't be your best move. Thus, your only real option here is to hit until you make a made hand of hard 17 or more, or soft 18 or more.

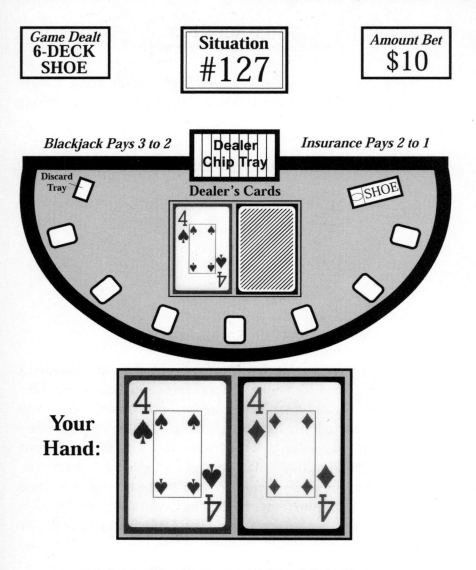

Situation #127

Blackjack Pays 3 to 2   Dealer Chip Tray   *Insurance Pays 2 to 1*

Discard Tray

SHOE

Dealer's Cards

Your Hand:

Variable House Rules in Play This Hand:

1. Double Down: Any two cards
2. Double Down After Splitting: Yes
3. Surrender Allowed: No
4. Dealer Soft 17s: Must hit

Situation #127

In a 6-deck shoe game, you have been dealt a pair of 4s against the dealer's 4. Of the options listed below, which is your best move?

My Options

A) Stand
B) Hit
C) Double down
D) Split
E) Surrender

Situation #127 Answer

You won't stand because you can improve this hand without breaking. You can't surrender, nor would you if you could. This leaves you with the options of splitting, hitting, or doubling down. If you split this hand, you'll have two possible 14s going against the dealer's possible 14, and that isn't a desirable goal. In fact, if you'll remember, you should never split a pair of 4s under any circumstances, whether in a shoe game like this or a single-deck game. The dealer's 4 is just at the fringe between bad hand and really bad hand. Your 8 total is just at the fringe of good hand and really good hand. The deciding factor here is that you are playing in a multiple-deck game. Because of the increased chance of drawing small cards in clumps, this is not a double down situation. You should just hit this hand. In a single-deck game, however, you will double down because of the truer fall of the cards.

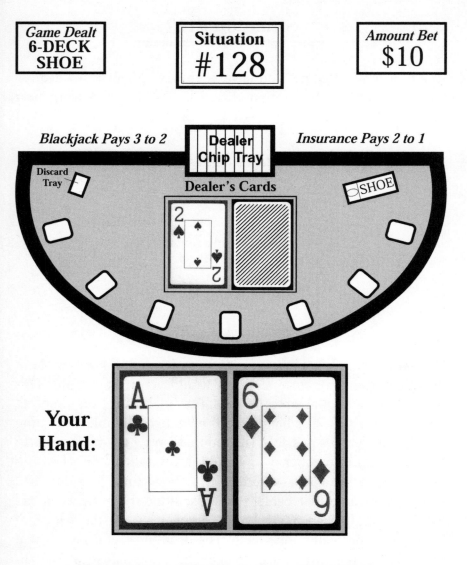

| Game Dealt 6-DECK SHOE | Situation #128 | Amount Bet $10 |

Variable House Rules in Play This Hand:

1. Double Down: Any two cards
2. Double Down After Splitting: Yes
3. Surrender Allowed: No
4. Dealer Soft 17s: Must hit

Situation #128

In a 6-deck shoe game, you have been dealt an Ace and a 6 for a soft 17 total against the dealer's 2. Which option below is your best play?

My Options

A) Stand
B) Hit
C) Double down
D) Split
E) Surrender

Situation #128 Answer

You won't be surrendering this hand because the rules don't allow it. You can't split it because it isn't a pair. So, should you stand, hit, or double down? If you'll take a look at the last of the Variable House Rules on the opposite page, you'll notice that the dealer has to hit a soft 17. Why do you suppose that is? That's right, because it's in the house's best interest to hit all soft 17s because the percentages favor that play. That means that you know you aren't going to stand on this hand, but you will hit or double down. When the dealer shows a 2, she'll make a made hand 65 percent of the time, and 51 percent of the time she'll make 18 or more. If you double down, there are more cards that'll give you 17 than any other total, which puts you at a slight disadvantage by doubling. Therefore, your best move is just to hit this hand in hopes of improving it. If you catch a 10, then you just stand. Ideally, you'll catch an Ace, 2, 3, or 4 and improve your hand. If you draw a 5 for a 12 total, you should hit once more. If you catch a 6, 7, 8, or 9, you should just stand, breaking hand against breaking hand.

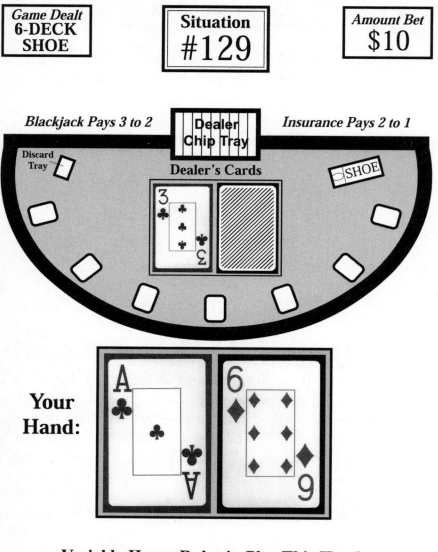

Game Dealt	Situation	Amount Bet
6-DECK SHOE	#129	$10

Blackjack Pays 3 to 2

Dealer Chip Tray

Insurance Pays 2 to 1

Discard Tray

SHOE

Dealer's Cards

3♣

Your Hand:

A♣   6♦

Variable House Rules in Play This Hand:

1. Double Down: Any two cards
2. Double Down After Splitting: Yes
3. Surrender Allowed: No
4. Dealer Soft 17s: Must hit

Situation #129

In a slight variation from situation #128, you have been dealt an Ace and a 6 for a soft 17 total against the dealer's 3 in a 6-deck shoe game. Which option below is your best play?

My Options

A) Stand
B) Hit
C) Double down
D) Split
E) Surrender

Situation #129 Answer

Once again, you can't surrender or split this hand, so you are left with standing, hitting, or doubling down. So, does the change from a 2 up card to a 3 up card make any difference? Yes. In situation #128, I mention—when considering the double down option—that the dealer, when showing a 2, would make a hand of 18 or more 51 percent of the time, which gives her a slight edge against your soft 17, so you shouldn't risk double the money. When the dealer shows a 3 up, however, the situation is reversed; she'll make an 18 or more only 49 percent of the time against your soft 17. In addition, she'll make a made hand 3 percent less with a 3 than a 2, 62 percent to 65 percent of the time, respectively. This slight drop in percentages is enough to swing the balance in your favor for doubling down rather than hitting.

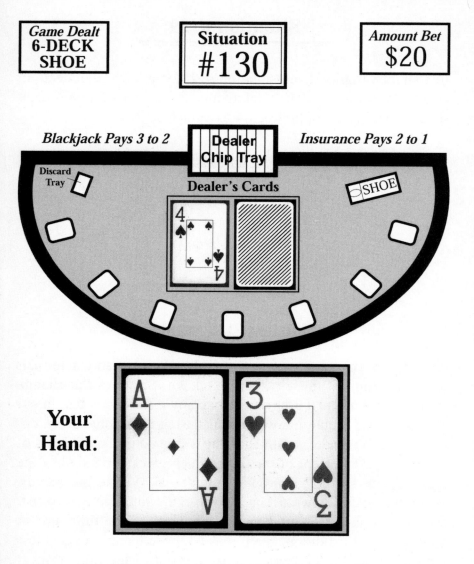

Game Dealt
6-DECK
SHOE

Situation
#130

Amount Bet
$20

Blackjack Pays 3 to 2

Dealer Chip Tray

Insurance Pays 2 to 1

Discard Tray

Dealer's Cards

SHOE

Your Hand:

Variable House Rules in Play This Hand:

1. Double Down: Any two cards
2. Double Down After Splitting: Yes
3. Surrender Allowed: No
4. Dealer Soft 17s: Must hit

Situation #130

In a 6-deck shoe game, you have been dealt an Ace and a 3 for a soft 14 total against the dealer's 4. Of the options listed below, which is your best play?

My Options

A) Stand
B) Hit
C) Double down
D) Split
E) Surrender

Situation #130 Answer

Since you don't have a pair, you can't split this hand. The rules don't allow for surrender (which you wouldn't take anyway). Obviously, with a soft 14, you won't stand since you can improve your hand without breaking. This leaves you with the options of hitting or doubling down. As I've mentioned numerous times already in this book, when playing in a shoe game, the tendency for small cards to come in clumps is greater than in a single-deck game. Given that fact, does it have an impact on this hand? Yes. While you could catch a small card and actually improve your hand, the dealer could catch one, too, and improve her hand to a made hand. And if you happen to catch a 10-count card here on a double down and the dealer makes a hand, you'll lose $40 instead of $20. Better just to hit this hand in this situation.

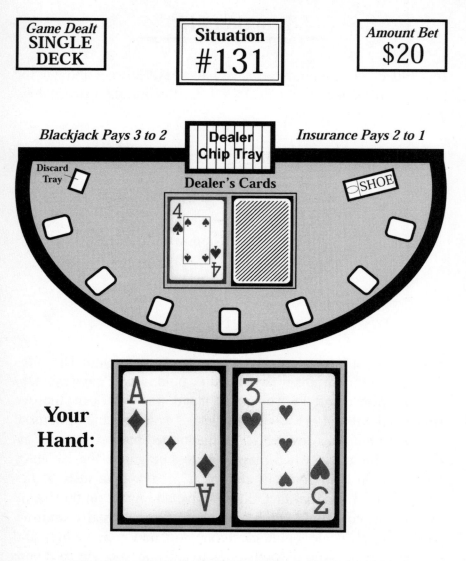

Game Dealt
SINGLE DECK

Situation #131

Amount Bet
$20

Blackjack Pays 3 to 2

Dealer Chip Tray

Insurance Pays 2 to 1

Discard Tray

SHOE

Dealer's Cards

Your Hand:

Variable House Rules in Play This Hand:

1. Double Down: Any two cards
2. Double Down After Splitting: Yes
3. Surrender Allowed: No
4. Dealer Soft 17s: Must hit

Situation #131

In a slight variation from situation #130, you have caught the same hand against the same dealer up card, but this time you are playing in a single-deck game rather than a shoe game. Of the options listed below, which is your best play?

My Options

A)   Stand
B)   Hit
C)   Double down
D)   Split
E)   Surrender

Situation #131 Answer

The question you are facing, then, is whether your strategy should change from a multiple-deck game to a single-deck game, and the answer is yes. By now you should be able to figure out why. Because you're in a single-deck game, the cards tend to run truer and not in large clumps of like ranks. That means when the dealer shows a 4 up—the third worst card she can catch next to a 6 and 5—she is in a weak position. Since you can more read-ily count on the big cards coming when they should (there are, you'll notice, no 10-count cards on the board yet) in a single-deck game, it is now to your advantage to double down rather than just hit this hand. While the gain in terms of units (18 in each 1,000 times you double down on this hand) is small, it is still a gain, and that is how you maximize your profits at black-jack.

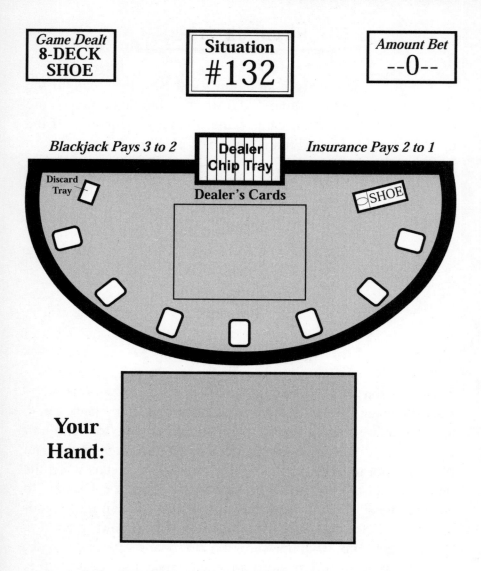

| Game Dealt
**8-DECK
SHOE** | **Situation
#132** | Amount Bet
--0-- |

Blackjack Pays 3 to 2   **Dealer
Chip Tray**   Insurance Pays 2 to 1

Discard
Tray

SHOE

Dealer's Cards

**Your
Hand:**

Variable House Rules in Play This Hand:

1. Double Down: Any two cards
2. Double Down After Splitting: Yes
3. Surrender Allowed: No
4. Dealer Soft 17s: Must hit

Situation #132

After six months of playing solid basic strategy blackjack, you have been able to attain a winning rate of about 80 percent of your sessions. Your success has been so good, in fact, that you've started working less at your regular income-producing job, relying on your blackjack winnings for partial support. Today, however, your session has been long and tough, and after four hours of playing, you are frustrated that you are up only $20, playing mostly $10 hands. Your rent and a few other bills are due, and you won't be getting your regular paycheck for several weeks. You have a $500 bankroll in your pocket and are considering raising your bets to the $50 level. What should you do?

My Options

A) Raise your bets to the $50 level in an effort to "make something happen."

B) Increase your bets somewhat to the $25 level.

C) Keep your bets at the same level.

D) Call it a day and go home.

Situation #132 Answer

Never, ever, *ever* gamble in order to make something happen, especially if you're doing so on a short bankroll. If you make bets in the $50 level with a $500 bankroll, you're betting 10 percent of your bankroll on one play, a *big* no-no. As I state in the beginning of this book, your bankroll should be fifty times your one-unit bet in order to ride out the occasional severe losing streak. If you've played for four hours and are frustrated, feeling pressured because of your bills, I'd call it a day and go home. Using gambling as a quick fix to financial problems is a surefire way to disaster.

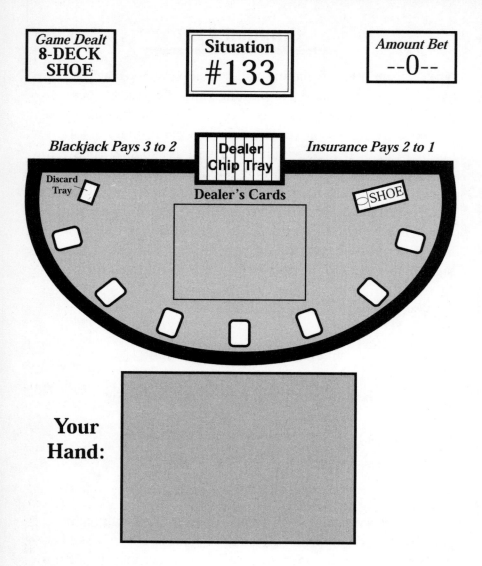

Game Dealt
8-DECK SHOE

Situation #133

Amount Bet
--0--

Blackjack Pays 3 to 2

Dealer Chip Tray

Insurance Pays 2 to 1

Discard Tray

Dealer's Cards

SHOE

Your Hand:

Variable House Rules in Play This Hand:

1. Double Down: Any two cards
2. Double Down After Splitting: Yes
3. Surrender Allowed: No
4. Dealer Soft 17s: Must hit

Situation #133

After a terrible fight with your wife (over a shortage of money, of course), you storm out of the house. You decide to get some fresh air and calm down by doing something you truly enjoy— playing blackjack. Once at the casino, you run into some friends, and they buy you a drink and listen to your marital woes as you play blackjack together. You only had $60 on you to begin with and lost it quickly, mostly on two double-down 20s when the dealer hit four-card 21s both times. Knowing she couldn't keep it up, you got another $200 from the cash machine and sat down to prove you could beat this dealer and win enough money to take home to your *irrational* wife. In the scenario just presented, how many mistakes did you make?

Situation #133 Answer

If you said ten, good for you. If you didn't see that many mistakes, here's the list: (1) Getting into a terrible fight with your wife. Talk things out, don't fight. (2) Storming out of the house. Running away doesn't solve problems. (3) Gambling while angry. Big no-no. (4) Drinking while gambling. Another big no-no. (5) Talking about your marital woes while gambling. Yes, it's human nature, but it's tacky and it's keeping you from concentrating on your gambling. (6) Starting with only a $60 bankroll. As you have found out, in gambling, anything can and will happen (like dealers hitting four-card 21s when you have 20). You need to be properly bankrolled before starting. (7) Playing in a shoe game instead of a single-deck game, which has better odds. (8) Using a fee-based ATM in a casino, which typically charges much higher than normal rates. (9) Trying to prove you can beat the house. Never gamble to prove anything. It'll make you do stupid things. (10) Not going home sooner to your wife and making up—with flowers.

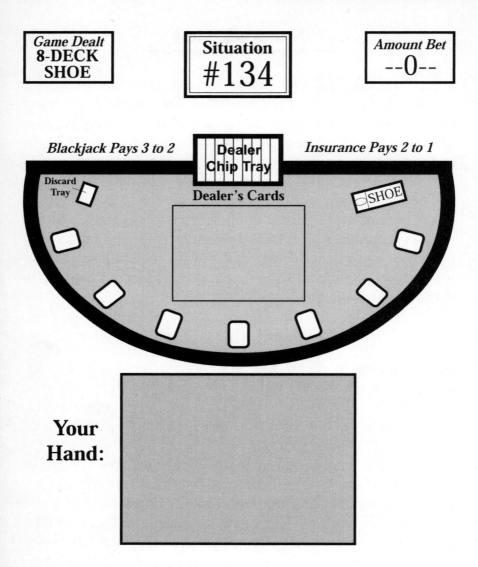

Your Hand:

<u>Variable House Rules in Play This Hand:</u>

1. Double Down: Any two cards
2. Double Down After Splitting: Yes
3. Surrender Allowed: No
4. Dealer Soft 17s: Must hit

Situation #134

You've become a pretty good basic strategy blackjack player and have decided to try your hand at card counting. You know that counters need to keep track of the Aces, so you decide to play perfect basic strategy in a shoe game so that you can practice counting the Aces, even though you won't be using the Ace count in any sort of betting strategy. You notice that the dealer consistently places the **cut card** 3/4 of the way back in the shoe, meaning that the dealer will deal about 6 decks of the 8-deck shoe before shuffling. After playing for seven shoes, your Ace count for the shoes is 11, 15, 14, 12, 12, 13, and 10 for an average of about 12.4 Aces per shoe. What conclusion(s) can you make as a beginning counter?

Situation #134 Answer

That you are most likely being cheated. I actually ran into this situation in a major casino in 1998 and reported it to the gambling commission but was never advised of the outcome. The casino is still in operation. You should receive, on average, about 24 Aces in 6 decks of a shoe game since an 8-deck shoe (if honest) will contain 32 Aces (4 per deck × 8 decks). Taking Aces out of the deck(s) cheats the players because it cuts down on the number of blackjacks (paying 3 to 2 to the player) that players can get. Also, cheating establishments sometimes add 5s or 6s to the deck to hurt players as well. When you find yourself in what seems to be this kind of situation, get up and walk out.

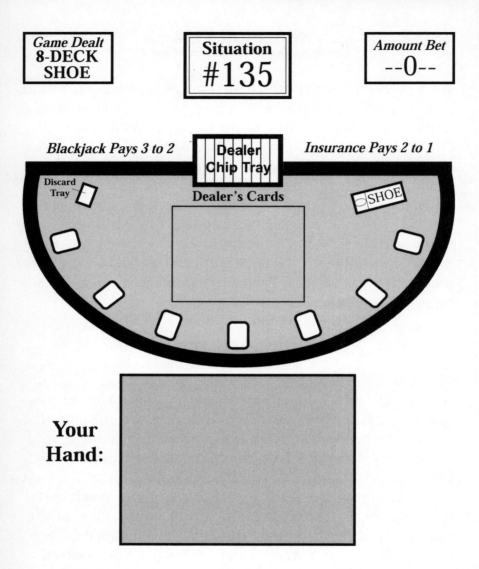

| Game Dealt
8-DECK
SHOE | Situation
#135 | Amount Bet
--0-- |

Blackjack Pays 3 to 2   Dealer Chip Tray   **Insurance Pays 2 to 1**

Discard Tray

Dealer's Cards

SHOE

Your Hand:

<u>Variable House Rules in Play This Hand:</u>

1. Double Down: Any two cards
2. Double Down After Splitting: Yes
3. Surrender Allowed: No
4. Dealer Soft 17s: Must hit

Situation #135

You're playing in a casino with only one other player at the table and happen to notice that the dealer has paid another player $55 for a $30 bet, in effect an extra $25 chip when it wasn't deserved. You don't say anything because the player—a big, rough-looking fellow—scoops up the chips very quickly and places them into his stacks, but now you decide to watch the handling of chips closer. Several hands later, the dealer again pays the same player too much, this time $50 for a $30 bet, the player having placed a $25 chip over the top of a $5 chip. Not sure what to do or say about this incompetent dealer, you look around and notice the pit boss several tables away. What should you do?

Situation #135 Answer

You should say nothing, at least not right there at the table. This person is not an incompetent dealer, she's a cheating dealer, and the player she's giving the money to is her confederate. They, too, have noticed that the pit boss is several tables away, which is why they got away with the player putting a $25 chip over a $5 chip, the opposite of what casinos require, making it look like a $50 bet to the *eye in the sky* (security cameras). The player quickly scoops up the chips so that those hired to watch for such things—pit bosses, security cameras, **floormen**, and so on—can't easily catch on to what the two cheats are doing. You should quietly and politely get up and leave the table. Then, report what you saw to another pit boss (in case this pit boss is in on the cheating). You also don't want the player to see that you're reporting him (the big, rough-looking fellow) because he just might have particular ideas about revenge and might have a partner sitting at another table who won't get busted. You need to report such behavior because, even though they're not cheating you, they might if the need arises, especially if the dealer is a **mechanic** (cheating dealer).

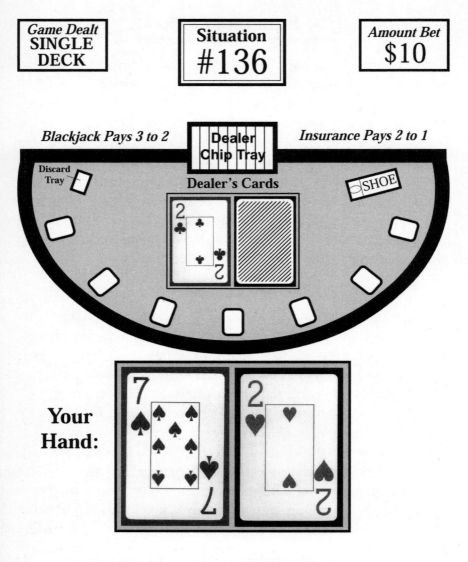

Game Dealt
SINGLE DECK

Situation
#136

Amount Bet
$10

Blackjack Pays 3 to 2

Insurance Pays 2 to 1

Dealer Chip Tray

Discard Tray

Dealer's Cards

SHOE

Your Hand:

Variable House Rules in Play This Hand:

1. Double Down: Any two cards
2. Double Down After Splitting: Yes
3. Surrender Allowed: No
4. Dealer Soft 17s: Must hit

Situation #136

You have received a 7 and a 2 for a 9 total in a single-deck game against the dealer's 2. Of the options listed below, which is your best play?

My Options

A) Stand
B) Hit
C) Double down
D) Split
E) Surrender

Situation #136 Answer

You can't split the hand because it isn't a pair. You can't surrender and wouldn't because you have a solid total against a breaking card. You won't stand on a 9 total because you can improve it without breaking. That makes your decision one of hitting or doubling down. As you've learned by now, the dealer will make a made hand 65 percent of the time when showing a 2. But she'll make a 20 or more (which is what is needed to beat you if you catch a 10-count card to your 9) only 25 percent of the time. Because of her 35 percent chance of breaking and just 25 percent chance of beating your 19, you should double down on this hand rather than just hit. In a multiple-deck game, however, you'd just hit and not double down because of the slightly increased chance the dealer has of making a made hand.

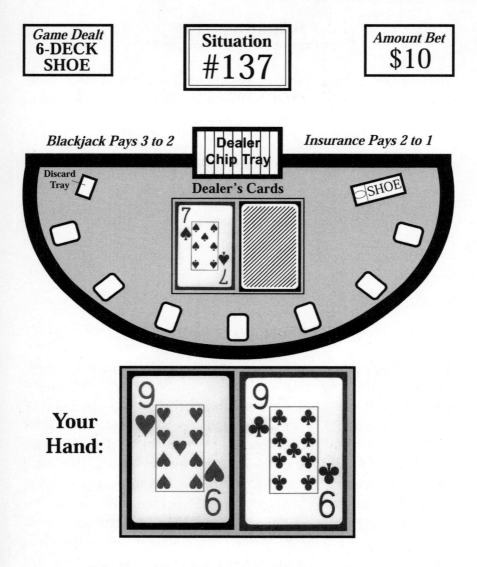

| Game Dealt 6-DECK SHOE | Situation #137 | Amount Bet $10 |

Blackjack Pays 3 to 2

Dealer Chip Tray

Insurance Pays 2 to 1

Discard Tray

SHOE

Dealer's Cards

7♠

Your Hand:

9♥   9♣

Variable House Rules in Play This Hand:

1. Double Down: Any two cards
2. Double Down After Splitting: Yes
3. Surrender Allowed: Yes
4. Dealer Soft 17s: Must hit

Situation #137

In a 6-deck shoe game, you have been dealt a pair of 9s against the dealer's 7. Of the options listed below, which is your best play?

My Options

    A)   Stand
    B)   Hit
    C)   Double down
    D)   Split
    E)   Surrender

Situation #137 Answer

You won't, of course, surrender this hand because it's a solid total. You also won't double down or hit it because you could easily break. That leaves you with the options of splitting or standing. In a single-deck game in which the cards run more true (i.e., you can expect the dealer to have a 10-count card in the hole), you would stand on this hand because your 18 will beat the dealer's possible 17 much of the time. If you split this hand in a single-deck game you'll realize a slight loss versus standing. In a multiple-deck game such as this, however, you should split this hand and play two hands against the dealer's 7 because there is a slight gain in units won. This is another of those borderline moves that won't cause the walls to come tumbling down if you go the wrong way, but if you want to maximize your units gained, you should split this hand in this situation in a shoe game. By doubling your units bet, you also take advantage of the fact that the dealer will break 26 percent of the time when drawing to a 7.

| Game Dealt 6-DECK SHOE | Situation #138 | Amount Bet $15 |

Your Hand:

Variable House Rules in Play This Hand:

1. Double Down: Any two cards
2. Double Down After Splitting: Yes
3. Surrender Allowed: No
4. Dealer Soft 17s: Must hit

Situation #138

In a 6-deck shoe game, you have been dealt a pair of 7s for a 14 total against the dealer's King. Of the options listed below, which is your best play?

My Options

    A)   Stand
    B)   Hit
    C)   Double down
    D)   Split
    E)   Surrender

Situation #138 Answer

This casino's rules don't allow surrender, so that option is out. You won't double down because you never double down on any hard total over 11. That leaves you the options of splitting, hitting, or standing. If you split this hand, you'll have two possible 17s against the dealer's possible 20. Not a good plan. So, should you stand or hit? If you have an excellent memory, you'll recall that early in this book I told you to stand on a pair of 7s against a 10-count card . . . in a *single-deck game*—because the only way to beat the possible 20 is for you to draw another 7 and you've already used up two of the four. In a multiple-deck game, however, you would hit this hand because there are still plenty of 7s to go around. You should hit until you have a made hand (17 or more) or break trying.

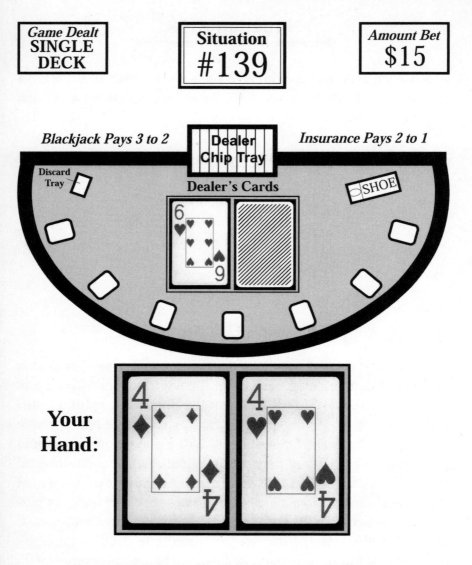

Game Dealt
SINGLE DECK

Situation
#139

Amount Bet
$15

Blackjack Pays 3 to 2

Dealer Chip Tray

Insurance Pays 2 to 1

Discard Tray

Dealer's Cards

SHOE

Your Hand:

Variable House Rules in Play This Hand:

1. Double Down: Any two cards
2. Double Down After Splitting: Yes
3. Surrender Allowed: Yes
4. Dealer Soft 17s: Must stand

Situation #139

In a single-deck game, you have been dealt a pair of 4s against the dealer's 6. Of the options listed below, which is your best play?

My Options

A) Stand
B) Hit
C) Double down
D) Split
E) Surrender

Situation #139 Answer

One hand you won't be surrendering is *anything* against a dealer's 6. Her chances of breaking are just too good. You won't be standing on this hand because you can still improve it without breaking. If you split this hand, you'll be playing two possible 14s against the dealer's possible 16. The only reason to split this hand would be to win twice as much money. If that's the case, why not double down and play only one possible 18 against the possible 16 instead of two 14s? In a single-deck game, in which you can count on the cards coming in truer fashion, you should double down on this hand, but in a shoe game, you should only hit because of the dealer's increased chances of catching a small card and making her hand. If you were to split this hand in a shoe game, you'd likely have to catch a small card, large card, small card, large card in that exact order to end up with two good hands, and the odds of catching four cards in that exact order aren't very good.

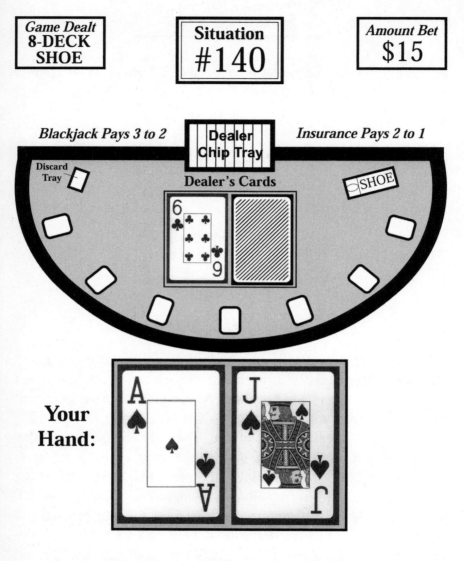

| Game Dealt
**8-DECK
SHOE** | Situation
#140 | Amount Bet
$15 |

Blackjack Pays 3 to 2   **Dealer Chip Tray**   *Insurance Pays 2 to 1*

Discard Tray   **Dealer's Cards**   SHOE

Your Hand:

Variable House Rules in Play This Hand:

1. Double Down: Any two cards
2. Double Down After Splitting: Yes
3. Surrender Allowed: Yes
4. Dealer Soft 17s: Must stand

Situation #140

In an 8-deck shoe game, you have been dealt an Ace and a Jack for a blackjack against the dealer's 6. During the deal, you notice the dealer carelessly flashing her hole card and it is a red 10. Since you know the dealer has a 16, and you can count your Ace as worth 1 or 11 (giving you the optional totals of 11 or 21), which of the below plays would be your best?

My Options

A) Take the blackjack payoff of 3 to 2 like normal.

B) Count your Ace as 1 for an 11 total and double down for a 2-to-1 payoff (better than a blackjack).

C) Surrender and convince the dealer you're insane.

Situation #140 Answer

If you chose option B, you might as well have chosen option C because they'll think you're insane anyway. As you learned earlier, you don't mess with 20s. Well, you really, really don't mess with 21s. Believe it or not, I've seen this play made many times by greedy players who think they're being smart. Think about it. You're already getting 3 to 2 for your blackjack. If you double down in order to try to increase the payoff to 2 to 1, you'll risk catching a small card, giving you an unmade hand, and there's nothing you can do about it because you only get one card when you double. How smart are you going to feel if you catch a 3 and the dealer flips a 5 in the hole and a face card for a 21 of her own? Don't monkey around with a blackjack. Take your money and be happy.

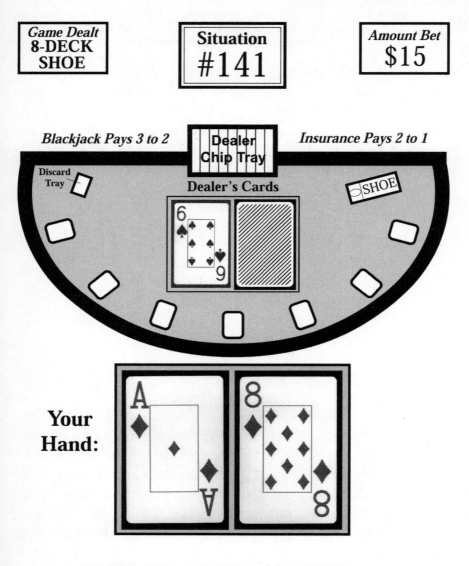

Your Hand:

Variable House Rules in Play This Hand:

1. Double Down: Any two cards
2. Double Down After Splitting: Yes
3. Surrender Allowed: Yes
4. Dealer Soft 17s: Must stand

Situation #141

In an 8-deck shoe game, you have been dealt an Ace and an 8 for a soft 19 total against the dealer's 6. Of the options listed below, which is your best play?

My Options

A) Stand
B) Hit
C) Double down
D) Split
E) Surrender

Situation #141 Answer

The dealer caught the worst card for her, a 6, so you won't be surrendering. You can't split the hand because it isn't a pair. Hitting would be pointless—even injurious, if you hit a small card and she makes her hand—since it would be very hard to improve on a 19. That leaves your options as standing or doubling down. Normally, you shouldn't mess around with a 19 because it's hard to improve the hand. The 6 up, however, gives reason for pause. You need to think, "Would I be better off by doubling?" And to that you would add, "In a shoe game?" Hmm. In a shoe game, you can't count on the 10-count cards coming with the degree of regularity that you can in a single-deck game. That means that you could likely catch a small card on your double down hand. It also means that the dealer could catch a small card and a large card (in either order!) and make a made hand, beating your double down hand that caught a small card (because the player only gets one card on a double down). Thus, in a shoe game, you should stand on a soft 19 against a 6, while in a single-deck game you *should* double down on this hand.

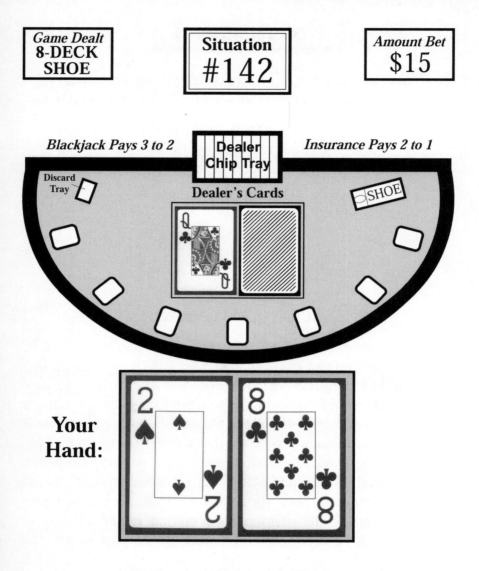

Game Dealt	Situation	Amount Bet
8-DECK SHOE	**#142**	**$15**

Blackjack Pays 3 to 2   **Dealer Chip Tray**   *Insurance Pays 2 to 1*

Discard Tray

Dealer's Cards

SHOE

Your Hand:

Variable House Rules in Play This Hand:

1. Double Down: Any two cards
2. Double Down After Splitting: Yes
3. Surrender Allowed: Yes
4. Dealer Soft 17s: Must stand

Situation #142

In an 8-deck shoe game, you have been dealt an 8 and a 2 for a 10 total against the dealer's Queen. Of the options listed below, which is your best play?

My Options

A) Stand
B) Hit
C) Double down
D) Split
E) Surrender

Situation #142 Answer

You've got a good starting total, so you won't surrender. You can't split the hand because it's not a pair. You won't stand because you can (and need to!) improve on a 10 without breaking. That boils it down to hitting or doubling down. As it stands now, you are looking at a possible 20 against a possible 20. A push, in other words. Since you're looking at a push, you would be at a disadvantage if you doubled down. Why? Because if you catch a 2, 3, 4, 5, or 6, you're stuck with your total of 12–16. If the dealer has a 2 through a 6 in the hole, she can (must) hit until she gets a 17 or busts trying. In effect, by doubling down, you don't get the opportunity to draw out on a bad hand while the dealer does. Just hit this hand until you get 17 or more, or break trying.

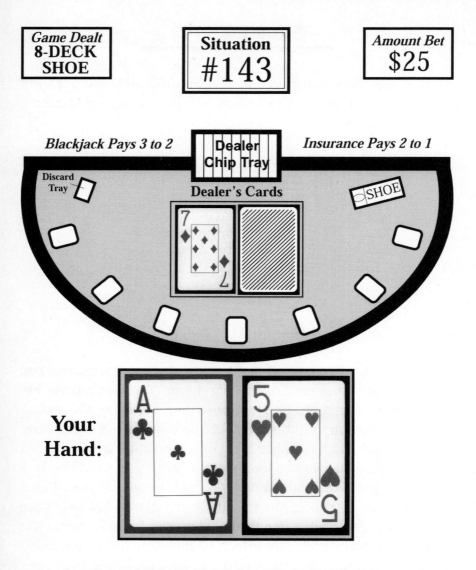

| Game Dealt 8-DECK SHOE | Situation #143 | Amount Bet $25 |

Blackjack Pays 3 to 2   Dealer Chip Tray   Insurance Pays 2 to 1

Discard Tray

Dealer's Cards

SHOE

Your Hand:

Variable House Rules in Play This Hand:

1. Double Down: Any two cards
2. Double Down After Splitting: Yes
3. Surrender Allowed: Yes
4. Dealer Soft 17s: Must stand

Situation #143

In an 8-deck shoe game, you have been dealt an Ace and a 5 for a soft 16 total against the dealer's 7. Of the options listed below, which is your best play?

My Options

A) Stand
B) Hit
C) Double down
D) Split
E) Surrender

Situation #143 Answer

You're not going to surrender because you have a number of ways to improve this hand without breaking, and the dealer's 7 is the weakest of up cards for a made hand. You can't split because you don't have a pair. You're not going to stand because the dealer has a possible 17 and you only have a 16. That leaves you with doubling down or hitting. The problem with doubling down on this hand is that if you catch a 6, 7, 8, 9, 10, Jack, Queen, or King, you still won't have a made hand, and at twice the price. Even an Ace only puts you in a position for a push. Therefore, your best move here is just to hit until you get a hard 17 or more, or a soft 18 or more.

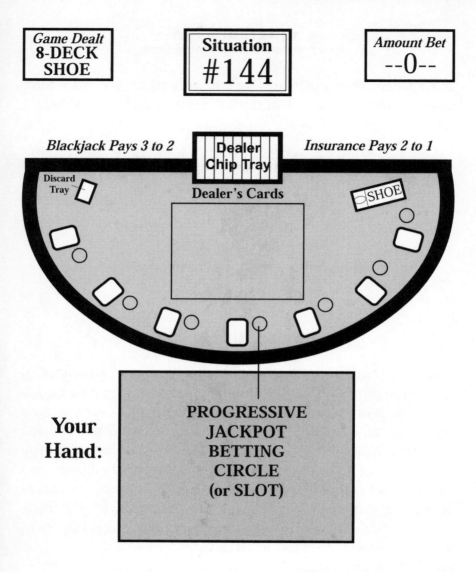

| Game Dealt **8-DECK SHOE** | Situation **#144** | Amount Bet **--0--** |

Blackjack Pays 3 to 2   Dealer Chip Tray   **Insurance Pays 2 to 1**

Discard Tray

Dealer's Cards

SHOE

Your Hand:

PROGRESSIVE JACKPOT BETTING CIRCLE (or SLOT)

Variable House Rules in Play This Hand:

1. Double Down: 10 and 11 only
2. Double Down After Splitting: No
3. Surrender Allowed: No
4. Dealer Soft 17s: Must hit

Situation #144

After sitting down at the blackjack table, you prepare to make your wager. You notice that next to the betting square is a small circle labeled JACKPOT. When you inquire as to its purpose, the dealer explains that it is a side bet for a large, continually growing, progressive jackpot, which now stands at $86,331. The cost is $1 per hand, regardless of the size of your main bet, and it is optional. Should you play this progressive jackpot or not?

Situation #144 Answer

The progressive jackpot wager is a gimmick bet. Some casinos use a chip slot instead of a betting circle in which the chip is placed on edge into a slot with a red light that illuminates to indicate that a particular player is in on the jackpot bet for that hand. Yes, somebody eventually wins it, but it often goes unclaimed for months at a time. The fact that the jackpot stands at more than $86,000 should tell you that. Also, not all the money placed on progressive jackpot wagers is returned to the players, only a portion of it. The casinos (surprise!) take a cut out of the bet. To win the jackpot, a player must catch a certain kind of hand such as four Aces or four 7s in his first four cards. The progressive jackpot is usually utilized in a shoe game, which in itself represents a bit of an advantage for the casino. And if you look closely at the variable house rules in a progressive jackpot game, you might find the rules are more restrictive to the player.

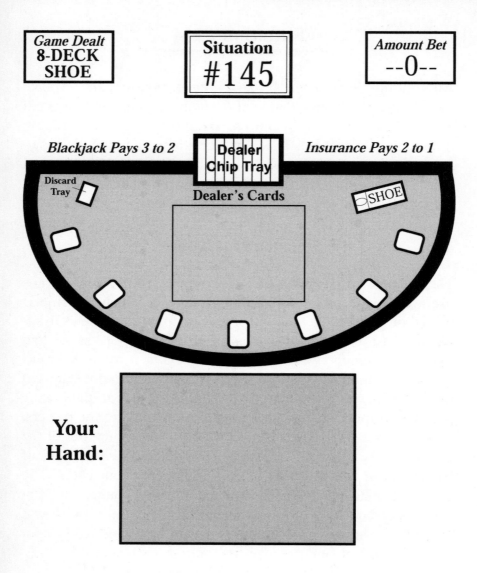

Your Hand:

Variable House Rules in Play This Hand:

1. Double Down: Any two cards
2. Double Down After Splitting: Yes
3. Surrender Allowed: Yes
4. Dealer Soft 17s: Must stand

Situation #145

You've come to a small local casino located inside a bowling alley for a night out. There are only about a half-dozen tables in operation: two feature Pai Gow, one has Caribbean Stud, one has Three-Card Poker, and the remaining two have Spanish 21, but no regular blackjack tables. You think about playing Spanish 21 but aren't sure about the game, so you ask the dealer what the rules are. She tells you they're the same as regular blackjack with two variations: First, all the number 10 cards are removed from the decks, leaving only the Jacks, Queens, and Kings as 10-count cards. Second, all player 21s are paid immediately, so if the dealer later comes up with a 21, the player still wins and doesn't have to settle for a push. Should you play this game?

Situation #145 Answer

By removing all the number 10s from the shoe, the casino has just given itself a huge (as in, Godzilla-huge) boost in its house edge. One of the real advantages a player has over the house in *real* blackjack is that you get paid 3 to 2 on all blackjacks, while the house only collects **even money**. Since you'll get a blackjack on average once in every 21 hands, this is an important boost in terms of units won. A blackjack requires an Ace and a 10-count card. By removing all the 10s, the house has cut the number of potential player blackjacks by 25 percent. And don't be misled by the rule that provides players to be paid on all 21s immediately. How often do you really push with the dealer on 21s? Not that often, and it will be even less with the 10s gone from the shoe. Don't play any of this casino's gimmick games with their high house edge.

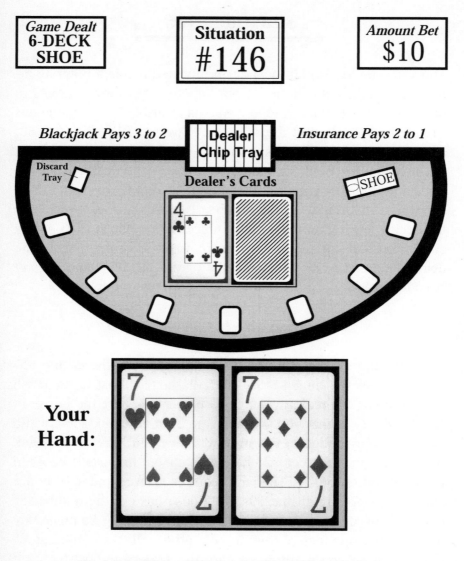

Game Dealt
6-DECK SHOE

Situation #146

Amount Bet
$10

Blackjack Pays 3 to 2

Insurance Pays 2 to 1

Dealer Chip Tray

Dealer's Cards

Discard Tray

SHOE

Your Hand:

Variable House Rules in Play This Hand:

1. Double Down: Any two cards
2. Double Down After Splitting: Yes
3. Surrender Allowed: No
4. Dealer Soft 17s: Must stand

Situation #146

In a 6-deck shoe game, you have been dealt a pair of 7s for a 14 total against the dealer's 4. Of the options listed below, which is your best play?

My Options

A) Stand
B) Hit
C) Double down
D) Split
E) Surrender

Situation #146 Answer

Any time you receive a pair, your first thought should be, "Should I split this hand?" In the case of 4s, 5s, and 10-count cards, you know automatically that you will never split them. In the case of Aces and 8s, you know you should always split them. As for the other ranks, it depends on the dealer's up card. When you analyze the possible benefits (as in this hand), you should think, "Would I be better off with two possible 17s against the dealer's possible 14, or one 14 against the dealer's 14?" In this case the answer is easy, go with two possible 17s, because playing a 14 against a 4 would require you to stand on an unmade hand (which is what you would do if your hand was 8-6, 9-5, or 10-4). To maximize your units won, you have to make the smart move every time.

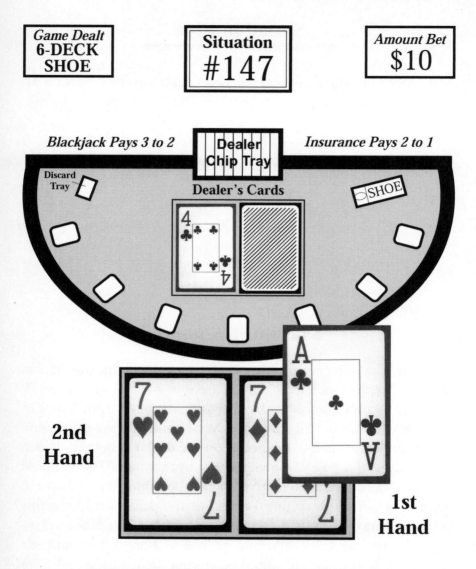

Game Dealt
6-DECK SHOE

Situation #147

Amount Bet
$10

Blackjack Pays 3 to 2

Dealer Chip Tray

Insurance Pays 2 to 1

Discard Tray

SHOE

Dealer's Cards

2nd Hand

1st Hand

Variable House Rules in Play This Hand:

1. Double Down: Any two cards
2. Double Down After Splitting: Yes
3. Surrender Allowed: No
4. Dealer Soft 17s: Must stand

Situation #147

After splitting the hand in situation #146, you receive an Ace on your new first hand for a soft 18 total. Of the options listed below, which is your best play?

My Options

A)   Stand
B)   Hit
C)   Double down
D)   Split
E)   Surrender

Situation #147 Answer

Your thought process now is one of deciding what to do with a soft made hand against the 4. You should know by now that a 4 up is the third worst card for the dealer behind the 6 and 5, and the 4-5-6 cards collectively are often suitable for doubling down against. While you shouldn't mess with 20s and 19s, you should mess with this soft 18 by doubling down. In the first place, you stand a good chance of catching a 10-count card for another 18, but for twice the money. You might also catch an Ace, 2, or 3, all of which will improve your hand. In the second place, the dealer will break, on average, about 40 percent of the time when showing a 4. And of the times she doesn't break, she will make a 17 an additional 13 percent of the time, meaning that you have the edge 53–47 percent on outright winning, and 65–35 percent on either winning or pushing. This is a huge percentage in gambling terms.

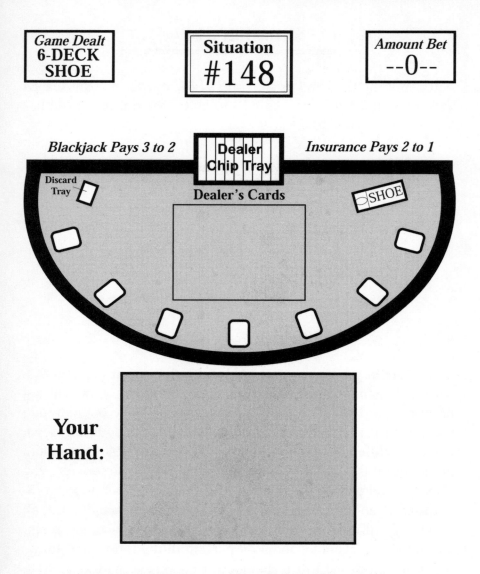

Game Dealt
6-DECK
SHOE

Situation
#148

Amount Bet
--0--

Blackjack Pays 3 to 2

Dealer
Chip Tray

Insurance Pays 2 to 1

Discard
Tray

Dealer's Cards

SHOE

**Your
Hand:**

Variable House Rules in Play This Hand:

1. Double Down: Any two cards
2. Double Down After Splitting: Yes
3. Surrender Allowed: No
4. Dealer Soft 17s: Must stand

Situation #148

You come to the casino with $500, intent on playing $10 hands as your standard one-unit bet. In short order, however, you lose $200, or 40 percent of your playing bankroll, your normal loss-limit amount. You know you told yourself that if you lost $200 you would end your playing session for the night, but because it happened so quickly, you are now rethinking your earlier decision to leave if you hit the target loss amount. Should you stay or should you quit for the night?

Situation #148 Answer

While many professional gamblers I've known set limits on how much they would win in a session before calling it quits, *all* professional gamblers I've known have set limits on how much they'd lose before calling it a day, and there's a reason. It's called *controlling your losses*. Sometimes no matter what you do, how well you play, or what you try, things just don't work out and you lose. The best session winning rate I ever achieved was about 85 percent which means that 15 percent of the time I lost, no matter what. One way to control your losses is to get up and leave the tables, which is what I would recommend to a novice player. You don't want to get yourself into a situation where you're playing to get even or playing angry. A loss-limit amount is one of the ways to prevent such a situation from arising. Establishing and sticking to a predetermined loss-limit amount requires **discipline**, the same kind of discipline it takes to play perfect basic strategy, the very essence of what you've been learning throughout this book.

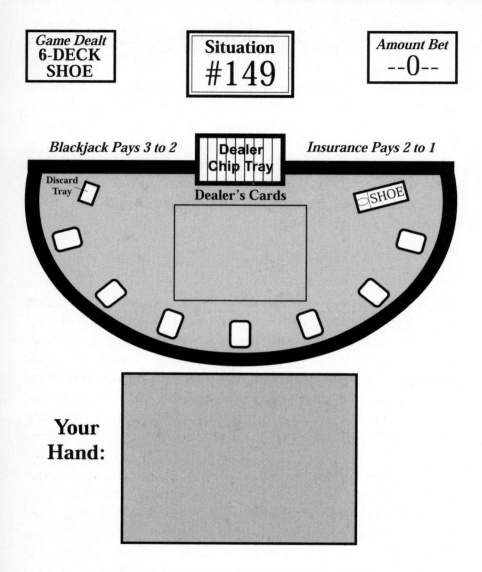

| Game Dealt 6-DECK SHOE | Situation #149 | Amount Bet --0-- |

Blackjack Pays 3 to 2   **Dealer Chip Tray**   Insurance Pays 2 to 1

Discard Tray

Dealer's Cards

SHOE

Your Hand:

Variable House Rules in Play This Hand:

1. Double Down: Any two cards
2. Double Down After Splitting: Yes
3. Surrender Allowed: No
4. Dealer Soft 17s: Must stand

Situation #149

Your have no intention of becoming a professional gambler, you just want to learn good basic strategy so that when you go on your three times a year minivacation with your friends to Vegas or take your gambling cruise you can do better at blackjack, maybe even come home a winner. As part of your pre-trip gambling strategy, you remind your friends to "take only what you can afford to lose." Is this strategy good or bad?

Situation #149 Answer

On one level (the surface), this sounds like good strategy. You don't, after all, want to lose the rent and grocery money. However, this is actually bad strategy and I'll tell you why. This sort of thinking ("I can afford to lose [$X] on this trip.") sets you up for making it okay to lose your designated amount. Literally, 98 percent of my friends who take a weekend trip to Vegas or go on a gambling cruise will make this or a similar remark to me. They are predisposed to losing an "acceptable" amount. Rubbish. By telling yourself that it's okay to lose a certain amount in your pursuit of a fun time, you're subliminally giving yourself permission to do borderline or outright foolish things, like drinking while playing, betting out of proportion to your bankroll, or making foolish bets to begin with. Many people can't wait to experience the lights, the action, and the best of everything that Vegas has to offer, and they'll even play their last few bucks in the slots at the airport as they wait for their plane. There is a reason that Vegas's motto is, *What happens here, stays here.* It's because a lot of what happens there is stupid and foolish, including the gambling habits of most players. Don't fall into the trap. Go there with a mind-set to win, not lose an acceptable amount.

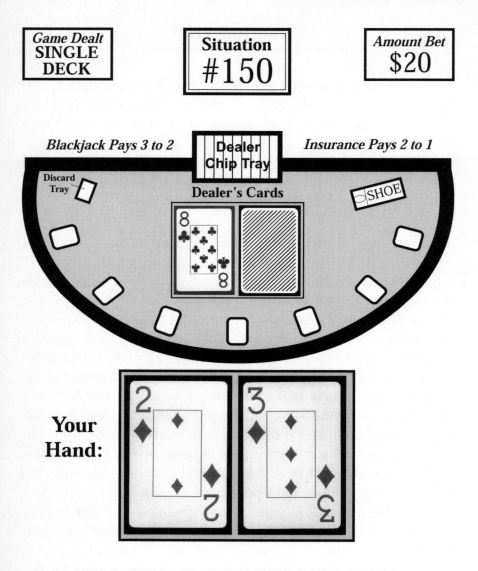

Game Dealt
SINGLE DECK

Situation
#150

Amount Bet
$20

Blackjack Pays 3 to 2   **Dealer Chip Tray**   *Insurance Pays 2 to 1*

Discard Tray

Dealer's Cards

SHOE

Your Hand:

Variable House Rules in Play This Hand:

1. Double Down: Any two cards
2. Double Down After Splitting: Yes
3. Surrender Allowed: Yes
4. Dealer Soft 17s: Must stand

Situation #150

In a single-deck game, you have been dealt a 2 and a 3 for a 5 total against the dealer's 8 up. How many more cards are you going to draw at a minimum, and how many could you draw at a maximum?

Situation #150 Answer

This exercise is designed to make you think ahead. Since the dealer has an 8 showing, we have to play her for an 18. That means that we have to hit our hand until we get at least a hard 17 or soft 18. There is no way to reach either with one more card, so the minimum number of cards you'll have to draw are two. As for the maximum, you could draw as many as eight more cards if you hit—in order—2, 2, 2, Ace, Ace, Ace, Ace, and 3, giving you an 18 total. If this were a shoe game, you could theoretically draw 10 more cards until you held a hard 17, by drawing three deuces and six Aces.

If you figured this one out correctly, call your travel agent and book your flight to Vegas 'cuz you're ready, baby! And don't forget to take this book along with you so that you can study in your room between playing sessions. But then you probably already figured that one out, too. Good luck!

Glossary: The Terminology of Blackjack

action: (1) The total dollar amount *bet* by a player on a *hand* or in a *session*. (2) Gambling, as in "He likes the action more than he likes to win."

advanced strategy: A system of playing *blackjack* used by advanced players and usually consisting of some form of card counting. Advanced strategy is not employed in this book.

anchor: See *third base*.

bank: Money (or *chips*) belonging to the *house* that is used to operate and back a casino game such as *blackjack*. Blackjack is a house-banked game, meaning that players compete against the house, and is unlike poker, which pits players (and their individual money) against each other.

bankroll: A player's money that is used to back his gambling *action*.

bar: To ban or exclude a player from playing in a club or casino. Casinos sometimes bar *blackjack* players for a variety of reasons, including the suspicion that they are card *counters*.

basic strategy: The perfect, mathematically optimal way for a *blackjack* player (particularly beginners and intermediate players) to play every *hand* without counting cards and based on long-term probabilities. This book concerns itself entirely with the playing of perfect basic strategy.

bet: The amount of money wagered on a hand.

betting ratio: Also called betting spread. The highest to lowest amounts *bet* by a player. For example, the lowest bet would always be one *unit*, whatever that amount happened to be, while the highest bet might be four or five units during a particular playing session.

betting spot: The place on a *blackjack* table where the player places his wager.

black: (1) Slang term for a $100 casino chip because typically $100 *chips* are black in most casinos. (2) Slang term for the clubs or spades suits.

blackjack: (1) The most common name for the game of 21. Technically speaking, in the game of blackjack, the deal rotates to a new player when he scores a blackjack. Since the deal does not rotate from the *house dealer* in a casino game, the game played in a casino is actually 21. (2) A hand containing an Ace and 10-count card on the first two cards dealt to either the dealer or a player. Also called a *natural*. If both the dealer and player have a blackjack on the same hand, the hand is a *push*.

break: The act of exceeding a count of 21 when *drawing* cards in *blackjack*.

break it down: The act of breaking down a large stack of *chips* into smaller, more manageable (and countable) stacks or into stacks of like denominations.

burn: The *dealer*'s act of taking a card out of play and placing it in the discard tray. Called burning a card.

bust: (1) The act of exceeding a count of 21 when drawing cards in *blackjack*. (2) Losing all one's money, as in "I've gone bust."

buy-in: The amount of cash exchanged for *chips* with the *dealer* before the initiation of play.

cage: The cashier's office in a casino where *chips* are always turned in for cash and where sometimes can be purchased for cash.

cash out: The act of turning in all one's *chips* for cash and leaving the gaming area.

casino countermeasures: Any of a number of moves taken by a casino in order to win back money lost to a *blackjack* player. These measures might include changing *dealers* frequently, speeding up the action, reshuffling before it's necessary, and closing some partially filled tables in order to force winning players to move to another full table, thereby getting less hands.

casino rate: A special hotel room rate offered to a casino's better customers to encourage their continued patronage.

check: See *chips*.

chips: Also called checks. Chips of varying denominations are used in *blackjack* (and all casino games) to both place *bets* and facilitate the exchange of wins and losses between the *house* and the players. Besides speeding up the game, the use of chips tends to make players feel they aren't betting "real" money, thereby making many players looser bettors.

color in: Also called color me in and color up. The act of exchanging all your smaller denomination *chips* for fewer higher denomination chips before leaving a table. This makes it easier for the player to carry his chips and keeps the *dealer* from having to have her chip *tray* restocked as often.

comp: A short term for "complimentary," usually when referring to casino products or services, especially drinks, meals, or rooms given by the casino to qualified players whose betting action they desire. The level of comp is usually in direct proportion to the *betting* level of the player.

counter: A *blackjack* player who uses any of a variety of counting systems to keep track of certain cards that have been dealt from a deck or *shoe* in order to gain a strategic *betting* advantage. Counters typically seek to find a deck or shoe that is disproportionately *rich* in 10-count cards in order to increase their bets and, ultimately, their winnings.

cut: The act of separating one portion of a deck or *shoe* and placing it on top of the remaining portion. The act of cutting the deck seeks to reassure players that the deck isn't stacked against them.

cut card: A blank card, usually made of plastic and solid in color, that is used to *cut* the deck. The *dealer* will offer the cut card to the players, in turn, until one of them elects to cut the deck. The player takes the cut card and inserts it into the deck to a place of his choosing. The dealer then places the bottom portion of the deck (or *shoe*) on top and *burns* one card before dealing to the players. A second cut card is usually placed in the deck or shoe by the dealer about three quarters of the way down to indicate the point at which she needs to reshuffle.

dead card: A card already played or discarded, or one that has fallen onto the casino floor and declared dead by the floor person.

dealer: The casino employee who deals the *blackjack* game, handles all the betting action, and sees that the rules are followed at her table.

discipline: The unwavering commitment to playing *blackjack* with a sound *basic strategy*, regardless of emotion or temporary setbacks due to a run of bad luck.

double deck: A game of *blackjack* that utilizes two decks of cards. Occasionally found, but not as prevalent as single-deck games or games utilizing a 5-, 6-, or 8-deck *shoe*.

double down: The player option of doubling one's *bet* after looking at the first two cards. If a player chooses to double down (also called simply double), he automatically receives one—and only one—more card. In playing perfect *basic strategy*, a player will double down when it is to his strategic advantage to do so. The act of doubling down at the appropriate time is one of a *blackjack* player's most powerful weapons.

double down after splitting: A *blackjack* option that allows a player to double down after splitting a pair. Not offered in all casinos.

draw: To receive more cards after the original two cards.

drop: The amount of player cash from the purchase of chips dropped by the *dealer* into her *drop box*.

drop box: A small box that is attached to the underside of a blackjack table under the drop slot and into which the *dealer* places all the cash used to purchase *chips*, *markers*, casino receipts, and any other casino paperwork necessary to record the *action* at that table.

dumping off: The act of a dishonest *dealer* who dumps off extra *chips* to a confederate player who wins a hand, usually by placing a larger, undeserved denomination *chip* under a smaller one so that the *pit boss* and *eye in the sky* can't easily see her cheating *action*.

early surrender: The opportunity for a player to take back half his *bet* before the *dealer* looks at her hole card to ascertain whether she has a *blackjack*. Not offered in all casinos. See also *surrender*.

edge: To have an advantage at a game or in a hand. Depending on the situation, sometimes the *house* has the edge and sometimes the player has the edge.

even money: A *bet* that will get you back the same amount you wagered plus your original wager if you win the bet. Most *blackjack* hands pay even money, although a *natural* blackjack typically pays 3 to 2 and a winning *insurance bet* pays 2 to 1.

eye in the sky: The casino's video surveillance system composed primarily of cameras installed in the ceiling above the gambling tables and that are routed to a separate viewing room where security employees monitor the table action, mostly in an effort to identify cheats and *counters*.

face card: Any Jack, Queen, or King. Also called *paint* cards, since the cards resemble portrait paintings.

fill: The act of replenishing a *dealer's* *chip tray*. When a fill is brought to the table by casino security personnel, the dealer or *pit boss* will usually require that all players remove any *bets* that happen to be on the table in case some of the fill chips accidentally spill onto the table, thereby causing confusion over whose chips are whose.

first base: The first player seat at a *blackjack* table and to the immediate left of the *dealer*. Always the first player to be dealt cards, assuming a player occupies the seat.

five-card Charlie: A bonus (usually 2 to 1) paid in some casinos when a player attains a hand of 21 or less in five cards. Not seen often.

five-count system: A counting system in which the player keeps track of the number of 5s played in order to gain a strategic *betting* advantage.

flash: The quick exposure of the *dealer*'s down card, usually done unintentionally by careless dealers. This act is also performed by dishonest dealers who are acting in confederation with a player at the table (usually seated in first- or *third-base* positions), or in confederation with several players, one of whom might actually be seated at a table behind the dealer and who signals his partner(s) at the cheating table as to the dealer's down card.

flat bet: A *bet* that remains the same, *hand* after hand, regardless of the condition of the deck or a players' winnings or losses.

floorman: A casino employee who supervises a designated area or number of tables. Sometimes called a *pit boss*. Also called more simply "floor" by *dealers* when they need his or her attention on a matter.

foreign checks: *Chips* from another casino. Sometimes honored by competing casinos, sometimes not.

front loader: Term for a careless blackjack *dealer* who accidentally exposes her *hole card* when dealing.

front money: Cash required by a casino to be placed on deposit with the establishment in order to receive *comps* and other services.

green: (1) Slang term for a $25 casino *chip* because typically $25 chips are green in most casinos. (2) Slang term for the felt that covers the top of a *blackjack* table.

Griffin Agent: An employee of the Griffin Detective Agency who is hired by one or more casinos to identify cheaters, dishonest *dealers*, and card *counters*.

grifter: A gambler who cheats.

grinder: A gambler who eeks out his profit (living) by *betting* small amounts, usually at the lower limits.

hand: (1) The first two cards dealt to either a player or the dealer. (2) The complete playing out of all players' and the *dealer*'s *hands* in a *round*.

hard total: Also called hard hand. Any *hand* whose total could put you over 21 with the addition of one more card, as opposed to a *soft total*. For example, a hand of 9–6 would total 15. This is a hard 15 since the addition of any card from a 7 through a King would put you over 21. If, however, you held an Ace and a 4, your total would be a soft 15, since no one card could put you over 21. If a 7 through a King were to come on a soft 15, you would simply count your Ace as worth 1 instead of 11, thereby protecting your hand from *busting*.

heads-up: The act of playing a *dealer* one-on-one, that is, being the only player at a table. Also called head-on.

heat: As in "The heat's on." Term used to indicate the casino's awareness that a player is either cheating or counting cards. Professional *blackjack* players avoid the heat by playing in such a manner so as not to attract attention and/or moving frequently from casino to casino.

high roller: A gambler who plays for high stakes at his game(s) of choice. Being a high roller shouldn't be equated with being skillful, but rather only being able to play for large amounts of money. Many high rollers are very poor gamblers but crave the *action*, and casinos are only too happy to provide them with that action as well as lucrative *comps* in order to make the high roller feel special. Most large casinos have whole departments dedicated to seeking out and securing high rollers from around the world.

hit: To request another card from the *dealer*. This can be done by speaking or by using any of several hand motions allowed by the casino. Verbally, a player would say "Hit" or "Hit me."

hold: The ratio of the amount of money won by a casino to the amount of money dropped. For example, if in a day's time the casino dropped $80,000 and paid out $65,000 at the *cage*, the day's hold would be $15,000.

hole card: The *dealer*'s bottom (face-down) card, which is not exposed until all the players at the table have completed the *betting action* on their *hands*.

hot: Said of a *dealer* or player who is on an uncommon streak of good luck. Also can refer to the table at which the streak is happening.

house: Another term for the casino or gambling establishment.

house advantage: Also called *house edge*. (1) The mathematical advantage—usually referred to as a percentage—that a casino holds over a player at a game of chance. In *blackjack*, some *hand* situations have a house (casino) advantage and some a player advantage, depending on the cards. (2) A strategic advantage held by the house over the player. For example, the biggest strategic advantage that the house holds over the player is that the players all have to act on their hands before the *dealer*. If a player *busts* and then the dealer busts later on the same hand, the player still loses.

hustling: The act of a coy (and sometimes not so coy!) *dealer* who solicits tips at the table.

index: The number in the corner of a playing card that indicates its rank.

insurance: A *betting* option for the player when the *dealer* shows an Ace as her *up card*. When the dealer sees she has an Ace up, she will ask, "Insurance?" and then give all the players a chance to make an insurance wager. A player who desires to take insurance must place up to half of his original bet next to that original bet. Once the insurance betting option closes, the dealer will check to see if she has a 10-count card in the hole for a *blackjack*. If she does, then she takes away all the losing player bets (original bets) and then pays 2 to 1 on any winning insurance bets placed. If the dealer does not have a blackjack, she collects all insurance bets placed by the players. Casino employees would have you believe that what you should always do is insure a good hand, such as an 18, 19, or 20. In actuality, insurance is a bad percentage bet unless you are a proficient card *counter* and the bet you are really making is whether you think the dealer has a blackjack. *Never take insurance* unless you are a proficient card counter.

junket: A short gambling trip, often organized by a casino or travel agency, and sometimes paid for or partially subsidized by the casino for qualified gamblers. Typically, a gambler must commit to purchasing a minimum dollar amount of *chips* ($500 is common) once they arrive at the casino.

leak: Any *dealer* weakness that costs the *house* money, such as exposing her hole card or accidentally overpaying the players.

loss limit: A predetermined amount of money (or portion of a bankroll) a *blackjack* player is willing to lose before ending a playing session.

marker: A special casino document used by a player to get extended credit, either because he already has money on deposit with the casino or because he has been given a predetermined amount of credit by the casino.

Martingale system: A *betting* system in which the player attempts to win a certain incremental amount by doubling his bet every time he loses. The flaw in the Martingale system is that casinos place maximum betting limits on their *blackjack* tables; therefore an extended losing streak of even eight or nine *hands* will reach the maximum limit and prevent the player from catching up. A very poor system, indeed.

match play coupon: A promotional coupon given away by casinos that allows a player to match the amount of his *even-money bet* on a single wager at casino expense. For example, if the player chooses to bet $10 with his coupon, he will collect $20 (for a total of $30) if he wins the bet. The coupon is removed from play, win or lose, after the *hand*.

mechanic: An experienced cheating *dealer* who is proficient at (typically) dealing *seconds* (the second card from the top so he can deal the top card to whomever he wants) or from the bottom of the deck. To do so, he somehow needs to know what that card is.

minus (or negative) count: A number that indicates to a card *counter* that the deck or *shoe* contains disproportionately more small cards than 10-count cards. A high minus count would be a disadvantage to the player when placing a new *bet*.

money management: The process whereby a *blackjack* player properly controls both his *bankroll* and *betting* systems in order to prevent devastating losses and to maximize his winnings when on a *hot* streak.

multiple-deck game: A *blackjack* game that employs the use of more than one deck, typically two, four to six, or eight.

natural: A hand totaling 21 by virtue of an Ace and a 10-count card on the first two cards dealt, that is, a natural *blackjack*.

negative swing: A protracted period of losing *hands* or *sessions*.

nickel: Slang term for a $5 casino *chip*.

Northern Nevada rules: A variance in *blackjack* rules that is often seen in the Reno/Lake Tahoe area as opposed to the rules used in Las Vegas and Atlantic City (and now, almost everywhere else in America!). Generally speaking, Northern Nevada rules allow a player to *double down* on only 10 or 11 and not any two-card total as is allowed elsewhere.

odds: The probability of winning a particular wager.

paint: See *face card*.

pair: Holding two cards of like rank, such as two 6s or two 8s. In *blackjack*, because all *face cards* are worth 10, even a *hand* of King-Jack would be considered a pair of 10s for purposes of *splitting*.

past posting: The cheating act of adding *chips* to, or removing chips from, one's wager after the cards are seen.

pat hand: Holding a hand of hard 17 up to 21, that is, holding a hand in this range that you would stand pat on and not *draw* another card.

peeking: A maneuver used by a cheating *dealer* in order to see the top card and help him determine if he needs to deal *seconds*.

penetration: The percentage of a deck or *shoe* that is dealt before reshuffling by the *dealer*. In an effort to combat card *counters*, casinos will often instruct their dealers to penetrate only 40–60 percent of a deck or *shoe* before they must reshuffle.

perks: Small *comps* received by a player from a casino.

pit boss: A casino employee who oversees the play at a small group of tables, or pit, usually 3–10 in number. The pit boss acts as the supervisor of the *dealers* and handles all *betting* disputes, takes care of player *comps*, and keeps a watchful eye out for cheating players and dishonest dealers.

pitch game: A game of blackjack in which the *dealer* holds either a single or *double deck* in her hand and pitches the cards to the players.

player advantage: The strategic advantage a player holds over the *house* (casino). Players actually hold a number of strategic advantages over the house, such as the option of *standing* on a bad (*busting*) hand, while the *dealer* must *hit* such hands until she attains at least a hard 17 (or busts trying); *doubling down* and *splitting pairs*, neither of which the house can do; *surrender*, *early surrender*, and taking *insurance*, advanced moves not available to the house; playing of multiple hands when it is advantageous to do so; and increasing or decreasing one's *bets*, depending on what the situation calls for. Taken in combination—and when used properly and fully—all these player advantages give the skilled blackjack player an advantage over the house, and casinos know this, which is why they sometimes indiscriminately bar good (or winning) players.

plus (or positive) count: A number indicating to a card *counter* that the deck or *shoe* contains disproportionately more 10-count cards than small cards. A high plus count would be in the player's favor when placing a new bet.

point count: (1) The total value of a player's hand. (2) A card *counter's running count* in a *blackjack* game.

poor deck (or *shoe*): A deck or shoe that is disproportionately short in Aces and 10-count cards. A poor deck favors the *house*.

press: As in pressing your *bet*. To increase your betting amount after a win or several wins, usually double the original amount.

push: A hand that is a tie between the *dealer* and player in which neither wins nor loses the hand and the *bet* is returned to player.

quarter: Slang term for a $25 casino chip. (See *green*.)

red: Slang term for a $5 casino *chip* because typically $5 chips are red in most casinos. (See *nickel*.)

rich deck (or *shoe*): A deck or shoe that is disproportionately long in Aces and 10-count cards. A rich deck favors the player.

round: (1) The period of time between the first and last cards dealt by a *dealer* from a deck or *shoe* before reshuffling. (2) A designated number of *hands* dealt by all dealers in a blackjack tournament. (3) The period of time between the first card dealt and the playing out of the dealer's hand.

running count: A *point count* used in counting systems and maintained by *blackjack counters* as each card is dealt.

seconds: As in dealing seconds. The act of a cheating *dealer* to deal the second card from the top in order to deal the top card to either herself or a designated cohort at the table.

session: A period of playing time in which a *blackjack* player either wins his goal amount, loses his limit amount, or completes a predetermined time period.

shill: A person employed by a casino to generate *action* at the tables, usually with casino money. Oftentimes a shill is a very attractive woman who the casino hopes will attract men to a table.

shoe: The rectangular box on a *blackjack* table that contains all the undealt cards in a game utilizing four or more decks. Single- and *double-deck* games are dealt out of the *dealer's* hand.

shoe game: A game of *blackjack* in which the *dealer* distributes the cards to the players by sliding them out of a multiple-deck storage box called a *shoe* that sits on top of the blackjack table to the dealer's left.

short shoe: A *shoe* that contains fewer 10s and/or Aces than it should and/or sometimes more [4s, 5s, or 6s] than it should, utilized by a cheating establishment because both these situations lend an advantage to the *house*.

shuffle: The mixing of the cards before the deal. Technically called the riffle.

silver: Slang term for silver dollars or metal $1 casino gaming tokens.

sky: Slang term for the ceiling area above the gaming tables. Also called *eye in the sky* because of the many cameras located in the ceiling used by security personnel to monitor play at the tables.

snapper: A *natural blackjack*.

soft total: Also called soft hand. A hand in which an Ace is counted as 11. See *hard total*.

split: A *blackjack* option in which the player can *split* his two like-valued cards and create two new *hands* to play instead of one. When a player splits his hand, he must place an additional *bet* equal to his original bet for the second hand. If, for example, a player has a pair of 8s, splits them, and then *draws* another 8 to either hand, he may split them again for an additional like bet. Most casinos allow players to split their hands up to three times with the exception of Aces, which are usually allowed to be split only once with a limit of one card to each Ace.

spread: (1) To play more than one *hand* at a time. In doing so, a player must bet at least twice the minimum required *bet* to play two hands, five times the minimum to play three hands, and ten times the minimum to play four hands. Occasionally a casino will relax these standards, especially when a player making large wagers wants to play any number of hands he chooses at a table by himself. (2) When a *dealer* fans the deck(s) out on the table to let the players all inspect the decks to make sure that all cards are present. This is usually done when new decks are put into play.

stand: The option a *blackjack* player exercises when he chooses not to *draw* any more cards to his hand.

steaming: A term used to describe a player who is playing while angry, usually after suffering a large loss or series of losses.

stiff: A poor hand, usually a hard 12 to 16 in which the player stands little chance of winning.

stop-loss plan: A predetermined strategy to end a playing *session* if a certain level of money loss has occurred.

study chart: Any of the charts or tables included in this book that a player can and should make use of to refresh his memory as needed in order to play perfect *basic strategy*.

surrender: Also called late surrender. A *blackjack* option that allows the player to surrender half of his original wager for the privilege of not playing out the *hand*. This option is typically exercised when the player's hand is very poor and the *dealer*'s *up card* is very strong. In late surrender, if a dealer has a blackjack, the player loses his complete bet. Not offered at all casinos. See also *early surrender*.

table maximum: The largest *bet* allowed by a casino on a single *hand* of *blackjack*. Table maximums vary widely.

table minimum: The smallest *bet* required by a casino on a single *hand* of *blackjack*. Table minimums vary.

tapped out: Said of a player who has lost his entire bankroll.

ten rich: Said of a deck or *shoe* that has a disproportionately high number of 10-count cards to smaller cards. A term used by card *counters* and close observers as to which cards have fallen from the deck or shoe. Ten poor would be the opposite of ten rich.

third base: The last player seat at a *blackjack* table and to the immediate right of the *dealer*. Always the last player to be dealt cards, assuming a player occupies the seat. Third base is usually the most desirable seat at a blackjack table to a blackjack professional because while in that seat he holds it within his power to take or not take cards as he desires and because no other player can act after him and adversely affect the card count.

toke: A tip given to a *dealer* or other casino employee, or a bet placed by a player on behalf of the dealer in addition to his own bet. Thus, if the player wins the hand, so does the dealer.

tray: The *dealer's* *chip* tray.

trends: The tendencies of the cards as they're dealt during a playing *session*. Advanced card *counters* can take advantage of card trends.

true odds: The ratio of times that one event can be expected to occur as opposed to another event occurring.

unit(s): The dollar amount of a player's basic *bet*. Many professional *blackjack* players bet from one to five units most of the time, no matter what one unit happens to be. In a betting range of $5 to $25, $5 would represent one unit, whereas $25 would represent five units.

up card: The *dealer* card which is turned up for the players to see and which is placed on top of the other (down) card. The *up card* is extremely important to a blackjack player because all basic strategy is based on the player's hand and the dealer's up card.

washing: The term given to the face-down mixing up of a new deck or decks of cards by the *dealer*.

white: Slang term for a $1 casino chip because typically $1 chips are white in most casinos.

win goal: Also called win limit. A predetermined amount of winnings set by the player after which he will typically end his playing *session*.

wired hand: Holding two cards of the same value in your hand, usually 10s for a total of 20.